"Transformational coaching enabled me to become a more effective leader, which resulted in the release of huge energy into the business from our people and tripled profitability."
John Duggan, former Chairman and Chief Executive, Gazeley

"The principles outlined in this book have provided an impetus for change in business that helps improve employee job satisfaction and delivers improved results."
Patrick Murphy, former Chairman, Ryanair

"Coaching is a proven way to achieve success and this book excels in laying out that path and, crucially, how to measure the impact along the way. This new edition is itself the highest-performing player in its field."
Juliet de Baubigny, Senior Partner, Kleiner Perkins Caufield & Byers

"My organization is passionate about harnessing the potential of the finest ingredients. The *Coaching for Performance* program enabled me to apply that passion to our greatest resource – our people."
Sandeep Verma, Managing Director, Liz Earle

"Organizations whose leaders adopt a coaching style get to market first and serve their customers, employees, and shareholders best. This book is essential reading for every leader – from the CEO to each digital transformation practitioner."
Martin Toth, Co-Founder, Danowsky Gruhn Toth & Partner

"For those implementing Lean, *Coaching for Performance* puts empathy, heart, and purpose right at the center of it, and gives practitioners a turbo boost to improve performance."
Caroline Healy, Senior HR Manager, Medtronic

"Performance Consultants are without doubt the market leaders in coaching globally. This new edition brilliantly shows how success comes from holistically maximizing the potential of people, and strong ethical principles, rather than a narrow focus on profit."
David Sanders, Founder, CleanTech Advisory, former Director, Carbon Trust

"*Coaching for Performance* has become a bible of the art, process and understanding of coaching."
David Hemery CBE DL, Olympic gold medalist, Founder of 21st Century Legacy

"This new work offers great wisdom and will help take coaching in organizations to a whole new standard and relevance. Not only a must-read but a must to act on."
Robert J. Kriegel Ph.D., author of international bestseller
If It Ain't Broke BREAK IT!

"*Coaching for Performance* should be required reading for anyone interested in power."
Jane Renton, author of *The Economist: Coaching and Mentoring*

Coaching for Performance

The principles and practice of coaching and leadership

SIR JOHN WHITMORE

PERFORMANCE CONSULTANTS INTERNATIONAL

NICHOLAS BREALEY
PUBLISHING
London · Boston

First published in Great Britain in 1992 by Nicholas Brealey Publishing
An imprint of John Murray Press
An Hachette UK Company

Fifth edition first published in 2017

7

Design by Craig Burgess

A CIP catalogue record for this title is available from the British Library

ISBN 978-1-47365-812-7
Ebook ISBN UK 978-1-85788-409-8
Ebook ISBN US 978-1-47364-457-1

Typeset in Celeste by Palimpsest Book Production Ltd, Falkirk, Stirlingshire

Printed and bound in Great Britain by CPI Group (UK) Ltd, Croydon CRO 4YY

Nicholas Brealey policy is to use papers that are natural, renewable and
recyclable products and made from wood grown in sustainable forests.
The logging and manufacturing processes are expected to conform to
the environmental regulations of the country of origin.

Nicholas Brealey Publishing
John Murray Press
Carmelite House
50 Victoria Embankment
London EC4Y ODZ
Tel: 020 3122 6000

Nicholas Brealey Publishing
Hachette Book Group
Market Place Center, 53 State Street
Boston, MA 02109, USA
Tel: (617) 263 1834

www.nicholasbrealey.com
www.coachingperformance.com

Contents

CONTENTS

Foreword

It has been a privilege to participate in the development of a number of the world's most important companies, firstly in the automotive sector, and ultimately leading three major financial institutions both as CEO and chairman. Few were steady state though, ranging from rapid growth situations to corporate recoveries requiring firm and urgent resolution.

This brings two memories. The first is success, not only in financial or market terms, but also in the creation of high-energy organizations with vibrant cultures, achieved through enlightened leadership and the release of the previously untapped energy of thousands of people across many countries. The second is sheer bewilderment as to why some companies faltered in the first place, and the realization that fixing them, while necessary, is not sufficient – we need to make sure it can't happen again.

When we reflect on what a company is, we tend to focus on strategy, market leadership, financial performance, and shareholder value. Frankly, while realistic and essential, this is all a bit technical and sterile. When finally I became responsible for the company as a whole, and was faced with the enormous complexity and uncertainty of steering a path to long-term success, I discovered that a company is more than a business: it is an ecosystem with an enormous impact on individuals, businesses, government, and society as a whole.

Leadership within extraordinary companies is based on principles. There is a tangible difference between a system governed by principles and one controlled by rules. Principles define the center of gravity, or the ideal state, or what is truly desired. Rules define the boundary of what is acceptable and in many cases limit the growth of what is possible. Running an organization by rules generally leads to a company operating at the boundary of what is tolerable, rather than fulfilling its potential. In this book, Sir John Whitmore and Performance Consultants wisely reveal how to use coaching to close that gap between what is only tolerable and what is possible in both human and organizational performance.

Embracing principles requires a strong ethical and emotional foundation and a long-term focus on the heart of what a business is trying to achieve. It creates an environment where people are inspired to learn, to succeed, to grow, and to do the right thing.

Outstanding companies focus on making a long-term and lasting contribution to all their stakeholders, as well as producing superior financial outcomes. Their leaders are very clear on why their people should devote their working lives to the adventure, why a customer should deal with them and not with another, why suppliers should give them priority, why the community should trust them, and why investors should choose them.

What we often forget, to the detriment of high performance, is our people and how we work together to make a company great. It is our people who serve customers, who design, build, and deliver products, and who create new ideas. It is our people who innovate and produce results, who choose to contribute their energies to a vision or cause beyond themselves.

As a banker, I appreciate all too well that a company needs to make a return; but what is clear today is that an organization is not simply a financial construction. A vibrant company is more than the sum of its parts and has a higher purpose that governs all decisions within the firm. Those companies that find their unique place in the world win over others that are not unique. Those with a sustainable reason for existing systematically win over those who do not.

I believe, like Sir John Whitmore himself, that each of us is on this planet to make a contribution to the world in our lifetime. People are searching for meaning and how they can make their own unique contribution. This is an age where humanity and community matter as well as financial returns. Finding this foundation underpins a longer-term philosophy.

As leaders, therefore, we need to take the actions necessary to earn long-term trust and commitment as a foundation for long-term value creation. Our actions and decisions must thus be socially beneficial, culturally desirable, ethically justifiable, economically feasible, ecologically responsible, and, above all, convincing and transparent.

Our responsibility as leaders is to create an exciting but safe adventure for our people, worthy of them devoting their lives to it. How people feel about working in the organization and how passionate and engaged they are in its agenda are what make the difference between good, great, and outstanding companies. Ultimately, our inner mindset and our outer leadership style determine how alive, energetic, and purposeful our organization is.

In this Fifth Edition of *Coaching for Performance*, Sir John Whitmore and Performance Consultants shine a light on what it takes to create high performance and unpick the myths around coaching. Leaders and employees the world over are truly fortunate to benefit from their enduring impact on our working lives.

John McFarlane
Chairman, Barclays plc
Chairman, TheCityUK

Preface

Our intention for this Fifth Edition is for it to be the must-have book for coaches, leaders, and entire organizations who want to create high-performance cultures. Four decades ago, Sir John Whitmore, the father of performance coaching, identified business as a potential force for good and driver of human evolution. He saw an opportunity to unite individual and organizational purpose to benefit people, profit, and planet – the hallowed "triple bottom line" – and this continues to be the driving force behind the work of Performance Consultants International which Sir John co-founded.

We partner with our clients to tap into the latent power of their people and create a culture that places awareness and responsibility at the heart of an organization. This updated edition reflects the progress of coaching in global business. Starting with the Chairman of Barclays, John McFarlane, in the Foreword, we share examples of such transformations and the resulting performance improvement, including benefits to the bottom line. By applying our philosophy, framework, and tools, Performance Consultants can demonstrate an average 800 percent return on investment through the impact of behavior change on the bottom line.

As McFarlane says, more and more people are looking for meaning and purpose at work that is "worthy of them devoting their lives to." Three billion of the world's 7.5 billion people are employed. In our global workshops, we ask people how much of their potential they bring to their workplace. The average answer, 40 percent, demonstrates a huge global productivity gap and an untapped reservoir of talent.

I myself left a successful career in banking: we were the top derivatives house globally, knocking the ball out of the park in terms of financial results. I was on the trading floor where the work was high energy, challenging, and fun. I took pride in hitting my target as part of a great team. Nonetheless, one day I woke up with a yearning for meaning and purpose in my life.

The transformation that John McFarlane led at ANZ bank is still the model for what is possible when you enable people to tap into the meaning and purpose of their work; it harnessed the potential of 35,000 employees and ANZ went from the bottom to the top of the league table of customer satisfaction. Companies can achieve so much more by investing in what they already have – their people.

The coaching profession owes Sir John Whitmore an enormous debt of gratitude for his extraordinary work. This new edition was completed shortly before his death which has been felt by many. He lived a remarkable life and I thank him personally for lighting the torch and passing it on to us. His vision, philosophy, and methodology have inspired millions of leaders and coaches to bring the best out of themselves and others. This book is an important part of his legacy; it has sold over a million copies and been translated into more than 20 languages.

The Fifth Edition will contribute to the continued professionalization of the coaching industry and clarify the huge benefits to leaders of adopting a coaching leadership style. At the same time, it will help to move investments in human capital from being perceived as a cost-center to a profit-center activity generating real value to business. For those who wish to go further with Coaching for Performance, e-learning, public, and in-house programmes are available at www.coachingperformance.com.

Finally, thank you to all members of our incredibly talented team who lead our work in over 40 countries around the world and have contributed their expertise and knowledge in bringing this edition up to date – fit for the future of coaching and business.

Tiffany Gaskell, MBA, CPCC, PCC
Global Director of Coaching & Leadership,
Performance Consultants

Introduction

The demand for change in business practice has never been greater than it is today. That the traditional culture of businesses has to evolve is hardly questioned now – the dot.coms have shaken up the way things have been done and are helping to redefine the relationship between organizations and their employees. In doing so, they are reaching into reservoirs of previously untapped performance. Bright sparks graduating from university have typically fought for internships at blue-chip corporations like Goldman Sachs. Now many of them dream of an internship at Google (Alphabet), Facebook, or the like, organizations that are doing things differently and pledging to provide a meaningful and exciting journey for their employees. This represents the next evolution of business, the reconnecting of business to its purpose, to its reason for being – after all, don't all businesses exist to serve a need? This Fifth Edition of *Coaching for Performance* will set out the reasons why all organizations need to embrace a new way of doing things, how coaching is central to that, and how it is a triple win for people, planet, and profit.

When I wrote the first edition in 1992, it was one of the first books specifically on coaching and the first on coaching in the workplace, and it has served to define coaching globally. Much more than that, it has fueled the adoption of coaching by organizations globally, and it is for this audience, people who want to apply coaching in organizations, whether as leader or coach, that the book is written. Originally, its purpose was to define and establish the root principles of coaching before too many people jumped on the fledgling coaching bandwagon, some of whom might not have fully understood the psychological depth and potential breadth of coaching, and where it fits into the wider social context. Without that understanding, they could easily distort the fundamental methodology, application, purpose, and reputation of coaching.

Coaching for Performance became the definitive book on coaching methodology for leaders, human resource departments, and schools of coaching globally, and now, while many other fine coaching books have added to the field of knowledge, by and large we all subscribe to a common set of principles. The coaching profession has expanded and matured beyond all expectations, and managed its start-up and early teething troubles with dignity and little pain. When we started Performance Consultants in the early 1980s, we were one of the only purveyors of coaching in Europe; now there are upward of 1,000 coaching businesses and more than 10,000 coaches in Europe involved in business, education, healthcare, charities, government departments, and every other activity imaginable. And indeed, Performance Consultants has spread its activities to 40 countries around the globe.

There is a growing number of professional associations of coaches and it is gratifying to see that, in the main, they are cooperating rather than competing. Robust accreditation, qualifications, standards, and ethics are being agreed and monitored in a very responsible way, thanks in large part to the International Coach Federation (ICF) and other coach accreditation bodies. Coaching has moved from a cottage industry to a well-respected profession and has several journals dedicated to it. It is our intention at Performance Consultants to continue to champion the professionalization of this industry. As I pass on the mantle of pioneering coaching in organizations to my younger colleagues, I acknowledge that there is a long way still to go, but I am delighted with the work we have already done and the difference we have made in organizations. Testimony to this is the fact that this book is now in over 20 languages, including Japanese, Chinese, Korean, Russian, and most European languages.

A note of caution: Poor practice in coaching leads to the danger of its being misrepresented, misperceived, and dismissed as not so new and different, or as failing to live up to its promises. My intention for this book is to keep the record straight and eliminate the surrounding weeds by describing and illustrating what coaching really is, including the psychological roots it stands on, what it can be used for, and how it creates the ultimate leadership style for driving thoughtful, performance-enhancing measures.

What is new in this edition?
This Fifth Edition is the product of more years of coaching experience, of course, and more importantly the exploration of evolutionary trends

in human attitudes, beliefs, and behaviors, and in consciousness itself. It reflects the advancement of this knowledge and the maturing of the coaching industry.

CREATING HIGH PERFORMANCE

The fact that *Coaching for Performance* focuses on creating high performance might seem obvious to all. What I am keen to underline throughout this edition, though, is that the principles of coaching can be applied to any type of activity and will have the impact of raising performance. What I mean by performance is the result of reducing interference and increasing potential. I have illustrated this by including practical examples and also chapters on specific applications, such as Coaching for Lean Performance and Coaching for Safety Performance.

Additionally, this Fifth Edition launches The Performance Curve, a model that maps the culture of an organization and relates this to the conditions for low, medium, or high performance. The Performance Curve enhances understanding of how coaching creates a high-performance culture and thereby revolutionizes the traditional approach to organizational culture. This is the new frontier for coaching and leadership development.

PRACTICAL ACTIVITIES, CASE STUDIES, AND EXAMPLE DIALOGUES

In this edition, I have sought to make The Practice of Coaching (Part III) even more practical. It includes the original chapters on questioning, listening, and the GROW model, revised and updated with activity boxes containing exercises from our gold standard Coaching for Performance programs that are run globally. These practice activities will help you develop the foundational skills of coaching through experience, which is the learning style that we advocate and which is proven to be most effective. After all, one can be completely versed in the theory of coaching, but not be able to coach in practice at all. Additionally, I share new example workplace dialogues and new case studies to demonstrate how coaching creates high performance and to show the practical application of a coaching style in day-to-day leadership. These sample coaching conversations draw on the extensive experience my colleagues at

Performance Consultants and I have had in working with organizations globally and the many thousands of participants of our programs, in the years since the book was first published.

GROW FEEDBACK FRAMEWORK AND PERFORMANCE MANAGEMENT

I have completely overhauled the chapter on Will to include feedback, because it is crucial for high performance. So many of our clients are looking to focus on continuous improvement and learning and to move away from traditional approaches to performance management. They are thankful and relieved when we introduce their leaders to our GROW Feedback Framework, which applies a coaching approach to completely transform feedback and performance management. Whether you are already familiar with the GROW model or not, I am certain you will be delighted by the GROW Feedback Framework.

MEASURING THE BENEFITS AND ROI OF COACHING

Like education, motivation, and management, coaching needs to keep up with psychological development and understanding of how people bring the best out of themselves. For years I have been banging the drum about the astonishing effects of coaching in the workplace and how coaching leads to optimal performance. There is always a time lag between what is known in some circles and full adoption by the crowd. Performance Consultants is opening the doors to share its methodology and examples concerning the evaluation and measurement of coaching. I have completely updated the chapter on the benefits of coaching to share our way of measuring the benefits and return on investment (ROI), which we know is widely seen to be the holy grail of coaching in organizations.

COACHING GLOSSARY

A Glossary of Coaching Terms has been included so that readers can explore and test the universe of coaching skills. The glossary is taken from the highly esteemed Coaching for Performance workshop, which is accredited by the ICF and considered the gold standard for those who wish to develop leadership ability.

QUESTION BAGS

Finally, there is a section of Question Bags at the back of the book. This is a useful resource for dipping into as you find your way with coaching. Having questions (rather than answers!) at the ready is the fastest way to learn the new skill and rewire your neural networks. After a while, your questions will trip off the tongue.

Go for it!

Contrary to the appealing claims of *The One Minute Manager*, there are no quick fixes in business. Good coaching is a skill, an art perhaps, that requires a depth of understanding and plenty of practice if it is to deliver its astonishing potential. In this book I will show you why coaching is key to creating a high-performance culture and how to do it. Reading the book will not turn you into an expert coach, but it will get you started and help you to recognize the enormous value and potential of coaching, and perhaps set you on a journey of self-discovery that will have a profound effect on you and your organization's success, your sporting and other skills, and the quality of how you relate to others at work and at home.

As with any new skill, attitude, style, or belief, adopting a coaching ethos requires commitment, practice, and some time before it flows naturally and its effectiveness is optimized. Some people will find this easier than others. If coaching is already your style, I hope this book will help you take what you already do to greater heights, or provide you with a fuller rationale for what you do intuitively. If it has not been your style in the past, I hope that the book will help set you on some new ways of thinking about leadership, about performance, and about people, and provide you with some coaching guidelines within which to begin your practice. I am frequently asked what people can do to maintain and raise their skill in their coaching work. My answer is to practice, practice, and practice, but with greater awareness of yourself and other people, and with commitment to your own continuing personal development.

There is no one right way to coach. This book is no more than a companion to help you decide where you want to go and to introduce you to some routes toward your goal. You will have to explore the territory for yourself, since no one but you can begin to map the infinite variety in the landscape of human interplay in your life. The richness of that landscape can turn coaching and leadership into a personal and unique art form with which to decorate, appreciate, and enjoy your place of work.

Individuals can evolve and transform their work and lives if they decide to embark on a personal developmental journey. Organizations can evolve and transform the work and lives of their people if they decide to embark on an organization-wide development journey. In practice the coaching process fosters evolution at every stage, for evolution emerges from within and can never be taught in prescriptive ways. Coaching is not teaching at all, it is about creating the conditions for learning and growing. Go for it!

A Note to the Reader

This book is intended for two audiences, leaders and coaches (and those aspiring to be either or both). Let me outline what I mean.

By leaders, I mean people leaders and managers in organizations. For them, this is a handbook to develop their own style of high-performance leadership. Leaders do not generally want to become certified coaches, but knowing how to lead in a coaching style that unlocks potential and delivers the highest level of performance is a skill that is increasingly being taught the world over. Indeed, it is the pathway to a new breed of leaders and a type of leadership that befits the twenty-first century. My ambition is that these skills become the norm, that old habits that do not enable people to fulfill their potential are replaced. As more and more organizations embrace a coaching style of leadership, organizations will become the platform through which people achieve their potential, and the relationship between organizations and people will finally evolve to become symbiotic.

By coaches, I mean people who deliver formal coaching sessions to people in organizations, commonly called 1:1 coaching or executive coaching. In this group are both internal coaches (who are employed full time by the organization) and external coaches (who are independents contracted by the organization). I believe it is crucial that this group of people learn to coach in the context of an organization, as that is where they will be operating, and this is what *Coaching for Performance* is about. It is also about combining the magic of coaching with the nuts and bolts of business to create a wholly powerful experience – both for the organization and for the coachee.

Throughout this book I use the term "coach" to describe both leader and coach, because organizations and leaders we work with often develop the term "leader coach" to demonstrate that they are practicing a completely different type of leadership or management that takes their abilities to a whole new level. I have written Chapter 15 specifically for internal and external coaches, to explain how to bring all the skills together to conduct a formal coaching session. Otherwise, where there are specific skills that are solely applicable to leaders or coaches, I point these out in the text.

For simplicity, I have used the term "coachee" for the person who is being coached, be they a peer, team member, leader, or coachee in a formal coaching session.

The quality of coaching taught throughout the book is high – standards and quality are key. The workplace dialogues are intended to reflect the coaching level required of an ICF Associate Certified Coach. For leaders used to a different style, questions such as "When do I tell?" often arise. I invite you to play with the tools described in the book, to build your competence with them. Once you have this, you will find your own authentic leadership approach. Leaders we work with find it is helpful to tell colleagues they are developing their leadership skills and trying new things so that there is an understanding and support around the change in behaviors that are experienced.

Whether you are a leader or a coach who wants to coach in organizations, this is the book for you!

PART I

Coaching Is Bigger Than Coaching

1   What Is Coaching?

Coaching focuses on future possibilities, not past mistakes

Despite the existence of the International Coach Federation (ICF) with members in 138 countries, if you look up "coach" or "coaching" on the Oxford Dictionaries website, you'll be none the wiser as to what all these people are up to. It offers two definitions. The first mentions a bus used for longer journeys, a railway carriage, and traveling. The second includes sports instruction or training, private tuition, and extra teaching. It might surprise you to learn that the first is more relevant. Coaching is all about a journey and nothing about instruction or teaching. It is as much if not more about the way things are done as about what is done. Coaching delivers results in large measure because of the powerful working relationship created, and the means and style of communication used. The coachee does acquire facts and develops new skills and behaviors, not by being told or taught but by discovering from within, stimulated by coaching. Of course, the objective of improving performance is paramount, and how that is best achieved and sustained is what this book reveals.

The Inner Game

Let us take a look at the birth of modern-day coaching. Timothy Gallwey was perhaps the first to demonstrate a simple but comprehensive method of coaching over four decades ago. A Harvard educationalist and tennis expert, he threw down the gauntlet in 1974 with a book entitled *The Inner Game of Tennis*, which was quickly followed by *Inner Skiing* and *The Inner Game of Golf*.

The word "inner" was used to indicate the player's internal state or, to use Gallwey's words, that "the opponent within one's own head is more formidable than the one the other side of the net." Anyone who has had one of those days on the court when you can't do anything right will recognize what he is referring to. Gallwey went on to claim that if a coach can help a player to remove or reduce the internal obstacles to performance, an unexpected natural ability to learn and to perform will occur without the need for much technical input from the coach.

The Inner Game Equation

To illustrate this, Gallwey created a simple Inner Game Equation which, with the benefit of hindsight, we can see very effectively summarizes the objective of modern coaching:

$$\text{Performance} = \text{potential} - \text{interference}$$
$$P = p - i$$

Both the Inner Game and coaching focus on improving performance (P) by growing potential (p) and by decreasing interference (i).

Internal obstacles are often more daunting than external ones.

At the time Gallwey's books first appeared, few coaches, instructors, or professional sportspeople could believe his ideas, let alone embrace them, although players devoured them eagerly in bestseller-list quantities. The professionals' ground of being was under threat. They thought that Gallwey was trying to turn the teaching of sport on its head and that he was undermining their egos, their authority, and the principles in which they had invested so much. In a way he was, but their fear exaggerated their fantasies about his intentions. He was not threatening them with redundancy, merely proposing that they would be more effective if they changed their approach.

The essence of coaching

We can see from all this that Gallwey *had* put his finger on the essence of coaching. Indeed, my definition of coaching describes the link to the Inner Game and all it stands for: **Coaching is unlocking people's**

potential to maximize their own performance. It is helping them to learn rather than teaching them. After all, how did you learn to walk? Did your mother or father instruct you? We all have a built-in, natural learning capability that is actually disrupted by instruction.

This idea was not new: Socrates had voiced the same concept some 2,000 years earlier, but somehow his philosophy got lost in the rush to materialistic reductionism of the last two centuries. The pendulum has swung back and coaching, if not Socrates, is here to stay for a century or three yet! Gallwey's books coincided with the emergence of a more optimistic psychological model of humankind than the old behaviorist view that we are little more than empty vessels into which everything has to be poured. The new model suggested we are more like acorns, each of which contains within it all the potential to be a magnificent oak tree. We need nourishment, encouragement, and the light to reach toward, but the oaktreeness is already within us.

If we accept this model – and few people now contest it – the way we learn, and more importantly the way we teach and instruct, must be called into question. Unfortunately, habits die hard and old methods persist, even though most of us know their limitations. It may be harder to give up instructing than it is to learn to coach.

Let me extend the acorn analogy a step further. Oak saplings, growing from acorns in the wild, quickly develop a single, hair-thin tap root to seek out water. This may extend downward as far as a meter while the sapling is still only 30cm tall. When grown commercially in a nursery, the tap root tends to coil in the bottom of the pot and is broken off when the sapling is transplanted, setting back its development severely while a replacement grows. Insufficient time is taken to preserve the tap root and most growers do not even know of its existence or purpose.

When transplanting a sapling, the wise gardener will uncoil the tender tap root, weight its tip, and carefully thread it down a long, vertical hole driven deep into the earth with a metal bar. The small amount of time invested in this process so early in the tree's life ensures its survival, and allows it to develop faster and become stronger than its commercially grown siblings. Wise business leaders use coaching to emulate the good gardener.

In the past, the universal proof of the success of new coaching methods was hard to demonstrate because few people had understood and used them fully. This is now changing and I hope that the additional models I have included in this book will support this further. However, many coaches have been unwilling to set aside old, proven ways for long enough to reap the rewards of new ones. Recently, as much through necessity as progress, employee engagement has been proven to be linked to performance, and so all the behaviors that underpin engagement – which are all coaching behaviors, such as collaborating, meaningful goal setting, delegating, and accountability – have found their way into business language and, more importantly, into behavior too.

Mentoring

Since I am defining coaching, I should perhaps mention mentoring, another word that is now common in business parlance. The word originates from Greek mythology, in which it is reported that Odysseus, when setting out for Troy, entrusted his house and the education of his son Telemachus to his friend, Mentor. "Tell him all you know," Odysseus said, and thus unwittingly set some limits to mentoring.

Some people use the term mentoring interchangeably with coaching. However, mentoring is very different to coaching, because coaching is not dependent on a more experienced person passing down their knowledge – in fact, this undermines the building of self-belief which creates sustained performance, as we shall discover. Instead, coaching requires expertise in coaching, not in the subject at hand. That is one of its great strengths. And something that coaching leaders grapple with most – but is key – is to learn when to share their knowledge and experience and when not to.

Mike Sprecklen was the coach and mentor to the famous all-conquering British rowing pair Andy Holmes and Steve Redgrave. "I was stuck, I had taught them all I knew technically," Sprecklen said on completion of a Coaching for Performance workshop many years ago, "but this opens up the possibility of going further, for they can feel things that I can't even see." He had discovered a new way forward with them, working from their experience and perceptions rather than from his own. Good coaching and leading, and good mentoring for that matter, can and should take a coachee beyond the limitations of the coach, leader, or mentor's own knowledge.

Inner Business

Many years ago I sought out Tim Gallwey, was trained by him, and founded the Inner Game in Britain. We soon formed a small team of Inner Game coaches. At first all were trained by Gallwey, but later we trained our own. We ran Inner Tennis courses and Inner Skiing holidays, and many golfers freed up their swings with Inner Golf. It was not long before our sporting clients began to ask us if we could apply the same methods to prevailing issues in their companies; IBM was the first. On the ski slopes of the Alps, leaders discovered a revolutionary way of learning to ski using the Inner Game and wanted us to help them bring this approach to their work. What is of note here is that the simple methods could be readily applied to almost any situation. Of course, the rest is history – we pioneered this new approach in business, which we called "performance coaching." All the leading exponents of business coaching today graduated from this and have been profoundly influenced by the Gallwey school of coaching.

Since 1982, Performance Consultants has built and elaborated on those first methods and adapted them to the practical issues and conditions of today's business environment. Indeed, our team has partnered with clients to apply coaching to such diverse topics as employee engagement, Lean methodology, and safety. We have specialized in teaching leaders to coach and transform organizations and also in providing expert coaching for executives and for business teams. Although coaches have to compete with one another in the market, they tend to be friends and not infrequently work together. This in itself speaks highly of the method, for it was Gallwey who suggested that your opponent in tennis is really your friend if they make you stretch and run. Opponents are not friends if they just pat the ball back to you, as that will not help you to improve your game, and isn't that what we are all trying to do in our different fields?

Although Gallwey, my more senior colleagues in Performance Consultants, and many others who now practice coaching in the business arena cut our teeth in sport, coaching in sport itself has changed little overall. It remains significantly behind the methodology of coaching that is virtually universal in business today. That is because when we introduced coaching into business four decades ago, the word was new in that context and did not bring with it the baggage of a long history of past practice. We were able to introduce new concepts without having to fight old prejudices and practitioners of old coaching.

That is not to say that we met no resistance to coaching in business; we still do at times from people who have remained strangely insulated from or blind to change. Coaching as a practice in business is here to stay, although the word itself might disappear as its associated values, beliefs, attitudes, and behaviors become the norm for everyone, as I explore in this book. My hope is that this Fifth Edition will lay the foundation for this to occur.

Mindset and Maslow

Gallwey was building on the work of others. In the 1940s, American psychologist Abraham Maslow broke away from the tradition of delving into pathology to try to understand human nature. He studied mature, complete, successful, and fulfilled people, and concluded that we could all be that way. In fact, he asserted that this was the natural human state. All we had to do, in his opinion, was to overcome our inner blocks to development and maturity. Maslow, along with Carl Rogers and others, was the father of the more optimistic wave of psychological thinking that is still in the process of displacing carrot-and-stick behaviorism as the best way of leading and motivating people. Psychological optimism is essential if we are to fully embrace coaching as the leadership style of the future.

Maslow is best known in business circles for his Hierarchy of Needs. This model suggests that our most basic need is for food and water, and that we will care for little else (except possibly a mobile phone!) until that physiological need is met. Once we have secured a supply of food and water, we begin to concern ourselves with items such as shelter, clothing, and safety. And once we have met, at least in part, these physical needs, we begin to focus on our social needs, including the need to belong to a grouping. These needs are met in part by our family, but later we also meet them in pubs, clubs, and teams.

FIGURE 1: *Maslow's Hierarchy of Needs*

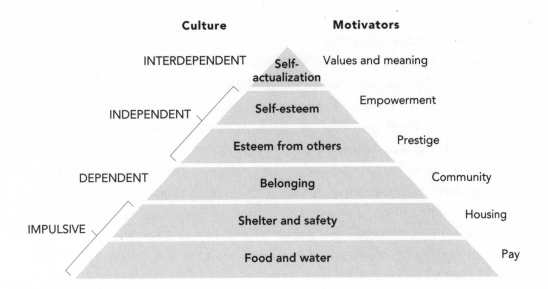

Next we seek to satisfy our desire for respect and admiration – the need for esteem from others – by display and by competing for power, victory, or recognition. These emotional needs are eventually displaced by a subtle shift to the need for self-esteem, or as I prefer to call it, self-belief (the bedrock of coaching and the prerequisite for high performance). Here we demand higher standards of ourselves and look to our own criteria by which we measure ourselves, rather than to how others see us. In terms of mindset, we have become **independent**.

Maslow's highest state was the self-actualizing person, who emerges when both the esteem needs (respect from others and belief in self) are satisfied and individuals are no longer driven by the need to prove themselves, either to themselves or to anyone else. These latter two needs are personal and are free of any external dependency. Maslow called the final stage self-actualiz*ing* rather than self-actualized, because he saw it as a never-ending journey. The primary need associated with self-actualizers is the need for meaning and purpose in their lives. They want their work, their activities, and their existence to have some value, to be a contribution to others. They are **interdependent**. I will discuss this vital performance leap from independence to interdependence in the next chapter.

MOTIVATION AT WORK

People will seek to engage in those activities that help them to meet their needs. They are likely to be only partially conscious of this process. Work has naturally developed in ways that do help meet those needs, and now it has to develop to the next level. At the basic level, work does meet people's primary needs by giving them an income with which they can feed, water, clothe, and house their families. Furthermore, work offers promotion, prestige, pay grades, and even a company car via which to solicit the esteem of others. The normal motivator used in work, rewards in various currencies, goes some of the way to meeting the survival needs, the belonging needs, and even the lower of the two esteem needs. Very clever so far.

However, society today is collectively seeking need satisfaction higher up the hierarchy to include meaning and purpose. Companies are beginning to reflect changes at that level.

SELF-BELIEF

Whereas Maslow used the collective term "esteem needs" and made the important distinction between esteem from others and self-esteem, I prefer to use the terms "status and recognition" for the former and "self-belief" for the latter.

Self-belief is not created by prestige and privilege, which are more symbolic than substantial. It is built when someone is seen to be worthy of making choices. Promotion without genuine empowerment and the opportunity to express potential is counterproductive. While telling negates choice, disempowers, limits potential, and demotivates, coaching does the opposite.

MILLENNIALS SEEK MEANING AND PURPOSE

Some employees, especially younger ones, are showing signs of seeking self-actualizing needs. They want their work to be of value and to have meaning and purpose, and traditional organizations are losing out as a result. These organizations must understand that lining the pockets of shareholders is no longer seen as meaningful. Companies are obliged to consider more carefully their ethics and values and the needs of all their stakeholders, including employees first and foremost, but also customers, the community, and the environment.

These are the issues that leaders and employees on the workshops we run are raising more and more frequently. Companies are seeking a change of leadership style, and employees are demanding it. If these young and, in Maslow's terms, more mature employees are not to become disaffected, the changes need to get underway immediately. So important is this issue, and so enormous will be the benefits to performance and ultimately to the triple bottom line of people, profit, and planet, that in this edition I have reorganized the book to address it more fully.

THE CHOICE OF LEADERSHIP BEHAVIOR
While millennials are demanding this change in leadership style, leaders do not know how to provide it. Our experience shows that the development of employees is the lowest priority of four criteria that cause us to adapt our leadership behavior in the moment. At the head of the list comes time pressure, then fear, and next comes the quality of the job or the product, leaving employee development a poor fourth. Shortage of time and excess fear drive us into command and control, while the quality of work and the need for development demand coaching.

It comes as little surprise that coaching is sometimes sidelined by short-termism and the urgency of the need to provide shareholder returns. However, the wake-up call has been sounded in the changing expectations of younger employees. At job interviews they want to know what training and development opportunities and what style of leadership they can expect. They do not seek – and nor do they want – a job for life, and they will leave a job if their needs are not met. And those needs are for things that will help their self-belief, such as a coaching leadership style.

Leadership style needs to evolve
Most business leaders today have reached Maslow's status and recognition level – and this is where they can do the most harm. They are often arrogant, assertive, domineering, and self-important. They will do anything

to get more pay; they don't need or deserve it, but it is a way of measuring and asserting their status.

However, if a business leader does escape the trap and progress to the next level, the need for self-belief, the leadership news gets better. Leaders who aspire to be there, or are there, will really try to do the right thing, rather than trying to *appear* to do the right thing or to do things right. Only being authentic gives the feel-good factor that accompanies self-belief. What this is all about, of course, is the emergence of broader altruistic values – leading for others rather than for oneself.

Leadership by people any lower than this on the scale has a selfish element regardless of the other skills they might possess. Such leadership is only useful to those they lead if those employees happen to have the same aspirations. And while leaders at the level of self-belief are well motivated, they might seek to be a little more high profile than a leader who has reached the next level – self-actualizing. This is sometimes called the level of service. Service is often seen as the answer to the search for meaning and purpose, something that people used to gain from their religion but now look for elsewhere, including while at work. Service to others manifests in a wide spectrum of forms, is very fulfilling, and is the universal way to meeting this need. One of the leaders of a multinational manufacturing company who attended an in-house program we ran for global leaders said: "I have realized that my job is to develop people every day, and I love it!" Learning a coaching style enabled him to tap into the potential of his people.

Toward the end of his life, Maslow added the level of self-realization. However, as I have said, development is a journey, not a destination. Some recent commentators also define self-actualizing more modestly and flatter business leaders by suggesting that they, and indeed many others, are at this level. I do not share that view. As far as I am concerned, in order to earn the title of leader a person must have evolved beyond the status and recognition level and beyond self-interest. Aspiring leaders will hone their leadership skills at lower levels while they are growing into the job, but their power to exercise control over others should be constrained until they have grown up.

The good news is that change is in the air, evolution marches on despite expected resistance, environmental concerns are becoming integrated into business strategy as opposed to being a tick-box exercise for appearances, and this is further driven by consumer and public demand for transparency, which is becoming more effective at policing business excesses, often via the internet. Evolution is key if we are to rise to the challenges of the twenty-first century. Coaching is the mechanism of transformation.

The need toward which a large segment of modern society is beginning to move is that of self-belief and independence, with a few people yearning for self-actualization and interdependence. Traditional businesses and management methods of command and control which create dependence are very poor at meeting this need, and that is what has to change. In fact, I believe that leaders fail to do so principally because they have simply never been taught how. The only way they learned was by being told. Adult learning theory tells us that adults learn in a completely different way to children. Self-belief is central to this. Coaching is adult learning in practice and is both what leaders need and the direction in which leadership style needs to travel.

In essence coaching is about partnership, collaboration, and believing in potential. I will take a close look at the principles of coaching in Part II, and explain my central premise that coaching and high performance come out of **awareness** and **responsibility**. To achieve this requires the foundation coaching skills of **powerful questioning** and **active listening** and a framework of compass for our coaching – the **GROW** model – all of which I explain in Part III. But first let's turn our attention to the attributes of a high-performance culture.

2 Creating High-Performance Cultures

Enabling a coaching culture generates high performance

What are the implications for organizations whose leaders adopt a coaching leadership style or who work with a coach on a 1:1 basis? Those leaders will, indisputably, create the conditions for a high-performance culture. The evolutionary journey of our species has reached the stage at which the hierarchies of the past are being replaced by a new form of devolved leadership and collective responsibility. Could it be that the coaching profession has grown so fast because it meets this broader need for self-responsibility, which, after all, is its principal product? Could the coaching profession have emerged to be a midwife for a new era, or is that too grand a notion? Could the only thing limiting us be the size of our vision and our own self-limiting beliefs?

Coaching is bigger than coaching

The Conference Board CEO Challenge® 2016 survey shows that attracting and retaining top talent and developing the next generation of leaders are the top most pressing concerns of global CEOs. This bodes well for change to happen, and human capital is now widely valued as one of the most important contributors to a company's sustainable performance and growth. In the wider context, corporate wealth and influence are such that organizations are more powerful than governments when it comes to the big social and environmental issues of our time. Manny Amadi, CEO of C & E Advisory, highlights this issue when he says: "The burden of economic fundamentals is now such that government on its own can't fulfill its social obligations. On the other side, the sheer power and influence of businesses in the economy are now huge." Logic dictates that business leaders have an extraordinary part to play on the planet – in my mind it is an invitation to move along the evolutionary map from selfish adolescent to respected adult. An invitation to play a positive, indeed critical part in the lives of the people they touch and in their relationship with the planet itself. An invitation to lead the charge toward transformational change.

From what to what?

We need the capacity to take a whole-system approach that is a product of personal development, of moving from the old paradigm of fear to one of trust and of recognizing that humankind is evolving both socially and spiritually. Coaching is the enabler and a coaching culture creates the conditions for high performance, which I will explain when I introduce The Performance Curve later in this chapter. The culture of business has to change – but from what and to what?

Any new culture will have to deliver higher levels of performance, but also be far more socially responsible than ever before. No corporation is going to take the risks and suffer the upheavals involved in major change just for the sake of it, or merely to be nicer to employees; although perhaps it should. While culture change will be, and needs to be, performance driven, the definition of performance is much broader today. Competition and growth are both losing their currency; stability, sustainability, and collaboration are gaining traction. Those companies and individuals who don't change their ways from what has been acceptable in the past to what will be acceptable in the future won't survive in our oversubscribed, fractured, and unstable markets. With opportunities for promotion and pay increases shrinking in most sectors, how does a business maintain, manage, and motivate its employees?

Expressions such as "our people are our greatest resource," "we must empower all our employees," "releasing latent potential," "downsizing and devolving responsibility," and "getting the best out of our people" have become clichés. Their true meaning remains as valid today as when they were coined, but all too often they are hollow words. They are talked about far more than acted on. Coaching for Performance is just what it says – a means of obtaining optimum performance – but one that demands fundamental changes in attitude, in leadership behavior, and in organizational structure.

Of course, there are also pragmatic reasons for change, such as growing global competition forcing the pace toward leaner, more efficient, agile, and responsive organizations and teams. The pace of technological innovation frequently results in leaders finding that they don't have time to learn the skills of the teams they employ. Globalization, demographic changes, the further integration or disintegration of Europe, immigration, and the multiple effects of the internet and instant communication oblige businesses to change their ways.

However, in my view by far the biggest challenge to hit business comes from the demands for legal and social responsibility that follow the expert consensus that climate change is both real and man-made. It is imperative that we find ways for businesses to succeed that are in harmony with the planet. The conduct and the success of organizations are inextricably bound to global, social and psychological, environmental, and economic factors to a far greater extent than ever before. In addition, the commercial and financial demands made by businesses, and their power, mean that they also profoundly influence the surrounding cultures, and those cultures are increasingly exercising their consumer power and hitting back.

A NEW STYLE

Most of the organizations we work with approach us because they are seeking to improve performance and have embarked on a process of fundamental change – or at least they would like to. They have recognized that, if they are to achieve real performance improvement, their leaders must adopt a coaching style. These companies have already identified that coaching is the leadership style of a transformed culture, and that as the style changes from directing to coaching, the culture of the organization will begin to change. Hierarchy gives way to partnership and collaboration, blame gives way to honest evaluation and learning, external motivators are replaced by self-motivation, protective barriers fall as teams build, change is no longer feared but welcomed, satisfying the boss becomes pleasing the customer. Secrecy and censorship are replaced by openness and honesty, pressure of work becomes challenging work, and short-term fire-fighting reactions give way to longer-term strategic thinking. Table 1 lists some of the characteristics of the emerging high-performance culture, but each business will have its own unique mix and priorities.

TABLE 1: *Attributes of a high-performance culture*

Old culture	New culture
Growth	Sustainability
Imposed rules	Inner values
Fear	Trust
Quantity	Quality
Excess	Sufficiency
Teaching	Learning
In/dependence	Interdependence
Success	Service
Control of nature	Natural systems
Degradation	Re-creation

INVOLVEMENT

There is another factor in the performance equation, subtler perhaps, but so pervasive that some people find it hard to put their finger on – for now it is being labeled "populism." There is a growing awareness that is leading people to demand more involvement in the decisions that affect them, at work, at play, locally, nationally, and even globally. Decisions made by traditional authorities, governments, and other institutions previously immune to challenge are being called into question and sometimes brought to book by the media, pressure groups, and concerned individuals. Is this not what was happening within the former Soviet Union and the Eastern bloc, leading to the collapse of communism from 1989 to 1991? The revolutionary wave of the Arab Spring (or Democracy Spring) that began in Tunisia in 2010 was fueled by people wanting to bring down the regime. In today's society it is easier to get a hearing than ever before, and cracks are appearing in impregnable citadels' dubious respectability. Those who have something to hide may hunker down and snarl, but the majority of thinking people welcome this kind of change, even if it does generate some feelings of insecurity. Of course, the demand to be heard can lead to some unexpected consequences, such as in 2016, when swathes of alienated people on one side of the Atlantic voted for the UK to exit the European Union (the so-called Brexit) and on the other for Donald Trump as President of the United States.

ENDING THE BLAME CULTURE

Companies often talk about getting rid of the "blame culture" – but just as often they take no action. Blame is endemic to business and endemic to a dictating philosophy and, let's face it, it is a natural human tendency. But blame is about history, fear, and the past. We need to refocus on aspiration, hope, and the future. Not only does the fear of blame inhibit even the most calculated risk taking, it blocks honest recognition, identification, and acknowledgment of the inefficiencies in a system. Blame evokes defensiveness – defensiveness reduces awareness. Appropriate adjustments cannot be put in place without accurate feedback. Fundamental culture change will not happen if blame comes along too. But most businesses, and most people, will have great difficulty leaving blame behind.

REDUCING STRESS

There is another good reason for increasing self-responsibility at work. Work-related stress is said to be reaching epidemic levels. According to a joint report by the European Foundation for the Improvement of Living and Working Conditions and the European Agency for Safety and Health at Work, workers in countries with more job autonomy experience less stress than those with equally demanding jobs but less autonomy. This in itself suggests an urgent need for change toward working practices that encourage personal responsibility.

But what is the reason for this correlation between stress and lack of personal control? Self-esteem is the life force of the personality, and if that is suppressed or diminished, so is the person. Stress results from long periods of suppression. Offering someone choice and control wherever possible in the workplace acknowledges and validates their capability and their self-esteem. A leadership style which fails to do this increases stress: "lack of coaching" and "low self-esteem" were among the main sources of job stress identified by the Canadian Union of Public Employees, for instance.

PERSONAL RESPONSIBILITY IS KEY TO SURVIVAL

However, for many people the fear of change, any change, looms large. This is not surprising when you consider there is little we can do to prepare our children for the world they are going to live in. It certainly won't be as we have known it, but we don't know how it will be. Yet this is not just about external change, it is internal change that will enable flexibility and adaptability to cope with whatever will be. When much of what we know and love is in flux, full acceptance of personal responsibility becomes a physical and psychological necessity for survival.

Introducing The Performance Curve

In the past, I have advocated examining what an individual's process of psychological development can tell us about the direction in which companies, communities, and cultures are evolving, and the stages through which they will pass on the journey. What sets this out very simply is a model that my colleagues at Performance Consultants have created called The Performance Curve, which I am eager to introduce here in this Fifth Edition of *Coaching for Performance*.

The late management professor Peter Drucker is credited with saying that "culture eats strategy for breakfast." I could not agree more: culture is key, and yet very few organizations take a proactive approach to creating and measuring their culture. *The Conference Board CEO Challenge* also confirms that "across the spectrum, the cultural DNA of an organization is critical to success, from operational efficiency to better customer service, to greater talent attraction and retention, to higher levels of business performance and breakthroughs in innovation."

It is on the collective prevailing mindset of the culture that The Performance Curve focuses, and how this creates the conditions for performance (see Figure 2). The greatest influencers of an organization's culture are its leaders, so it is not surprising that studies by the Hay Group and others show that leadership behavior affects bottom-line performance by up to 30 percent. It is the leaders who are the gatekeepers to performance, and it is the lever of leadership behavior that we focus on in this book.

In The Performance Curve, each of the four stages is represented by an overall cultural mindset (shown in italics). As you look at this developmental model of performance, it helps to recall Maslow's Hierarchy of Needs from Chapter 1. Also, Gallwey's Inner Game Equation; above the line depicts interference decreasing, below the line potential increasing as performance improves. Each mindset creates distinct organizational characteristics and relates to a certain level of performance. As you look at the model, reflect on what mindset you operate from on a daily basis.

Of course, what The Performance Curve looks at is the maturity of an organization's behavior, not the maturity of an organization's management systems. However, we can extrapolate what we would likely find and have done so in Table 2.

The question to ask of course is: What is the culture of your team or organization? When thinking about this, it is important to bear in mind that you are looking for the prevailing mindset within your organization or your team. It might be the case that different parts of your organization operate on different parts of the curve. The Performance Curve is a useful tool for coaches to explore the prevailing cultural ethos and mindset with their coachees and for leaders to explore that of their culture. Once people become aware of their current mindset and the direct link between mindset and performance, they can choose to change. Awareness really is curative, as we shall explore in Part II.

FIGURE 2: *The Performance Curve*

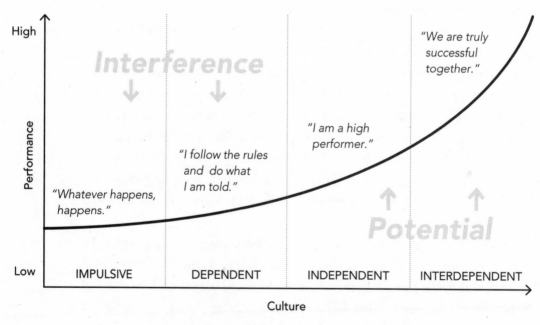

Each incremental move to the right yields bottom-line results

TABLE 2: *The Performance Curve: Four stages of organizational development*

	Impulsive	Dependent	Independent	Interdependent
Quick glance	• *"Whatever happens, happens."* • Lack of systems and structure • Haphazard and inconsistent leadership	• *"I follow the rules and do what I am told."* • Hierarchy • Leaders that command and control	• *"I am a high performer."* • Systems support individual goals • Leaders that empower	• *"We are truly successful together."* • Meaning and purpose unite • Teams that self-govern
Performance	Low	Low–medium	Medium–high	High
Maslow's motivators	Survival	Belonging	Esteem	Self-actualization
Inner Game	High interference Low potential	High–medium interference Low–medium potential	Low–medium interference Medium–high potential	Low interference High potential
What does the culture look like?				
Prevailing cultural mindset	"Whatever happens, happens."	"I follow the rules and do what I am told."	"I am a high performer."	"We are truly successful together."
Cultural characteristics	Minimal awareness and responsibility. The organization reacts to situations as they arise. Feels unpredictable. Little communication, engagement and development. Survival mentality.	Low–medium awareness and responsibility. The organization is focused on maintaining stability and following the rules. Individuals focus on process and task completion with little opportunity for autonomy. Strong sense of group identity; people feel the need to fit in. Strong one-way communication and varying levels of recognition. Low engagement and trust. Risk averse mentality.	Medium–high awareness; high responsibility for own performance. The organization supports innovation and individual development. People believe they can make a difference with their own actions. Individuals may focus on achieving own goals above team or organization goals. Work–life balance may be hard to reach. Two-way communication and engagement. Achievement mentality.	High awareness and responsibility – self and others. Strong coaching culture. Teams feel strong sense of ownership for high performance and believe this can only be achieved by the group. People engage with others to understand diverse viewpoints, and display high levels of trust, care, and collaboration. Continual authentic communication and feedback. Collective potential mentality.

TABLE 2: *The Performance Curve: Four stages of organizational development (cont.)*

Organizational systems	Fundamental systems not in place; roles and responsibilities unlikely to be defined. No aligning factors.	Systems and processes focus on efficiency and tend to be rigid; strict application of rules. Aligning factors are rules and targets.	Systems support continuous improvement and learning, and individual goals. Aligning factors are values and standards.	Principle-led adaptive systems underpin agility, continual, collective learning, and support performance at every level. Aligning factors are shared vision, meaning, purpose, and direction.
Connection to organization's vision and purpose	No connection. No consistent vision.	Low connection. The vision extends to the pursuit of profit; would be strengthened by including people, e.g., *"We aim to be the biggest telecoms company in the world."*	Medium–high connection. The vision encompasses people and profit; would be strengthened by extending to the planet, e.g., *"We are dedicated to enhancing our customers' lives through connection."*	High connection. The vision embraces people, profit, and planet, e.g., *"With great courage, integrity, and love we embrace our responsibility to co-create a world where each of us, our communities, and our planet can flourish, while celebrating the sheer love and joy of food."**
What are leaders doing?				
Leadership style	Haphazard and inconsistent. Leader may be enthusiastic but does whatever it takes to succeed short-term, often getting involved in everything. Little focus on long-term vision and direction.	Command and control – transactional. Leader may focus on a clear hierarchy to get work done and to maintain stability and consistency. Leaders may display territorial behaviors, competing between themselves. Tendency to blame.	Delegating – enabling individual transformation. Leader is acquiring a coaching mindset, empowering individuals to perform, focusing on creating efficient high performance, adaptability, and continuous learning.	Partnering and supporting – collaborative, collective transformation. Leader takes a support/servant role, creating a coaching culture and inspiring high-performing, self-governing teams with a focus on the common good.

* Whole Foods Market – the other visions have been created for illustrative purposes

TABLE 2: *The Performance Curve: Four stages of organizational development (cont.)*

Leader's impact	Leader's behavior causes confusion, frustration, and stress.	Leader is (albeit unknowingly) limiting people's potential. Fear of failure can crush initiative and creativity and lower engagement.	Leader enables individuals to achieve goals and be accountable. Teamwork is encouraged.	Leader inspires and enables great teamwork and commitment. Community spirit pervades the organization within the context of serving a higher purpose.
Interference for leaders and how to address	Short-termism. This leader reacts to each situation from a position of fear, which creates an inconsistent short-term experience. This leader needs to focus on becoming self-aware as well as developing fundamental strategic, management, and leadership skills.	Judgment and lack of trust. This leader sees themselves as the expert and other people as right or wrong, which creates a polarizing effect. Believing that people's intentions are good and using curiosity instead of judgment will move the culture from fear to trust, evolving to the next stage of the curve.	Control. This leader retains a level of involvement and may be too attached to their personal agenda. Focusing on letting go of control, setting aside their personal agenda, and working for the common good means the leader can support the transition to interdependence and a focus on the collective.	Self-importance. This leader may experience lapses in the levels of higher consciousness at which they generally operate. For example, tipping from self-belief into "guru status" and not listening to feedback, or experiencing inconsistencies in living their ethical standards. This leader must work to keep in balance, and stay grounded and open to feedback, so as not to revert to any of the earlier stages.
How 1:1 coaching or a coaching leadership style will improve performance	Coaching for awareness and responsibility of personal impact, development of key management skills.	Coaching for enabling empowerment and ownership further down the organization to improve agility and adaptability.	Coaching for widening perspective and inspiring collaboration.	Coaching for collective performance, unity, and social responsibility – taking time to consciously create the direction of travel, to continuously develop and improve while maintaining balance.

A COACHING MINDSET CREATES HIGH PERFORMANCE

So how is it that coaching creates high performance? How do we know that high performance is correlated with an **interdependent**, integrated culture? How is all this proven?

Answers to these questions come from our work with multinational clients, the most recent example of which I'd like to share with you here. Linde AG, one of the leading gas and engineering companies in the world, approached us to bring in a safety performance culture across its plants. As the team looked into the work Linde was already doing, they were enormously impressed by the extent to which it was measuring its culture. This is something that we at Performance Consultants have long believed needs to be done universally but, as I've already said, few companies do it. When the team examined why Linde was so sophisticated in measuring its culture, they found the answer: people's lives were at stake.

Companies like Linde are what are termed "high reliability organizations" (HROs), organizations that seek to sustain error-free performance despite operating in complex and hazardous conditions where the consequences of a mistake could be catastrophic; a life-and-death situation. Other types of organizations that would be regarded as HROs include oil companies, airline carriers, air control authorities, nuclear power generators, and petrochemical plants.

Our team investigated the work done by HROs and others in the area of "safety maturity" and found that extensive work had indeed been conducted. Safety maturity models look at the maturity of an organization's safety behavior by assessing its safety culture. There are many models, variously mapping safety results across anything from three to eight stages of behavior maturity, as Foster and Hoult report. Looking through the lens of coaching, each of those stages relates to human development and the levels of Maslow's Hierarchy of Needs (see Chapter 1) and William Schutz's theory of interpersonal behavior in teams (see Chapter 17). They also correlate with the leader's level of emotional intelligence. As with individuals, cultures are seen to develop in stages.

Safety maturity models focus on safety, but the team recognized the principles of Gallwey's Inner Game in there and realized that the work on safety could be extended to include a view of the overall performance of an organization. Gallwey's equation states that performance can be enhanced by decreasing interference – inner obstacles such as fear, doubt, self-criticism, and limiting beliefs or assumptions. The command-and-control structure of traditional management creates interference because, by definition, what people are doing is following the rules of what they have been told. There is little room for the potential of the human being to come through, and the result is that both performance and enjoyment levels will be low. Thus, as a top-down, command-and-control approach is replaced by a coaching style of leadership, interference decreases, potential can emerge, and performance will improve.

This is where The Performance Curve differs from the safety models. We have shifted the focus from safety performance to apply it to one key overall indicator, performance. By looking at The Performance Curve, organizations or individuals can have an immediate idea of where they are operating, either from the perspective of "this is the culture of my organization" or "this is the culture I create." From that awareness, they will gain insight into what needs to change in order to improve performance.

Perhaps the best-known safety maturity model is DuPont's Bradley Curve. The story of how it came about will give some insight into how an organization's cultural maturity has a direct impact on general performance. In the 1990s, chemical giant DuPont set out to establish why some locations were performing better than others in terms of operating safely. Its team talked to between 500 and 1,000 workers at each of its sites around the world, across the organization. Their survey showed that there was a direct correlation between the group's culture and how safe, how productive, and how profitable it was. In other words, they found that as culture matured, performance improved across the board. Inspired by Stephen Covey's Seven Habits, Verlon Bradley, manager of DuPont's Beaumont plant, established that he could correlate the behaviors found at each site with Covey's framework of dependence, independence, and interdependence, and map them to safety performance. Of course, Covey was exploring a model of individual development and his genius was that he translated this so articulately and practically into leadership effectiveness. Later, in 2009, DuPont conducted a study based on data collected in the previous 10 years across 64 industries in 41 countries, which demonstrated a direct correlation between the strength of the organization's safety culture and its injury frequency rate and sustainable safety performance, exactly as predicted by the Bradley Curve. The 2009 study on safety serves to reinforce its earlier survey, which showed that cultural maturity is correlated with high organizational performance.

Linde had completed a company-wide culture survey of its 65,000 employees using DuPont's Bradley Curve and found that it was in the dependent sector of that model. One member of the Linde Engineering team, James Thieme, Global HSE Manager, had been on our public Coaching for Performance workshop and realized that a coaching leadership approach mirrored the behaviors required of an interdependent culture. After securing an internal program sponsor, Kai Gransee, Head of Construction & Commissioning HSE, who also saw the link, Thieme approached us to partner with his team and bring these behaviors into his organization. Through a mix of in-person workshops for senior leaders and self-paced e-learning for managers and supervisors, the team taught Linde's people a coaching approach to safety. Let me give an example of what this looks like in practice.

MOVING FROM HIERARCHY TO COACHING FOSTERS LEARNING AND RESPONSIBILITY

In a **dependent** culture, such as that found at Linde, people follow rules. The prevailing mindset of managers is "if only they would do what I tell them" which leads to blame and judgment being rife. After all, when we think someone has done something wrong, what is our first response? The natural human tendency is to criticize or blame. Research by psychologist John Gottman shows that when criticism becomes pervasive it leads to relationship failure. In fact, criticism is such a negative communication style that it is likened to the first of the Four Horsemen of the Apocalypse, in reference to the allegorical figures from the Bible whose arrival heralds the end of the world. Gottman's research into marital relationships revealed the reason for this: if blame and criticism are a prevalent communication style and this doesn't change, relationship failure can be predicted with over 90 percent accuracy.

How this manifests in organizations is that it breaks down relationships and blocks learning. This is described by Andrew Hopkins in his book *Failure to Learn* about the BP Texas City refinery explosion in 2005, which killed 15 workers and injured more than 170 others. Hopkins says: "It is an interesting feature of human psychology that, once we have found someone to blame, the quest for explanation seems to come to an end." He adds that this is a false conclusion, because no one has found out why those people did those things in that way. The learning has been blocked. We can clearly see therefore how the prevailing mindset of the leaders creates the conditions for lower performance.

What leaders can do instead is use the coaching skill of curiosity – the antidote to blame. When behaviors like blame cease, interferences like fear and self-doubt decrease. In teaching general coaching principles and practices, our training at Linde highlighted behaviors like judgment and blame, which raise interferences to learning, and taught as alternatives the interdependent behaviors of curiosity and partnering, which raise potential. In this example, we can see Gallwey's Inner Game Equation in action. The impact of this was a staggering 74 percent decrease in incidents with clear benefits to people, planet, and profit. In terms of The Performance Curve, that is a significant tangible improvement in performance. Each incremental shift in mindset toward interdependence leads to improved performance.

Another example of an organization consciously looking to move from a dependent culture is tire manufacturing company Michelin. They ran a successful initiative to replace hierarchy with trust at production plants in six countries. Andrew Hill of *The Financial Times* says team members in Le Puy-en-Velay, France, now describe their leaders as coaches. Product line team leader, Olivier Duplain admits that not issuing orders feels like losing power, "But we get 10 times as much back from the team." Not surprisingly, CEO Jean-Dominique Senard has announced a plan for the whole group – more than 105,000 employees, at plants in 17 countries – to become more agile and more responsive to customers based on empowerment and responsibility.

An interdependent mindset equals a high-performance mindset

The Performance Curve finally depicts what many people in human development have known for a while: a coaching leadership style is the enabler for a high-performance culture, because it shifts the organizational mindset to interdependence. Maslow in his hierarchy described the conditions for self-actualization, which correlate to interdependence. And Stephen Covey in *The Seven Habits of Highly Effective People* said: "As we look at the terrain ahead, we see that we are entering a whole new dimension. Whether you are the president of a company or the janitor, the moment you step from independence into interdependence in any capacity, you step into a leadership role."

The invitation is for leaders to develop themselves to be able to lead interdependent organizations in which people can grow and fulfill their potential. By enabling an interdependent culture, organizations tap into the potential of every employee and change the very relationship between employees and organizations. This is the cutting edge of coaching and organizational development.

I have one big question still looming: Why aren't all organizations actively measuring their culture? HROs such as Linde have no choice but to take a proactive approach to culture – for them it is literally a matter of life and death. I believe that in the future all companies will measure and take a proactive approach to their culture. After all, if you can't measure it, you can't manage it.

Now that you understand how important coaching for performance is, and also how coaching really is bigger than coaching, let's explore the principles of coaching – the attitudes and behaviors that underpin high performance.

PART II

The Principles of Coaching

3   Coaching Is Emotional Intelligence in Practice

Emotional intelligence (EQ) is twice as important as cognitive ability (IQ) in predicting outstanding performance
Daniel Goleman

Coaching is a way of being

Coaching is not merely a technique to be wheeled out and rigidly applied in certain prescribed circumstances. It is a way of leading and managing, a way of treating people, a way of thinking, a way of being. Roll on the day when the word "coaching" disappears from our lexicon altogether and it just becomes the way we relate to one another at work, and elsewhere too. Why, you may ask, do I advocate coaching as the fundamental way of operating? Why is it so impactful for leaders to be coached and to incorporate coaching skills to create their own coaching leadership style?

Transformational coaching is the practice of emotional intelligence. Before examining what that means, I invite you to do a quick activity. Being aware that emotional intelligence will be high in key people who have positively influenced your life will help you to understand its power. The following activity is an exercise we use in our workshops that you can do now to experience the impact of emotional intelligence on yourself. Note down your own answers before you read further.

Recall someone you loved being with when you were younger – not a parent, but perhaps a grandparent, a teacher, or a role model. When you were with this person:	**ACTIVITY:** *Experiencing Emotional Intelligence*
1. What did they do that you liked so much?	
2. How did you feel?	
Think about the person's attitudes and behaviors. Write down your answers.	

Having run this exercise all over the world, we find that people everywhere have broadly the same response. The commonality of the characteristics and qualities that people recall remains true regardless of country or culture. Do you see your answers or similar in this list?

The person . . .	I felt . . .
• Listened to me	• Special
• Believed in me	• Valued
• Challenged me	• Confident
• Trusted and respected me	• Safe, cared for
• Gave me time and full attention	• Supported
	• Fun, enthusiasm
• Treated me as equal	• Self-belief

Of course there are other responses too, but these are the most consistent. Becoming more emotionally intelligent or choosing appropriate behaviors is not about checking a list of your competencies and behaviors against an academic ideal. It is much simpler to practice by recalling your special older person and comparing yourself with what they would think or do under this or that circumstance. They had loads of emotional intelligence, so use them as a role model. And reflect on these questions: What would people say about you? How do you make people feel?

Emotional intelligence is the ability to relate to others from a paradigm of trust, rather than one of fear, and it therefore sits firmly in the interdependent sector of The Performance Curve, which generates high performance. It was not until 1995 that Daniel Goleman's book made emotional intelligence not only acceptable, but desirable to the point of necessity in business. Goleman's research indicated that high emotional intelligence (what he termed EQ or EI) confers a significant performance advantage on leaders. It found that emotional intelligence is twice as important, 66 percent to 34 percent, as academic or technical knowledge for success at work – for everyone, not just leaders, and in terms of both relationships and productivity. For leadership roles, the ratio is even greater and accounts for more than 85 percent of "star performance" in top leaders. Everyone began to want some. It is a prerequisite for a professional coach and it is key to being a great leader.

Emotional intelligence can be described as interpersonal intelligence or, even more simply, as personal and social skills. Goleman and others have defined many competencies, including self-confidence, empathy, adaptability, and being a change catalyst, which can be grouped neatly into four domains: self-awareness, self-management, social awareness, and relationship management. That sounds straightforward enough and all of us combine these skills to some degree. Emotionally intelligent people just embody them more fully than others.

EMOTIONAL INTELLIGENCE AS A LIFE SKILL

If emotional intelligence is such an important life skill, and school is supposed to prepare children for life, it is an inexcusable omission that all schools do not include classes in it. The assumption is, of course, that such social skills are learned through social interaction with peers and adults, and that they cannot or need not be taught. This is erroneous on both counts. In fact, school would provide an ideal environment for developing the emotional intelligence of young people, through play, structured interactive exercises, and coaching.

Awareness

One-to-one coaching or teaching a group of leaders to adopt a transformational coaching style is the most powerful way to develop the emotional intelligence competencies that have been shown to create high performance. It all starts with one of the key pillars of coaching: awareness (see Figure 3). The reason for this is that awareness is curative: humans are natural learning systems. Once we become aware of something, we have the choice to change it. Awareness has various aspects:

- **AWARENESS OF SELF – understanding why you do what you do**
Learn to recognize your human tendencies, internal interferences, and biases in order to consciously choose responses rather than reacting. This will lead to improved performance by self-managing and overcoming your inner obstacles to achieving your potential.

• **AWARENESS OF OTHERS – seeing the person behind the performance** Learn to spot people's strengths, interferences, and motivations in order to manage relationships and inspire and collaborate successfully with individuals and teams. Improve social skills by getting curious about, listening to, and partnering with those you work with.

• **AWARENESS OF ORGANIZATION – creating a positive impact on the culture** Learn to align individual, team, and organizational goals and develop a coaching style which leads to high performance, learning, and enjoyment.

FIGURE 3: *Transformational coaching is the practice of emotional intelligence*

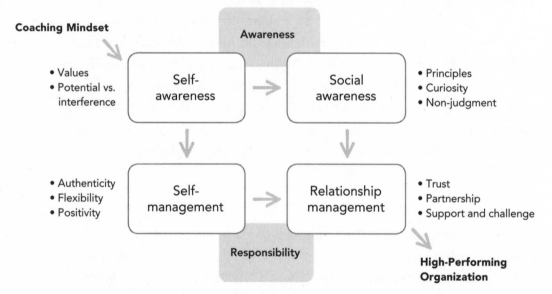

Spiritual intelligence

No sooner had we digested the impact of emotional intelligence than several new books appeared advocating the merits of spiritual intelligence (or SQ, as it became known). Spiritual in this sense is not a religious concept, but is defined by authors Ian Mitroff and Elizabeth Denton as "the basic desire to find ultimate meaning and purpose in one's life and to live an integrated life." Meaning and purpose are the drivers for Maslow's level of self-actualization and the mindset of interdependence. In their book on spiritual intelligence, Danah Zohar and Ian Marshall quote a 36-year-old businessman describing his crisis of meaning in his corporate life:

I am managing a large and successful company here in Sweden. I have good health; I have a wonderful family, a position in the community. I suppose I have "power." But still I am not certain what I am doing with my life. I am not certain I am on the right path doing the job that I do.

He explained that he was very worried about the state of the world, especially the condition of the global environment and the breakdown of the community. He felt people were avoiding the real scale of the problems facing them. Big businesses like his were especially guilty of not addressing such problems. "I want to do something about it," he continued. "I want, if you like, to use my life to serve, but I don't know how. I just know that I want to be part of the solution. Not the problem."

As John McFarlane says in the Foreword to this book: "Our responsibility as leaders is to create an exciting but safe adventure for our people, worthy of them devoting their lives to." People want to be part of the solution and to do something meaningful with their lives. Organizations can tap into this by helping their leaders develop a coaching style. And external coaches can help develop a more emotionally intelligent leader through 1:1 coaching.

So what skills does the leader or coach need? Certainly, they need to develop the fundamental skills of asking powerful questions to raise **awareness** and **responsibility**, listening well, and following the GROW model, which are all described in Part III. To be most effective they need to move to a more advanced level of coaching. There is so much more to coaching which would take the leader and coach into the next evolution of themselves, and indeed the next evolution of the organization for which they work. An in-depth description of advanced coaching goes beyond the scope of this book, but some of the background and concepts that underpin our advanced coaching workshops are introduced in Part V.

We find that exercises like the following visualization activity help people to get in touch with the sort of leader they want to become. The leader they envision as their future self usually embodies emotional intelligence. Which attributes of emotional intelligence described earlier did your future self embody most? Thinking about the present, how much do you embody those attributes now? Pick one to focus on and bring more fully into your work. If you would like to do some coaching on this to develop yourself further, complete the self-coaching exercise in the Coaching Question Toolkit (Question Bag 1).

ACTIVITY:
Vizualization

Get into a comfortable position, sitting and with both feet on the floor. Notice how the ground feels under your feet. Roll your shoulders to loosen them. Notice your breath, breathing in and breathing out. As you breathe in, imagine that you are breathing in clarity and fresh air. As you breathe out, imagine that you are breathing out any worries or concerns. Take three deep breaths like that.

Now imagine you are walking down a street on a sunny day. Look around and notice what the street looks like and what it feels like to walk down this street. In a moment you are going to meet someone coming the other way. This person will be you in the future, your future self. Your future self is living their dream as a leader. As you walk along, you see this person, your future self, in the distance coming toward you. As you meet them, greet them. Notice how they greet you. Really look at this person. What do you notice? How do they behave? How they make you feel? Is there a question you want to ask them? If so, ask that question now and listen to hear the answer.

Now, say goodbye to this person and thank them for coming to meet you here today.

Take a couple of moments to come back to the present, starting by bringing your awareness back to how you are sitting. Next, wiggle your toes and fingers. And finally, feel perfectly refreshed, revitalized, and present. Write down what you wish to remember of the visualization as you bring it to a close.

GUIDING PRINCIPLES

What are the guiding principles that will help emotionally intelligent leaders create a meaningful and purposeful journey for their people?

• **Successful leaders of the future will lead in a coaching style rather than command and control** Talent retention is a vital issue and expectations about the way people are treated are rising fast. Prescription, instruction, autocracy, and hierarchy are losing traction and acceptability. Good people want more choice, more responsibility, and more fun in their lives, and that includes the workplace.

• **Leadership style determines performance and a coaching style delivers the highest performance** The relationship between performance and leadership style is well documented – see the previous chapter for further discussion on this. What business would not like better performance? This is widely accepted intellectually in organizations, in both public and private sectors, but they still struggle to embed and embody the behaviors they advocate. In many cases both leaders and followers collude to resist change, even though that benefits neither.

• **Helping others to build their awareness, their responsibility, and consequently their self-belief lays the foundation stones of their own future leadership capability** Leaders by definition have to make choices and decisions every day. To do so effectively, they require these fundamental personal attributes. Coaching builds leaders, and there is a lack of leadership today, in every sector, in every institution, and in every country.

• **The external context within which organizations operate is changing fast, due in large measure to circumstances outside the control of the company or even the country** Globalization, instant communication, economic crises, corporate social responsibility, and huge environmental issues are a few obvious examples, and there are many more. Coping with these, along with the speed of change itself, demands new leadership qualities.

The next chapter addresses how the role of leader as coach can help achieve this kind of high-performance culture.

4 The Leader as Coach

Leaders must be experienced as a support by their team, not as a threat

There is a paradox in coaching leadership, because the leader traditionally holds the pay check, the key to promotion, and also the axe. This is fine so long as you believe that the only way to motivate is through the judicious application of the carrot and the stick. However, for coaching to work at its best, the relationship between the coach and the coachee must be one of partnership in the endeavor, of trust, of safety, and of minimal pressure. The check, the key, and the axe have no place here, as they can serve only to inhibit such a relationship.

Can a leader be a coach?

Can a leader, therefore, be a coach at all? Yes, but as discussed in the previous chapter, coaching is emotional intelligence in practice and demands the highest qualities of that leader: empathy, integrity, and balance, as well as a willingness, in most cases, to adopt a fundamentally different approach to employees. Coaching leaders will also have to find their own way, for there are few role models for them to follow, and they may experience initial resistance from some of their employees, who might be suspicious of any departure from traditional management. They may fear the additional personal responsibility implicit in a coaching style of leadership. These problems can be anticipated and generally are easily coached away, but a different set of behaviors is required.

Traditional management

The polarities of management or the communication style with which we are familiar place an autocratic approach at one end of the spectrum, and laissez faire and hope for the best on the other. Traditional management rests in the dependent and independent stages of The Performance Curve, and can be illustrated as in Figure 4.

FIGURE 4: *Traditional management*

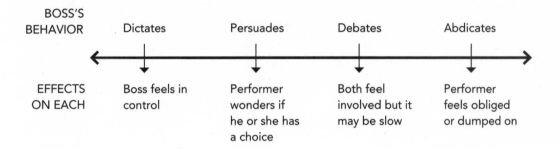

BOSS'S BEHAVIOR	Dictates	Persuades	Debates	Abdicates
EFFECTS ON EACH	Boss feels in control	Performer wonders if he or she has a choice	Both feel involved but it may be slow	Performer feels obliged or dumped on

DICTATES

When I was a little boy, my parents told me what to do and scolded me when I didn't. When I went to school, my teachers told me what to do and caned me if I didn't. When I joined the army, the sergeant told me what to do and God help me if I didn't, so I did! When I got my first job, my boss told me what to do too. So when I reached a position of some authority, what did I do? I told people what to do, because that is what all my role models had done. That is true for the majority of us: we have been brought up on telling, and we are very good at it.

The attraction of telling or dictating is that, besides being quick and easy, it provides the dictator with the feeling of being in control. This is, however, a fallacy. A dictator upsets and demotivates their employees, but those employees dare not show it or offer feedback, which would not have been heard anyway. The result is that they are subservient in the dictator's presence, but behave differently when their back is turned, with resentment, with poor performance at best, maybe by downing tools or even by sabotage. Dictators are anything but in control – they are deluding themselves.

There is another problem with the dictating end of the traditional management spectrum: recall. Quite simply, we do not remember very well something we are told. The matrix in Figure 5 is an oft-used part of training folklore, but it is so relevant that it warrants being included here.

It was a piece of research first carried out some time ago by IBM, and has been repeated, and the results confirmed, by other studies since. A group of people were divided randomly into three subgroups, each of which was taught something quite simple, the same thing, using three different approaches. The results speak for themselves and again reflect the adult learning theory that people learn best through experience. One issue they demonstrate that particularly concerns us here, however, is how dramatically recall declines when people are only told something.

FIGURE 5: *Recall scores after training*

	Told	Told and shown	Told, shown, and experienced
Recall after 3 weeks	70%	72%	85%
Recall after 3 months	10%	32%	65%

I well remember showing this to a couple of parachute-jumping trainers, who became very concerned that they taught emergency procedures only by telling. They hurried to change their system before they were faced with a terminal freefall!

PERSUADES

If we move along the traditional management spectrum to the right, we come to selling or persuading. Here the boss lays out their good idea and attempts to convince us how great it is. We know better than to challenge them, so we smile demurely and carry out their instructions. Nicer maybe, if a bit phoney, and it gives the appearance of being more democratic. But is it really? We still end up doing exactly what the boss wants and they get little input from us. Nothing much has changed.

DISCUSSES

When we get further along the line to discussing, resources are genuinely pooled and the good leader may be willing to follow a path other than their own option, provided it is going in the right direction. The late British industrialist Sir John Harvey-Jones, interviewed about team leadership for David Hemery's book *Sporting Excellence*, said:

> *If the direction everyone else wants is not where I thought we should go, I'll go . . . once the thing is rolling, you can change direction anyway. I may see they were right or they may realize it isn't the right place to be and head towards my preferred course, or we may both come to realize that we would rather be in a third alternative. In industry, you can only move with the hearts and minds.*

Attractive as democratic discussion may be, it can be time-consuming and result in indecision.

ABDICATES

The far end of the scale, just leaving their direct reports to get on with it, frees the leader for other duties and gives individuals freedom of choice. It is, however, risky for both. The leader has abdicated their responsibility, although the buck still stops with them, and individuals may perform poorly due to a lack of awareness of many aspects of the task. A leader may sometimes withdraw with good intent, wishing to force their employees to learn to cope with more responsibility. This strategy seldom serves its purpose, because if the direct report feels obliged to take responsibility, rather than choosing to do so, their personal ownership remains low and their performance will not reflect the benefit of the self-motivation that the leader hopes to generate.

COACHING

The majority of leaders will position themselves somewhere between these extremes, but coaching lies on a different plane altogether. It combines the benefits of both ends of the scale with the risks of neither (see Figure 6).

In responding to their leader's coaching questions, an individual becomes aware of every aspect of the task and the actions that are necessary. This clarity enables them to envisage the near certainty of success, and so to choose to take responsibility. By listening to the answers to the coaching questions, the leader knows not only the action plan but the thinking that went into it. They are now far better informed than they would be if they told the coachee what to do, and therefore there is greater alignment between the two. Since the dialogue and relationships in coaching are non-threatening and supportive, no behavior change occurs when the leader is absent. Coaching provides the leader with real not illusory control through the common understanding that has been created, and provides the coachee with real not illusory responsibility.

FIGURE 6: *A coaching leadership style*

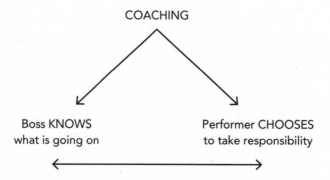

COACHING

Boss KNOWS
what is going on

Performer CHOOSES
to take responsibility

The role of the leader

What this discussion generates is: What is the role of a leader? Many leaders too frequently find themselves fire-fighting, struggling to get the job done. By their own admission, they are unable to devote the time they feel they should to long-term planning, to creating a vision, to taking an overview, to surveying alternatives, the competition, new products, and the like. Most importantly, they are unable to devote the time to growing their people, to employee development. They send people on a training course or two and kid themselves that that will do it. They seldom get their money's worth.

A leader's task is simple: to get the job done and to develop employees. Time and cost pressures limit the latter. Coaching is one process with both effects.

So how can leaders find the time to coach their employees? It is so much quicker to dictate. The paradoxical answer is that if leaders do coach their employees, the developing employees shoulder much greater responsibility, freeing leaders from fire-fighting not only to coach more, but to attend to those overarching issues that only they are required to address. So the activity of developing people represents enlightened self-interest rather than idealism that offers no added value. Sure, at times it will be all hands to the pumps and to hell with the niceties, but that is acceptable and accepted in a culture in which people feel cared for.

Leaders often ask me when they should coach, or at least how they should decide whether to coach or tell. The answer is quite simple:

• If **time** is the predominant criterion in a situation (e.g., in an immediate crisis), doing the job yourself or telling someone else exactly what to do will probably be the fastest way. But note that this is only time saving in the short term; in the long term this behavior creates dependency.

• If the **quality** of the result matters most (e.g., a full and detailed report needs to be created), coaching for high awareness and responsibility is likely to deliver the most.

• If maximizing the **learning** is predominant (e.g., a person doing something for the first time), clearly coaching will optimize learning and its retention.

• If buy-in and real **commitment** are necessary (e.g., implementing a service improvement), then coaching creates the possibility of this much more than telling, which is likely to achieve compliance, resistance, and a lack of ownership.

• If **engagement** and retention are important (e.g., high potentials, millennials), then coaching is the most effective approach to align individuals' wants, needs, and expectations with the organization's mission, thus creating meaning and purpose for people at work.

In most situations in the workplace, time, quality, and learning all have some relevance all of the time. The sad truth is that in most businesses, time takes precedence over quality and learning is relegated to a poor third. Is it surprising that leaders have such a hard time giving up telling, and that business performance falls far short of what it could and should be?

If leaders manage by the principles of coaching, they get the job done to a higher standard and develop their people simultaneously. It sounds too good to be true to have 250 days a year of getting the job done and 250 days a year of employee development per person, but that is precisely what a coaching leader does get.

On-the-job development

Each day, there are opportunities for on-the-job development. Let's look at an example of an employee, Sue, who is working on a task that had been discussed and agreed with her leader the previous week. She has a problem and goes to find her leader, Mo:

SUE: I did what we agreed but it isn't working.
MO: Try doing it this way instead then.

No coaching there. Sue is dependent on Mo for the answer and Mo is creating that dependent culture. But here is an alternative based on the coaching principle of interdependence:

SUE: I did what we agreed but it isn't working.
MO: I know you've put a lot of thought into getting it working. What do you think is the best thing to do next?
SUE: Well, I could go back to see exactly when the blockage occurs in case that shows up anything new.
MO: OK, that makes sense. Anything else?
SUE: Not at this stage, but if that doesn't work then I guess we'll need to take a look at the original calculations.
MO: Sounds like a good plan. You're getting there, Sue, even though it may feel like you're not. I know you will crack this. Let me know how it goes.

The next morning, Mo checks in with Sue:

MO: How did it go?

SUE: Pretty well, actually. I discovered that it was a timing issue and I now know what exactly needs to be changed to get it working.

MO: That's great! Your determination and incredible attention to detail have paid off. What needs to happen now?

SUE: I just need to persuade Sanjeev to change the code as soon as possible, but I know he's got a lot on right now.

MO: What do you think will persuade Sanjeev to make this a priority?

SUE: If you asked him to do it.

MO: Why don't you have a conversation with Sanjeev first? I sense that you have more influence than you think. Let's check in again before lunch.

SUE: OK, I'll give it a try.

Just before lunch, Sue lets Mo know how the conversation went:

SUE: I managed to get Sanjeev to make the code changes straight away and it's all working fine now.

MO: That's great news, Sue. Well done. What did you do to influence Sanjeev?

SUE: I asked him if he could help and explained how critical it was to get it working today.

MO: What was different to previous times you've tried to get Sanjeev to do something at short notice?

SUE: I asked him as opposed to telling him he had to do it. It was as simple as that.

MO: What you did was simple, yet very effective. What have you learned through this whole process?

SUE: To keep things simple and not to make assumptions about people.

In the alternative example, Mo embraces the two key principles of coaching, awareness and responsibility, which we will look at in Chapter 6. In this brief interaction Mo showed no blame or irritation, and helped Sue to solve the issue herself, believe in herself, and learn from the experience.

Also, Mo helped build this high-performance culture of interdependence by championing Sue to build stronger relationships with her peers.

The application of coaching

When and where do we use coaching and what for? As we have discussed, coaching is on-the-job development; a coaching mindset is a way of being and so is relevant whatever you are doing. As we shall explore in the next chapter, a coaching mindset is one where you see the coachee as equal to you and as having the capability of overcoming barriers and obstacles and fulfilling their potential. From that mindset, you are able to communicate honestly with that person, no matter what the subject is.

There are some obvious situations in the workplace where a coaching approach will enhance your conversation:

- Goal setting
- Strategic planning
- Creating engagement
- Motivating and inspiring
- Delegating
- Teamworking
- Problem solving

- Planning and reviewing
- Team and people development
- Career development
- Performance management
- Performance reviews
- Feedback and appraisals
- Relationship alignment

The list is endless, and the opportunities can either be tackled by using a highly structured approach, or by adopting a coaching leadership approach. In the latter, be aware that superficially the discussion might sound like a normal conversation and the term coaching might not be used. This is far more pervasive and perhaps more important, because it is the continuous awareness and employment of the underlying principles of coaching during the many brief daily interactions that occur between leaders and their people at work that results in on-the-job development. It is to this coaching style that we turn in the next chapter.

5   A Coaching Style: Partnership and Collaboration

Partnership and collaboration create self-confidence and self-governing teams

Let's explore the basic toolkit that you will need for coaching. The main characteristics of a coaching style are partnership and collaboration as opposed to command and control. Coaching is a conversation between equals. The ICF defines it as "partnering in a thought-provoking and creative process to maximize personal and professional potential." In this way, the coaching mindset immediately creates a culture of interdependence as opposed to the one of dependence created by traditional management. In what seems to be a global context of "doing more with less," it comes as a huge relief to leaders to learn how to engage the full potential and wisdom of their employees through partnership and collaboration, instead of constantly feeling pressurized to provide all the answers and steer the ship oneself. Leaders who have been on our coaching workshops tell us they feel a weight being lifted off their shoulders and less stress.

The coaching ethos

Coaching is a way of being that stems from a coaching ethos – a belief in the capability, resourcefulness, and potential of yourself and others which allows you to focus on strengths, solutions, and future success, not weakness, problems, or past performance. A coaching style of leadership requires that you connect at the human level, beyond the task – being before doing – and stop thinking that the leader is "the expert" who has to tell everyone else the best way to do things. Coaching is based on trust, belief, and non-judgment; it's a culture where "best practice" is not as you know it, where enjoyment is essential to learning and "upsets" are reframed as "set-ups" or opportunities. It is a place where all things are possible and collaboration is the ultimate enabler.

One CEO who participated in a public Coaching for Performance workshop, Luc Deflem of Securex, said: "It has changed the way we work – the way we interact as people. You get very strong at a personal relationship level and transform the interaction at executive level."

There are some basics that will set up and maintain a coaching mindset of partnering and collaboration, which this chapter will reveal.

Self-motivation

The secret of motivation is the holy grail that every business leader would dearly love to find. The carrot and the stick, those symbolic external motivators, are becoming less and less effective. Few leaders doubt that self-motivation would be better, but forcing someone to motivate themselves is a contradiction in terms. Self-motivation dwells within the mind of each individual, out of reach of even the chiefest of executives.

Ever since work began, people have resorted to a combination of threat and reward to get other people to do what they want. Fear is a forceful motivator, but also a powerful inhibitor of creativity and responsibility. Slavery is all stick and no carrot. Carrots help people perform better, for a while, but if we view and treat people like donkeys, they will perform like donkeys. We've tried washing the carrots, cooking them, and providing bigger ones too, and we've tried padding the stick or even hiding it, pretending we didn't have one, until we needed it once more. Again performance improves – a little.

After the recent global financial crisis, workers are facing constraints on pay increases and fewer opportunities for promotion. During a global economic downturn, staying employed is the best that many can hope for. We are desperate for higher performance and we are running out of carrots. So if the motivation system is failing us, we must fundamentally change our ideas about motivation. If people are really going to perform, they must be self-motivated. Leaders who adopt a coaching mindset will enable this to happen.

For an organization to achieve a truly collaborative culture in which people are self-motivated, there needs to be a belief that every individual is fully capable and resourceful. There is no room for "I'm the boss" mentality or the traditional notion of best practice, where I know what you should do based on my or other people's success. Collaboration is not compatible with "I'm the expert" or "this is the way we do things round here." American high jumper Dick Fosbury reached his potential precisely because his coach didn't insist that he follow best practice. Fosbury discovered as a schoolboy that by clearing the bar head first and backwards he could jump higher than the traditional straddle technique. Within a decade of him winning the 1968 Olympic gold medal, the scissor kick had been rendered old-fashioned and the great majority of Olympic high jumpers were using the "Fosbury flop."

Belief in potential

As a coach or leader, the effectiveness of what you do depends in large measure on your beliefs about human potential. The expressions "to get the best out of someone" and "your hidden potential" imply that more lies within the person waiting to be released. Unless you believe that people possess more capability than they are currently expressing, you will not be able to help them express it. Leaders must think of employees in terms of their potential, not their past performance. The majority of appraisal systems are seriously flawed for this reason. People are put in performance boxes from which it is hard for them to escape, either in their own eyes or those of their leader.

That our beliefs about the capability of others have a direct impact on their performance has been adequately demonstrated in a number of experiments from the field of education. In these tests teachers are told, wrongly, that a group of average pupils are either scholarship candidates or have learning difficulties. They teach a set curriculum to the group for a period of time. Subsequent academic tests show that the pupils' results invariably reflect the false beliefs of their teachers about their ability. It is equally true that the performance of employees will reflect the beliefs of their leaders. In order fully to partner and collaborate, you need to see people's potential, not their past performance.

Creating a culture of trust

I have argued the importance of leaders recognizing the potential that lies within each and every one of their people and of treating them accordingly. It is also critical that people recognize their own hidden potential and believe in themselves. We all think we could do better to some extent, but do we really know what we are capable of? How often do we hear or make comments such as "She is far more capable than she thinks"?

For example, Fred sees himself as having limited potential. He feels safe only when he operates well within his prescribed limit. This is like his shell. His leader, Ruth, will only give him tasks within that shell. She will give him task A, because she is confident Fred can do it and Fred is able to do it. She will not trust him to do task B, because she sees this as beyond Fred's capability. If she gives the task to the more experienced Jane instead, which is expedient and understandable, she reinforces or validates Fred's shell and increases its strength and thickness. To help Fred venture outside his shell, Ruth needs to set him the realistic challenge of task B and to support or coach him to success. She needs to suspend any limiting beliefs she has about Fred and trust that he is capable of more than past experience has shown.

Developing your emotional intelligence and the ability to trust is about how you see yourself and others in terms of **potential**, and how you deal with the **internal** and **external obstacles** that hinder the full expression of this potential.

I invite you to reflect on the three revealing questions in the following activity. Make sure you have noted your own answers before you read any further.

ACTIVITY:
What Blocks
Your Potential?

1. How much of your full potential do you bring to your work? Interpret the question as you like and then write down a percentage.
2. What gets in the way of your full potential being realized?
3. What is the main inner obstacle that prevents your potential from manifesting itself?

WHAT PERCENTAGE OF PEOPLE'S POTENTIAL MANIFESTS ITSELF IN THE WORKPLACE ON AVERAGE?

Individual answers given by delegates on Coaching for Performance workshops range from single figures to over 80 percent, but the average answer to the first question is 40 percent.

We also ask what evidence people have to support their figures. The three most consistent answers are:

- I just know I could be much more productive.
- How well people respond in a crisis.
- The things that people do so well outside the workplace.

WHAT EXTERNAL AND INTERNAL BLOCKS OBSTRUCT THE MANIFESTATION OF THE REST OF THAT POTENTIAL?

The external blocks most frequently cited are:

- The prevailing management style of the organization/my leader.
- The lack of encouragement and opportunity.
- My company's restrictive structures and practices.

The single universal internal block is unfailingly unanimous: **fear**, variously described as fear of failure, lack of confidence, self-doubt, and lack of self-belief (see Figure 7). I have every reason to suspect that this internal block is true. It is certainly true for me. In a safe environment people tend to tell the truth about themselves. If lack of confidence and so on are perceived to be true, then in effect they become the case anyway. The logical response would be to put every effort into building employees' self-belief, and coaching is tailor-made for that, but many businesspeople are anything but logical when the need for a change in management behavior is raised. They far prefer to hope for, look for, pay for, or even wait for a technical or structural fix, rather than adopting a human or psychological performance improvement, however straightforward it may be.

FIGURE 7: *Potential*

How much of our total potential do we normally express?	**40%**
What is the principal inner obstacle that prevents it manifesting itself?	**FEAR**

A coaching mindset

To coach successfully you have to adopt a far more optimistic view than usual of the dormant capability of all people – a coaching mindset. Pretending you are optimistic is insufficient, because you convey your genuine beliefs in many subtle ways. Building others' self-belief demands that you change the way you think about them and, in doing so, release the desire to control them or to maintain their belief in your superior abilities and thus make them dependent. One of the best things you can do for them is to assist them in not being dependent on you. After all, children's most memorable and exciting moments are often the first occasions on which they beat a parent at a game of skill. That is why in the early days parents sometimes allow them to win. They want their children to overtake them and they are proud when they do – would that leaders could be so proud when their team members do the same! You can only gain, through your team's greater performance and through the satisfaction of watching them and helping them grow. However, all too often you may be afraid of losing your job, your authority, your credibility, or your self-belief.

ADOPTING A COACHING MINDSET HELPS PEOPLE TO DISCOVER THEIR SELF-BELIEF

For people to build their self-belief, in addition to accumulating successes they need to know that their success is due to their own efforts. They must also know that other people believe in them, which means being trusted, allowed, encouraged, and supported to make their own choices and decisions. It means being treated as an equal, even if their job has a lesser label. It means not being patronized, instructed, ignored, blamed, threatened, or denigrated by word or deed. Unfortunately, much generally expected and accepted leadership behavior embodies many of these negatives and effectively lowers the self-belief of those being led.

What you think of a person will come through in your attitude and create an impact, even if you don't speak. Albert Mehrabian's research is the best known in this field. His work provided the basis for the often oversimplified statistics about the relative effectiveness of spoken communication versus the unconscious messages people are giving through their body, tone of voice, facial expressions, and movement. He found that when it pertains to feelings and attitudes:

- 7% of a message is in the words that are spoken.
- 38% of a message is in the way that the words are said, e.g., tone and rhythm.
- 55% of a message is in the facial expression.

To explore and experience different mindsets, try the activity below.

ACTIVITY:
Experience Different Mindsets

Find somewhere you won't be disturbed for three minutes. Think of someone you work with regularly and then try on each of the following mindsets in turn. Stay with each mindset for as long as you can before moving to the next, noticing what responses each evokes in you:

1. "I think this person *is* a problem."
2. "I think this person *has* a problem."
3. "I think this person is on a learning journey and is capable, resourceful, and full of potential."

What did you notice about the different mindsets?
What different feelings or emotions do they create in you?
What did you believe about the person's potential each time?
What changed in your attitude?
Which mindset do you tend to adopt on a daily basis?

Nearly all personal interaction involves feelings and attitudes of some kind, and a leader's communication is especially scanned for the emotions and meaning behind the words, so becoming aware of what you are really feeling is critical. Then you need to do the work to move from what may be your naturally skeptical or pessimistic view of life to a positive one.

To begin with, you might like to think of choosing a mindset like choosing to wear different colored glasses. While you see others, ourselves, and the world from the perspective of your own colored glasses, you have not just one but many colors to look through. There are colors that come and go and colors that seem to have been there forever. As soon as you recognize this, you are able to take control, self-manage, and make a conscious decision to adopt a coaching mindset.

I invite you to choose to **adopt the mindset that someone is capable, resourceful, and full of potential**, the essence of a coaching mindset. It will build their self-belief and self-motivation and enable them to flourish. And with that mindset, you can coach them to make their own powerful choices and find enjoyment in their performance and their success.

The underlying and ever-present aim of coaching is building the self-belief of others, regardless of the content of the task or issue. If leaders bear this principle in mind and act on it persistently and authentically, they will be staggered by the improvements in relationships and in performance that result. Think about how you build self-belief in your team members.

Intention

Another way in which you can consciously influence the success of a working relationship, a meeting, or a project is through **intentionality**. Whether you're wanting a quick conversation with a colleague or your entire team or planning a formal coaching session or performance review, set your intention for the meeting. Setting a clear intention for the outcome of the meeting will have an impact on its success. You could define intentions as your dreams for what could happen if nothing got in the way. It is important to set clear and specific intentions, because they will act as an anchor and a guide for you. Practice this skill with the next activity.

Take two minutes of quiet time before a meeting to set your intention by answering this question:

- **If the meeting were wildly to exceed your expectations, what would happen in it?**

Let go of any limiting beliefs you have about the meeting, your people, or yourself, and allow yourself to "dream" of the best you can possibly imagine. By placing your focus on a positive outcome and articulating this, you have set your intention for the meeting. Revisit your intention after the meeting, and notice how it showed up in your meeting. Practice doing this until it becomes a natural part of your toolkit.

ACTIVITY:

Set Your Intention

Conscious working agreements

When you consciously create your working environment, you are more productive, creative, and have better teamwork. Partnership and collaboration in a working relationship require a strong foundation built on clear expectations and agreement by conscious creation, not by default. Often you may dive into a project or a new work relationship without pausing to clarify roles, responsibilities, common goals, and optimal working agreements. Partnering to consciously create how to work together addresses these questions with a clear intention to create success. The conscious and deliberate design of a good working relationship at the start builds the respect, trust, and agreement that are essential to collaboration and high performance.

When deadlines are tight, it can be tempting to skip this whole process. Because of our human addiction to doing, it's quite normal to feel impatient when you first take the time to be conscious and intentional about relationships. However, once you've done it a few times, you'll feel uneasy when you don't do it.

Everyone has different assumptions about what things "should" look like. If you don't discuss them and you are working in a team, they will overshadow you in a negative way. Try out the following activity with a new team member, or use the exercise with someone you already work with to redesign and refresh the relationship. You can also do the activity as a group to create a strong team. For completeness, the questions are also in the Coaching Question Toolkit at the back of the book (Question Bag 2).

ACTIVITY: *Consciously Design Your Working Agreements*	Explore the following questions: • What would the dream/success look like for us working together? • What would the nightmare/worst-case scenario look like? • What's the best way for us to work together to achieve the dream/success? • What do we need to be mindful of to avoid the nightmare/worst case? • What permissions does each of us want from the other? • What will we do when things get hard? It's a flexible contract, so it's crucial to check in as time goes on, to revisit agreements and redesign them as needed by checking on these aspects: • What is working and what is not? • What do we need to change in order to make the relationship more effective, productive, or positive?

Permission

Another key element in maintaining partnering and collaboration is the use of **permission**. It builds trust and confidence, respects individual sensitivities, focuses attention, and prevents misunderstandings arising.

When you are talking to someone you like and trust, you tend to use permission naturally, both verbally and in your body language, for instance by asking "What if we do this?" When speaking to people you are in conflict with or threatened by, permission tends to be absent, and you might say "What I think we should do is this."

Permission is included in a conscious working agreement, but is also essential throughout our coaching. Often you believe you have a good suggestion to make or some valuable experience to offer. And when you do, it's a common human tendency to jump in with "You know what you should do . . ." or "I had the same problem and I fixed it like this . . ." Hold that thought and first ask permission to share what you know: "Would it be helpful if I shared what works for me?"

Another advantage of asking permission is that it makes people stop and listen to what you have to say, particularly in meetings. Offering the simple question "Can I add something to that?" can reduce a meeting room to expectant silence for two reasons:

- You are handing the other person control of the situation by asking permission.
- You are validating what the other person has said by offering to add to it.

And if a coaching style is something unfamiliar to your employees, before you switch your leadership style, gaining permission will help to get their buy-in: "I'm going to be trying a new coaching approach to the way we work. One change you'll notice is that I'll ask more questions to find out what you think. Are you ready to give it a go?"

See Question Bag 3 in the Coaching Question Toolkit at the end of the book for a number of different ways in which you could ask permission, and use them in your ongoing partnerships. Obtaining permission before trying something out that involves another person, or offering your own experience and perspective, is a good way of maintaining trust and rapport and, crucially, will keep the relationship balanced.

Get curious, not critical

Collaboration can be just a buzzword in some organizations. When the going gets tough, people can resort to criticism and blame, and Chapter 2 has already discussed how damaging these can be in any relationship. The antidote to criticism is curiosity. By getting curious rather than getting critical, you will ensure that partnership and collaboration are not derailed when things get tough. And there is much more to it than that – by getting curious about what has happened, you enable yourself to enter a whole new perspective, that of the person you are working with. This creates learning and discovery for both and, ultimately, alignment. I will revisit this in later chapters, especially Chapter 13, where sharing perspectives on performance is key to feedback and continuous learning. And it's not just judging another person's performance that is a problem. How often have you heard someone (perhaps yourself) say "I'm my own worst critic"? As hard a critic as people can be of others, they're often ten times harder on themselves. Recognizing and managing the inner critical voice, or as Gallwey calls it "the opponent within one's own head," is fundamental to coaching. In a non-judgmental, blame-free environment, you can learn from your mistakes and be willing to stretch yourself. A coaching ethos is positive and inspirational: it shines a bright light on what has worked well so far, what learning can be had from the past, and the pathway to the best that is possible in the future.

Judgment, criticism, and correction put people on the defensive. And these tend to go hand in hand with blame. Fear of judgment or blame is one of the key inhibitors to collaboration and high performance. Chapters 11 and 13 examine more closely the need to move away from judging and fault finding to description and objectivity.

So far I have discussed the link between coaching and emotional intelligence and defined what makes a coaching style so effective for building the self-belief and motivation a person needs to unlock their own potential. The next chapter explores the fundamental coaching principle that high performance comes out of high awareness and responsibility.

6   Awareness and Responsibility: Activating Learning

Building awareness and responsibility is the essence of good coaching and enables the activation of natural learning

Awareness and responsibility are without doubt two qualities that are crucial to performance in any activity. My colleague David Hemery, 400-meter hurdler and 1968 Olympic gold medalist, researched 63 of the world's top performers from more than 20 different sports for his book *Sporting Excellence*. In spite of considerable variations in other areas, awareness and responsibility consistently appeared to be the two most important attitudinal factors common to all – and the attitude or state of mind of the performer is the key to performance of any kind. Let's explore the meaning of each of these aspects.

The winning mind

In sports coaching, it used to be that technical ability and fitness commensurate with your sport were what coaches worked on. The mind was not universally recognized to be so crucial, but in any case that was what the performer was born with and the coach could not do much about it. Wrong! Coaches could and did affect the state of mind of their performers, but largely unwittingly and often negatively by their autocratic methods and obsession with technique.

These coaches denied their performers responsibility by telling them what to do; they denied them awareness by telling them what they saw. They withheld responsibility and killed awareness. Some so-called coaches still do, as do many leaders. They contribute to the performers' or employees' limitations as well as to their successes. The problem is that they may still get reasonable results from those they manage, so they are not motivated to try anything else and they never know or believe what they could achieve by other means.

Much has changed in sport and most top teams employ sports psychologists to provide performers with attitudinal training. If old coaching methods remain unchanged, however, the coach will frequently be unintentionally negating the psychologist's efforts. The best way to develop and maintain the ideal state of mind for performance is to build awareness and responsibility continuously through daily practice and the skill acquisition process. This requires a shift in the method of coaching, a shift from instruction to real coaching. Coaching for awareness and responsibility works in the short term for achieving a task, and it also works in the long term for a better quality of life.

A coach is not a problem solver, a counselor, a teacher, an adviser, an instructor, or even an expert; a coach is a sounding board, a facilitator, an awareness raiser, a supporter. These words should at least help you to understand what the role implies.

Awareness

The first key element of coaching is **awareness**, which is the product of focused attention, concentration, and clarity. Let us look for a moment at the *Concise Oxford Dictionary*: aware means "conscious, not ignorant, having knowledge." I prefer what *Webster's* adds: "aware implies having knowledge of something through alertness in observing or in interpreting what one sees, hears, feels, etc."

I am able to control only that of which I am aware. That of which I am unaware controls me. Awareness empowers me.

Raising awareness is one of the principles of coaching, because you can only respond to things you are aware of. If you are not aware of something, you won't respond to it. As Gallwey established with the Inner Game, becoming aware of something activates our built-in, natural learning capability. The first step is becoming aware.

Like your eyesight or your hearing, both of which can be good or poor, there are infinite degrees of awareness. Unlike eyesight or hearing, in which the norm is good, the norm of your everyday awareness is probably rather poor. A magnifying glass or an amplifier can raise your sight and hearing threshold way above normal. In the same way, awareness can be raised or heightened considerably by focused attention and by practice, without having to resort to the corner drugstore! Increased awareness gives greater clarity of perception than normal, as does a magnifying glass. While awareness includes seeing and hearing in the workplace, it encompasses much more than that. It is gathering and clearly perceiving the relevant facts and information, and developing the ability to determine what is relevant. That ability will include an understanding of systems, of dynamics, of relationships between things and people, and inevitably some understanding of psychology. Awareness also encompasses self-awareness, in particular recognizing when and how emotions or desires distort your own perception.

For example, if you start the day in a bad mood, you might arrive at work wearing "negative glasses" and behave rudely to a colleague. Your colleague in turn might react negatively to you and a bad relationship is formed. Alternatively, if you are self-aware, you will recognize the bad mood and can choose to put it aside and not inflict it on your colleagues.

AWARENESS LEADS TO SKILL

In the development of physical skills, the awareness of bodily sensations may be crucial. In the majority of sports, for example, the most effective way to increase individual physical efficiency is for the performer to become increasingly aware of the physical sensations during an activity. This is poorly understood by the majority of sports coaches, who persist in imposing their technique from outside. When kinesthetic awareness is focused on a movement, the immediate discomforts and corresponding inefficiencies in that movement are reduced and soon eliminated. The result is a more fluid and efficient form, with the important advantage that it is geared to the particular performer's body rather than the "average" body.

Teachers and instructors, or for that matter leaders, will be tempted to show and tell others to do something in the way they themselves were taught to do it, or the way "the book" says it should be done. In other words, they teach the student or employee their way and thereby perpetuate the conventional wisdom. While learning and employment of the standard or "right" way to do something will show initial performance benefits, the personal preferences and attributes of performers are suppressed. The performers' dependence on the expert is also maintained, which boosts the leaders' egos and their illusion of power, but won't free up their time.

The coaching alternative of raising awareness surfaces and highlights the unique attributes of the body and mind of each coachee, while at the same time building the ability and the confidence to improve without someone else prescribing how. It builds self-reliance, self-belief and confidence, and self-responsibility. Coaching should never be confused with the "here are the tools, go and find out for yourself" approach. People's normal level of awareness is relatively low. Left to your own devices, you may be liable to take an age to reinvent the wheel and/or to develop only partially effective methods that can consolidate into bad habits. So the awareness-raising function of the expert coach is indispensable – at least until or unless you develop the skill of self-coaching, which opens the door to continuous self-improvement and self-discovery.

No two human minds or bodies are the same. How can I tell you how to use yours to its best? Only you can discover how, with awareness.

What you need to increase your awareness of will vary. Each activity is geared to different parts of you. Sport is primarily physical, but some sports are highly visual too. Musicians require and develop high levels of auditory awareness. Sculptors and magicians need tactile awareness, and businesspeople require mental and people awareness, and certainly other areas too.

Non-judgmental awareness in itself is curative, which is where the magic lies. And there is a biological explanation for this in neuroscience. Brainwaves have different vibrational frequencies and they interact between the neurons within our brain. There are four major brainwave patterns, ranging from high to low frequency. We spend most of our working life in the higher frequency brainwaves of Alpha and Beta – our awareness is directed outward toward cognitive tasks. In order to heighten our awareness and access the potential within us, we need to be able to access other levels of brainwaves, such as Delta and Theta, at will. After all, as Einstein said, "Problems cannot be solved with the same mindset that created them." The benefits are plentiful, since by heightening your awareness you can more easily uncover and connect with your purpose.

In order to develop your awareness, I highly recommend meditation. We offer a form of meditation created by my colleague, Gita Bellin, whose work has transformed corporations globally. The practice is designed for leaders to create a high-performance mind, and we share how to learn this on our website, www.coachingperformance.com.

Awareness is something that develops quickly through simple practice and application, and through being coached. It is perhaps easier to relate to the following lay definitions:

- Awareness is knowing what is happening around you.
- Self-awareness is knowing what you are experiencing.

By becoming aware of something, you can change it. And you don't even need to expend effort on it, as your natural learning system – that part of you that learned to walk, to ride a bike, to speak – will naturally respond and adapt to new information. That is often why people say they have their best ideas in the shower. They have stopped being in busy Beta, they accessed other brainwaves, and "Eureka!"

INPUT

Another term may add to the understanding of what I mean by awareness: input. Every human activity can be reduced to input–process–output.

For example, when you drive to work you receive input in the form of other traffic movements, road and weather conditions, changing speed and spatial relationships, the sounds of your engine, your instruments, and the comfort, tension, or tiredness in your body. This is all input that you may welcome, reject, take on board sufficiently, receive in its intricate detail, or not even notice save for its major elements.

You may consciously be aware of your driving, or unconsciously acquire the input necessary to drive safely to work while you listen to the radio. Either way, you are receiving input. Better drivers will receive a higher quality and quantity of input, which provides them with more accurate and detailed information that they process and act on to produce the appropriate output, the speed and position of the vehicle on the road. However good you are at processing the input received and acting on it, the quality of your output will depend on the quality and quantity of the input. Awareness raising is the act of sharpening the acuity of your input receptors, often tuning your senses but also engaging your brain.

While high awareness is vital for high performance, you are blessed with a mechanism that continually seeks to lower your awareness to the level of "just enough to get by." While this sounds unfortunate, it is in fact essential if you are to avoid input overload. The downside is that if you do not raise your awareness and that of those you work with, you will deliver output at a minimal level. The skill of the coach is to raise and sustain awareness at the appropriate level and in those areas where it is required.

I define awareness as **high-quality relevant input**. I could add the word **self-generated** before that, but in a sense that is already implied, because input will simply not be high quality unless it is self-generated. The act of becoming engaged in something itself provides the quality. Consider the poverty of the image you receive if I say "The flowers out there are red," compared to the input you get when I ask you "What color are the flowers out there?" and you are compelled to see for yourself. Better still if I ask what color and what tone or shade. And knowing what is most relevant to coachees is key to knowing where to direct their focus of attention.

In this example, if the coachee were color-blind I would need to ask what shape the flowers are. One way gives a standard flower image, the other a detailed explosion of life in myriad subtle shades of red as it is at a particular instant. It is unique. In 15 minutes it will be different, for the sun will have moved. It will never be quite the same again. So self-generated input is infinitely richer, more immediate, more real. Higher than normal focused attention leads to higher than normal performance.

Another word that characterizes awareness is feedback – feedback from the environment, from your body, from your actions, from the equipment you are using, as opposed to feedback from other people. Change follows naturally and unforced once quality feedback or input is received.

Let's look at how raising awareness gives you different choices (and therefore responsibility) in practice. Silence your phone, get comfortable, relax, and follow the questions in the self-coaching exercise in the Coaching

Question Toolkit (Question Bag 1). You'll need about 20 minutes. While you completed the self-coaching activity, you might have noticed yourself becoming more reflective as you accessed other brainwaves to respond to the questions. I expect that you are closer now to achieving your goal. And you'll probably feel empowered and more confident because you have experienced that by asking yourself the right questions and listening to yourself, you can find your own solutions. The questions help raise your awareness, which encourages you to take responsibility for achieving your goal. The fact that you come up with your own solutions will also raise your confidence that you can achieve your goal. This is awareness in the act of being curative.

Responsibility

Responsibility is the other key concept or goal of coaching. It is also crucial for high performance. When you truly accept, choose, or take responsibility for your thoughts and your actions, your commitment to them rises and so does your performance. When you are ordered to be responsible, told to be, expected to be, or even given responsibility if you do not fully accept it, your performance does not rise.

Sure, you may do the job because there is an implied threat if you do not, but doing something to avoid a threat does not optimize performance. Feeling truly responsible invariably involves choice.

Let's look at a couple of examples.

BLAME

If I give you advice, especially if it is unsolicited, and you take the action but it fails, what will you do? Blame me, of course, which is a clear indication of where you see the responsibility lying. I have traded my advice for your responsibility, and that is seldom a good deal. The failure might even be attributable as much to your lack of ownership as to my bad advice. In the workplace, when the advice is a command, ownership is at zero and this can lead to resentment, surreptitious sabotage, or ownership of the reverse action. *You gave me no choice; you damaged my self-esteem; I cannot recover that through an action of which I have no ownership, so I take responsibility for an alternative action that will damage you. Of course, that course of action may damage me too, but at least I will have got my own back!* If this (unconscious) sequence in italics seems exaggerated to you, let me assure you that there are millions of workers with bad employers who would acknowledge having followed that track at one time or another.

CHOICE

Here is another example of the difference between the normal or imposed level of responsibility and high or chosen responsibility. Imagine a group of construction workers being briefed: "Peter, go and get a ladder. There's one in the shed."

What does Peter do if he finds no ladder there? He returns and says, "There's no ladder there."

What if I had asked instead, "We need a ladder. There's one in the shed. Who is willing to get it?"

Peter replies "I will," but when he gets there there is no ladder.

What will he do this time? He will look elsewhere. Why? Because he feels responsible. He wants to succeed. He will find a ladder for his own sake, his own self-esteem. What I did differently was to give him a choice, to which he responded.

One of our clients had a history of poor labor relations. In an attempt to improve these, I ran a series of courses for shop-floor supervisors. Although the company grapevine reported that our course was very enjoyable, the participants were invariably suspicious, defensive, even resistant at the outset. I recognized that their pattern was to resist anything senior leaders told them to do. They had been told to attend the course, and they would resist that too.

To defuse this unproductive situation, I asked them how much choice they had had about attending the course.

"None," they chorused.

"Well, you have a choice now," I said. "You have met your obligation to the company – you're here. Congratulations! Now, here is your choice. How do you want to spend these two days? You can learn as much as possible, you can resist, you can be as inattentive as you like, you can fool around. Write a sentence describing what you choose to do. You can keep it to yourself, if you prefer, or share it with your neighbor. I don't need to know and I won't tell your boss what you do. The choice is yours."

The atmosphere in the room was transformed. There was something like a collective sigh of relief, but also a release of energy, and the vast majority of supervisors then engaged at a high level of involvement. Choice and responsibility can work wonders.

> *Self-belief, self-motivation, choice, clarity, commitment, awareness, responsibility, and action are the products of coaching.*

These simple examples clearly illustrate how important choice is for the performance gain that occurs with full responsibility. That does not occur unless the coachee feels responsible. *Telling* someone to be responsible for something doesn't make them *feel* responsible for it. They may fear failure and feel guilty if they do fail, but that is not the same as feeling responsible. That comes with choice, which in turn demands a question. We will look at the construction of coaching questions in the next chapter. The following activity will help you reflect on what helps you to raise awareness and responsibility, and what holds you back.

1. Think of a colleague at work who is good at raising awareness and responsibility. What can you learn from their behavior for your own development? 2. What strengths do you want to develop with respect to raising awareness and responsibility in your colleagues?	**ACTIVITY:** *Raising Awareness and Responsibility*

Combining awareness and responsibility

Figure 8 illustrates the many-pronged, many-faceted nature of the benefits that spread through an organization when leaders coach in accordance with the two simple but powerful concepts of awareness and responsibility. Following any line of arrows from top to bottom illustrates the sequence of effects which leads to high performance.

FIGURE 8: *The benefits of a coaching leadership style*

Coach as expert

Regardless of the benefits, you may wonder whether coaches need to have experience or technical knowledge in the area in which they are coaching. The answer is no – not if they are truly acting as detached awareness raisers. If, however, coaches do not fully believe in what they are espousing – that is, the potential of the coachee and the value of self-responsibility – then they will think that they do need expertise in the subject to be able to coach. I am not suggesting there is never a place for expert input, but less good coaches will tend to overuse it and thereby reduce the value of their coaching, because every time input is provided the responsibility of the coachee is reduced. Your potential is realized by optimizing your own individuality and uniqueness, never by molding them to another's opinion of what constitutes best practice.

THE PITFALLS OF KNOWLEDGE

The ideal would seem to be an expert coach with a wealth of technical knowledge too. It is, however, very hard for experts to withhold their expertise sufficiently to coach well. Let me illustrate this further with an example from tennis. Many years ago, several of our Inner Tennis courses were so overbooked that we ran out of trained Inner Tennis coaches. We brought in two Inner Ski coaches, dressed them in tennis coach uniform, put a racket under their arms, and let them loose, with the promise that they would not attempt to use the racket under any circumstances.

Not entirely to our surprise, the coaching job they performed was largely indistinguishable from that of their tennis-playing colleagues. However, on a couple of notable occasions they actually did *better*. On reflection, the reason became clear. The tennis coaches were seeing the participants in terms of their technical faults; the ski coaches, who could not recognize such faults, saw the participants in terms of the efficiency with which they used their bodies. Bodily inefficiency stems from self-doubt and inadequate bodily awareness. The ski coaches, having to rely on the participants' own self-diagnosis, were therefore tackling the problems at their cause, whereas the tennis coaches were only tackling the symptom, the technical fault. This obliged us to do more training with the tennis coaches to enable them to detach themselves more effectively from their expertise.

A LEVEL DEEPER

Let us look at the same idea with a simple example from a business context. Georgina's leader saw that she did not communicate sufficiently with her colleagues in the next department, and knew that a weekly progress memo was the solution. Such a memo, however, would contain inadequate information so long as Georgina's resistance to communicating persisted. Instead of being satisfied with Georgina's agreement to send memos, the leader coached Georgina to discover and let go of her own resistance. The lack of communication was the symptom, but the resistance was the cause. Problems can only be resolved at the level beneath that at which they manifest themselves.

THE LEADER: EXPERT OR COACH?

It is hard, but by no means impossible, for an expert to be a good coach. Of course, expertise is invaluable for many other aspects of a leader's function, and the truth is that the leader is most likely to be an expert anyway. But take the case of a senior leader in an organization who does not have the same degree of technical knowledge as people in their team.

If they are a good coach, they should have no difficulty creating a high-performance culture, whether they have less technical depth or not. As soon as they do this, any credibility gap that may exist in the minds of some of their employees will disappear. As skills become more specialized and technically complex, which is a global trend, coaching is an absolute prerequisite for leaders.

PART III

The Practice of Coaching

7 Powerful Questions

Telling or asking closed questions saves people from having to think
Asking open questions causes them to think for themselves

It is questions rather than instructions or advice that best generate awareness and responsibility. It would be easy if any old question would do,
but it won't. We need to examine the effectiveness of various types of
question. To do so, I will use a simple analogy from sport. Ask anyone
what is the most frequently used instruction in any ball sport and they
will tell you: "Keep your eye on the ball."

In all ball sports it is certainly very important to watch the ball, but
does the command "Watch the ball" actually cause you to do so? No. If it
did, many more of us would be far better at our sport. We all know that
golfers hit balls further and straighter when they are relaxed, but will the
command "Relax" cause a golfer to feel more relaxed? No, it will probably
make them more tense.

If commanding a person to do what they need to do does not produce
the desired effect, what does? Let's try a question:

• **Are you watching the ball?** How would you respond to that?
Defensively, perhaps, and you would probably lie, just as you did at
school when the teacher asked you if you were paying attention.

• **Why aren't you watching the ball?** More defensiveness – or
perhaps a little analysis if you are that way inclined. "I am," "I don't
know," "because I was thinking about my grip," or, more truthfully,
"because you are distracting me and making me nervous."

Those are not very powerful questions, but consider the effect of the
following:

- Which way is the ball spinning as it comes toward you?
- How high is it this time as it crosses the net?
- Does it spin faster or slower after it bounces, this time, each time?
- How far is it from your opponent when you first see which way it is spinning?

These questions are of an altogether different order. They create four important effects that the other questions and commands do not:

- This type of question compels the player to watch the ball. It is not possible to answer the question unless they do that.
- The player will have to focus to a higher order than normal to give the accurate answer the question demands, providing a higher quality of input.
- The answers sought are descriptive not judgmental, so there is no risk of descent into self-criticism or damage to self-esteem.
- There is the benefit of a feedback loop for the coach, who is able to verify the accuracy of the player's answer and therefore the quality of concentration.

So, powerful questions promote proactive, focused thought, attention, and observation. This leads one to wonder why all those sports coaches persist in giving such an ineffective command as "Keep your eye on the ball." There are probably two main reasons: they have never considered whether it works or not, because it has always been done that way; and they are more concerned about what they say than about its effect on their pupil.

The heart of coaching

I have taken some time to explore this apparently straightforward act of watching a ball in order to illustrate by simple analogy the very heart of coaching. You must understand the effect you are trying to create – aware-ness and responsibility – and what you have to say/do to create that effect. Just demanding what you want is useless; you must ask **powerful questions**.

I have given a sporting example, but how would this work in the work-place? A good example comes from a 1:1 coaching engagement with an operations manager who managed 180 people. The manager, let's call him Stefan, found that people were not delivering what he had in mind and thought he had asked for. Using the principles of the sporting example I described – that coaching questions compel attention for an answer, focus attention for precision, and create a feedback loop – he got curious about what was happening in order to raise his awareness. In getting curious and asking questions, he found out what team members heard and was able to work with them on closing the gap. He called this exercise "What I Wanted and What I Got," and he discussed this regularly over his next few coaching sessions. As a result, he started to see higher performance in two distinct areas: site housekeeping improved and the quality of written work from management did too. This is the sporting example in action in the workplace – once Stefan had a different level of awareness about what was happening, he responded differently. At the end of the coaching engagement, he reflected on the impact of this coaching on himself: "I feel better, my team and I are much more aligned and I don't get frustrated and tempted to do it myself."

These examples are probably sufficient to convince you that awareness and responsibility are better raised by asking than by telling. It therefore follows that the primary form of verbal interaction from a good coach is in the interrogative. A key attribute of a coaching leadership style is the ability to ask powerful questions that focus attention and evoke clarity; questions that increase coachees' self-belief and self-motivation; questions that help coachees learn, grow, and achieve success. Now we need to examine how to construct powerful questions.

The function of questions

Questions are most commonly asked in order to elicit information. You may require information to resolve an issue for yourself, or if you are proffering advice or a solution to someone else. If you are a coach, however, the information in the answers is generally not for your benefit, and may not have to be complete. You only need to know that the *coachee* has the necessary information. The answers the coachee gives indicate to you, the coach, the line to follow with subsequent questions, while at the same time enabling you to monitor whether the coachee is following a productive track, in line with the purpose of the conversation or the coachee's agenda and the organization's objectives.

OPEN QUESTIONS

Open questions requiring descriptive answers promote awareness, whereas **closed** questions are too absolute for accuracy, and yes or no answers close the door on the exploration of further detail. They do not even compel someone to engage their brain. Open questions are much more effective for generating awareness and responsibility in the coaching process.

The following are all open questions:

- What do you want to achieve?
- What's happening at the moment?
- How would you like it to be?
- What's stopping you? What's helping you?
- What problems might there be?
- What could you do?
- Who could help you?
- Where could you find out more?
- What will you do?

INTERROGATIVE WORDS

The most powerful questions for raising awareness and responsibility begin with words that seek to quantify or gather facts, words like "what," "when," "who," "how much," and "how many." "Why" is discouraged since it often implies criticism and evokes defensiveness, and "why" and "how," if unqualified, both cause analytical thinking, which can be counter-productive. Analysis (thinking) and awareness (observation) are dissimilar mental modes that are virtually impossible to employ simultaneously to full effect. If the accurate reporting of facts is called for, analysis of their import and meaning is better temporarily suspended. If you do need to ask such questions, "why" questions are better expressed as "What were the reasons . . .?" and "how" questions as "What are the steps . . .?" These evoke more specific, factual answers.

FOCUS ON DETAIL

Questions should begin broadly and then focus increasingly on detail. This demand for more detail maintains the coachee's focus and interest. The point is well illustrated by the exercise of looking at a square foot of carpet. After observing the pile, color, pattern, and perhaps a spot or a stain, the carpet will hold little further interest for the observer and their attention will begin to wander to more interesting things. Give them a magnifying glass and they will look again in greater depth and for longer before becoming bored. A microscope could turn that little piece of carpet into a fascinating universe of forms, textures, colors, microbes, and even live bugs, sufficient to hold the eye and mind of the observer transfixed for many minutes more.

So it is in coaching. The coach needs to probe deeper or for more detail to keep the coachee involved and to bring into their consciousness those often partially obscured factors that may be important.

The focus of open questions can be increased by adding single words, for example:

- What **else** do you want?
- What do you **really** want?
- **Exactly** what is happening now?
- What **more** could you do?
- **Precisely** what will you do?

Your questions don't need to match the examples given here; incorporate the principles into words that are comfortable for you and appropriate to the situation. A casual "Then what?" can work instead of "Precisely what will you do?" And one of the most powerful coaching questions is simply "What else?"

Areas of interest
POWERFUL QUESTIONS FOLLOW THE COACHEE'S INTERESTS AND AGENDA

How, then, do coaches determine what aspects of an issue are important, especially if it is in an area about which they are not particularly knowledgeable? The principle is that questions should follow the interest and the train of thought of the coachee, not of the coach. Put another way, the coach should follow the coachee's agenda. If the coach leads the direction of the questions, this will undermine the responsibility of the coachee. But what if the direction in which the coachee is going is a dead end or a distraction? Trust that the coachee will soon find that out for themselves, or ask a question: "What would it be helpful for us to look at next?"

If coachees are not allowed to explore avenues in which they have an interest, the fascination is likely to persist and cause distortions or diversions in the work itself. Once they have explored their interests, they will be far more present and focused on whatever will emerge as the best path. Paradoxically, it may also be valuable for the coach to focus on any aspect that the coachee appears to be avoiding. So as not to break the coachee's trust and responsibility, this avenue of exploration is best entered into by a statement followed by a question: "I notice that you have not mentioned . . . Is there any particular reason for this?" "Are there any other problems?" invites the answer "No." "What other problems might there be?" invites more thought.

The following activity will help you to practice and reflect on the impact of powerful questions and how you can bring them into your work.

ACTIVITY: *The Use of Powerful Questions*	Look in the Coaching Question Toolkit at the end of the book and choose a couple of questions to start practicing with. 1. What did you notice the impact to be? 2. What steps will you take to use powerful questions?

BLIND SPOTS

Golfers and tennis players might be interested in the physical parallel to this principle. A sports coach might ask a performer which part of their swing or stroke they find most difficult to feel or be accurately aware of. It is most likely that in this "blind spot" lies a suppressed discomfort or flaw in the movement. As the coach seeks more and more awareness in that area, the feeling is restored and the correction occurs naturally, without resort to technical input from the coach. The curative properties of awareness are legion!

CRITICAL VARIABLES

In his book *The Inner Game of Work*, Gallwey says that when we focus our attention on the things that change and matter most to our desired outcome – the "critical variables" – our internal interference decreases and our performance improves. For example, he relates that boredom, stress, and resentment toward supervisors had led to low "courtesy ratings" among AT&T customer service operators. Rather than tell the operators to be more courteous, he coached them to identify and explore two critical variables for courtesy: how they listened and how they talked. They played a game that required them to listen more closely to the customer's voice and track the impact of their own responses on customer vitality. Their courtesy ratings went up. And as a result of their increased awareness, confidence, and enjoyment, their speed and accuracy also improved.

Avoid leading questions and criticism

Leading questions, the resort of many poorly trained coaches, indicate that the coach does not believe in what they are attempting to do. The coachee will quickly recognize this, and trust will be reduced. Better for the coach to tell the coachee that they have a suggestion they would like to offer, rather than attempt to manipulate the coachee in that direction. Questions that imply criticism should also be avoided, such as "Why on earth did you do that?"

To summarize, powerful questions:

- Create awareness and responsibility
- Follow the interest of the coachee
- Inspire creativity and resourcefulness
- Increase possibilities/vision
- Are goal oriented and solution focused
- Are non-judgmental

- Compel attention, thought, and observation
- Demand a higher degree of focus, detail, and precision
- Demand answers that show quality of thought, performance, and learning
- Are supportive and challenging/motivating
- Create a feedback loop

Question Bag 4 contains a list of the Top 10 powerful questions that I consistently find to be helpful in coaching. You will no doubt accumulate your own from your coaching experience. Above all, they must be authentic.

8   Active Listening

The Chinese character for "listen" says it all:
Ear = What you use to listen (hear)
King = Pay attention as if the other person were king (obey)
Ten and Eye = Be observant as if you had ten eyes (heed)
One = Listen with individual attention (attend to)
Heart = Listen also with your heart (in addition to ear and eye, hearken)

It is a luxury to be really listened to, to be truly heard. Most people are not good listeners; they were told to listen at school, not trained or coached to listen. Usually when people appear to be listening they are just waiting their turn to speak, and once they do they follow their own agenda. They might talk about something totally unrelated or else want to share their experience, thoughts, and opinions, or give advice. Just for a minute, recall how you felt the last time someone "listened" to you in this way.

Be attentive to answers

A coaching approach means being fully attentive to the coachee's answers to questions – what is said and the feelings conveyed. Trust will be lost if this doesn't happen, and the coach will not know the best question to ask next. Questioning must be a spontaneous process. Questions prepared mentally before they are asked will disrupt the flow of the conversation and not follow the interest or agenda of the coachee. If you are working out the next question while your coachee is speaking, they will be aware that you are not really listening. Far better to hear the person through and then pause if necessary while the next appropriate question comes to mind. And if you've really been listening, then your **intuition** will be your best guide.

WHERE IS YOUR ATTENTION?

Listening is a skill that requires concentration and practice. Yet strangely enough, few people have difficulty listening to the news or to a good radio play. Interest holds the attention. Perhaps you need to learn to be interested in others, to allow yourself to get curious. When you really do listen to someone, or when someone really listens to you, how appreciated it is. When you listen, do you really hear? When you look, do you really see? By that I mean make eye contact with the other person. Obsession with your own thoughts and opinions and the compulsion to talk, particularly if you are placed in any kind of advisory role, are strong. It has been said that since you were given two ears and one mouth, you should listen twice as much as you speak. Perhaps the hardest thing a coach has to learn to do is to shut up!

Words and tone of voice

What do you listen to and for? The coachee's tone of voice will indicate any emotion and you should listen for it. A monotone may signal low interest or repetition of an old line of thought. A more animated voice will hint at the awakening of new ideas and greater motivation. The coachee's choice of words can be very revealing: a predominance of negative terms or a shift toward formality or childish language has hidden meaning that can help the coach to understand and therefore facilitate effectively.

Body language

As well as listening, the coach needs to watch the coachee's body language, not with the purpose of making glib observations, but again to help with the choice of question. The coachee's high level of interest in the direction of the coaching may well be indicated by a forward posture. Uncertainty or anxiety in answers may be revealed by a hand partially covering the mouth while speaking. Arms folded across the chest often indicate resistance or defiance, and an open body posture suggests receptivity and flexibility. I am not going to go into the many aspects of body language here, but one guide is that if the words say one thing and the body seems to be saying something else, the body is more likely to indicate the true feelings.

Reflecting back

So there are listening, hearing, watching, and understanding, and coaches need to be self-aware enough to know which they are doing at any one moment. However clear the coach may feel, it is worth reflecting back to the coachee from time to time and summarizing the points being made. This will ensure correct understanding and reassure the coachee that they are being fully heard and understood. It also gives them a second chance to check on the veracity of what they have said. In most coaching sessions someone needs to take notes, but this can be agreed between the coach and the coachee. When I am coaching I like to take the notes so that the coachee is free to think.

Self-awareness

Finally, good coaches will be applying self-awareness to monitor carefully their own reactions, of emotion or judgment, to any of the coachee's responses that might interfere with the coach's necessary objectivity and detachment. Your own psychological history and prejudices – and no one is free of either – will influence your communication. And monitoring sensations in your own body, like tense shoulders or jitters in your stomach, can give you an insight into emotions that you've intuitively picked up from the coachee.

Transference

Projection and transference are the terms given to these psychological distortions that all those who teach, guide, coach, or lead others need to learn to recognize and minimize. Projection means projecting onto, or perceiving in, another person your own positive or negative traits or qualities. Transference is "the displacement of patterns of feelings and behavior, originally experienced with significant figures of one's childhood, to individuals in one's current relationships." In the workplace, one of the most common manifestations of this is authority transference.

In any perceived hierarchical relationship, leader/direct report or even coach/coachee, both parties' issues or unconscious feelings about authority will be operating. For example, many people give away their power to designated authorities – "they know, have all the answers, are more advanced," and so on – and make themselves small and childlike in the face of it. This might serve the wishes of an autocratic leader for dominance and dependence, but it works against the objective of coaching, which is to generate responsibility in the coachee.

Another common example of an unconscious transference reaction to authority is rebellion and covert sabotage of work goals. Individual transference will increase the collective frustrations and feelings of power-lessness wherever leadership style limits choice. One major motor manufacturer used to be able to assess the state of labor relations from the percentage of good parts dumped in the reject bins alongside the assembly line.

Countertransference

Countertransference, which is a further complication of transference, occurs when people in authority, leaders or coaches, themselves uncon-sciously react to transference from their own history by perpetuating dependence or rebellion. Good coaches will recognize their potential for this and compensate for the effects of all manifestations of transference by consciously working to empower coachees. If they do not, these distor-tions will creep into managerial or coaching relationships, with the long-term effect of seriously undermining what their leadership style is intended to achieve.

Active listening skills

Active listening skills are summarized in Table 3. The skills of reflecting/mirroring, paraphrasing, and summarizing show someone that you are listening to their words (the content), checking you have understood, replaying and perhaps checking in on the meaning of what's being said, and validating.

Try out your listening skills with the activity opposite.

TABLE 3: *Active listening skills*

Skill	Description
Reflecting/mirroring	Saying someone's exact words back to them.
Paraphrasing	Using slightly different word(s) which do not change the substance or meaning of what the other person said.
Summarizing	Repeating back what has been said but more briefly, without changing the substance or meaning.
Clarifying	Expressing succinctly the essence/core of what has been said and adding something valuable picked up intuitively from emotions or discrepancies in words or expressions of face or body that haven't been said in words, to generate insight and clarity for the speaker and check that you understood: "It sounds like . . . What would you say?"
Encouraging self-expression	Building trust and intimacy to encourage openness.
Suspending judgment, criticism, and attachment	Keeping an open mind. Judgments and criticism make people defensive and stop them from talking.
Listening for potential	Focusing on capabilities and strengths, not past performance or seeing someone as a problem. What could the person unleash if there were no limits?
Listening with heart	Listening to non-verbal messages such as voice tone, phrasing, facial expression, and body language. Listen attentively at the level of feeling and meaning (the intent) to hear the core/essence of what is being conveyed.

ACTIVITY:
Listening Skills

Recall a recent conversation that you did not initiate. Try to assess the quality of your listening skills.

1. Whose agenda did you follow? Did you give advice?
2. When someone next asks to discuss something with you, try actively listening to them and then assess yourself. Did you stay on their agenda? Did you use your intuition? Did you clarify and/or reflect what they say? Did you hold back your opinion or your advice? Did you suspend judgment? Did you help your colleague explore their own thoughts?
3. What are you learning about your listening skills?
4. What area of listening do you choose to focus on to develop?

Coaching requires you to be fully attentive to what the coachee is saying and the feelings they are conveying. A person can communicate one thing in words and yet betray something very different in tone of voice, body language, or facial expression. If you actively listen to someone you can feel "in tune" with them, as if you understand them at several levels at once, and even physically sense what they are sensing. You can then start to use your intuition, listening "behind" and "between" the words, and noting silences, tone of voice, energy levels, body language, and other emotional signals. Having laid the foundation skills with powerful questions and active listening, let us now introduce the GROW model, a structure for coaching conversations.

9   The GROW Model

Goals, Reality, Options, and Will

So far we have established the essential nature of awareness and responsibility for learning and for performance improvement. We have also looked at the context of coaching, at the parallels between coaching and leading, and at company culture and high performance. We have explored the role and the attitude of the coach, and we have considered powerful questioning and active listening as the primary forms of communication in coaching. We now have to determine what to ask questions about and in what sequence to ask them.

Formal or informal?

It is important at this point to stress that it is possible for coaching to be loose and informal, so much so that employees do not know they are being coached. For the everyday function of briefing and debriefing employees, nothing is better than coaching, but it should not be identified as such; it would just be effective leadership. In this case, coaching ceases to be a tool and simply becomes the way to lead people, in my opinion the most effective way. At the other end of the spectrum, a coaching session can be scheduled and structured in such a way that its purpose and roles are unambiguous. While the majority of coaching is of the former type, we will examine the latter in detail because, while the process is the same, the stages are more sharply defined.

One to one

For reasons of simplicity and clarity we will look at one-to-one or 1:1 coaching, although the format of team coaching or even self-coaching remains exactly the same. Both of these will be elaborated in later chapters. One-to-one coaching may take place between peers, between a leader and a direct report, between an erstwhile teacher and a student, between a coach and a coachee. One-to-one coaching can even be used in an upward direction, although generally covertly, by an employee on their boss. After all, as no one gets very far by telling their boss what to do, coaching upward has a much higher success rate!

A framework for coaching

Whether in a formal coaching session or when having an informal coaching conversation, the sequence of questions I suggest follows four distinct stages:

- **G**oal setting for the session as well as the short and long term.
- **R**eality checking to explore the current situation.
- **O**ptions and alternative strategies or courses of action.
- **W**hat is to be done, When, by Whom, and the *Will* to do it.

The sequence conveniently forms the mnemonic GROW, to which I will refer frequently. And since choice and self-motivation are critical to success, I like to emphasize the Will element in the final stage because it is here that intention turns into action and it is for this reason that I call it trans-formational: **Goal**, **Reality**, **Options**, and **Will**. See Figure 9 for the key questions to ask in each stage.

FIGURE 9: *The GROW model*

This sequence assumes that it is desirable to visit all four stages, which is usually the case when tackling a new issue for the first time. Often, however, coaching will be used to progress a task or process that has been

THE GROW MODEL | 97

discussed before or is already under way. In such cases coaching may begin and end with any stage. One of the things which makes GROW so effective is that the framework is flexible.

Origins of the GROW Model

When we brought the Inner Game to Europe in 1979, initially we coached tennis players and golfers. But we soon realized the value of the Inner Game for leaders in organizations. So we spent much of the 1980s developing the methodology, concepts, and techniques for performance improvement in organizations. Wanting to make a real difference to people's lives, we showed it was possible to improve performance, increase learning and enjoyment, and find a sense of purpose in work.

The management consulting firm McKinsey became a client of myself and other colleagues in the mid-1980s. Many of the programs we ran for McKinsey included experiential coaching work on tennis courts. The coaching was so successful at improving performance and unlocking potential that McKinsey asked Graham Alexander and myself to come up with an underpinning framework for coaching – a model on which to hang what was happening on the courts and elsewhere in the programs.

We decided to video ourselves and our colleagues coaching. We invited neurolinguistic programming (NLP) experts to look at what we did, and we held debriefs to try to discover what was happening and whether there was a model that played out in our unconscious competence. And there was, whether on the tennis court or in a business setting.

Initially we fitted this into something we called the 7S Coaching Model, because McKinsey had its existing 7S Framework. However, it was tortuous, and really it looked like 1, 2, 3, 4, or sometimes 1, 3, 4, or just 1, 2, 3. In the end, we came up with the acronym GROW for the four key stages we identified. We bounced it and a few other ideas off an internal communications person at McKinsey, who said they thought it would fly well. They liked it because it was simple and because it was actions and outcome focused. We had no idea of its significance at the time!

I became the first to publish the model when the first edition of this book went to press in 1992. Through the book's success and our international work, GROW became world famous and one of the most popular coaching models globally.

Goal first

It may seem strange to set **goals** before examining **reality**. Superficial logic suggests the opposite, as we surely need to know the reality before we can set any goal. Not so – goals based on current reality alone are liable to be negative, a response to a problem, limited by past performance, lacking in creativity due to simple extrapolation, in smaller increments than may be achievable, or even counterproductive. Short-term fixed goals may even lead us away from long-term goals. My experience with goal setting on team-training courses is that teams invariably set goals based on what has been done before rather than on what can be done in the future. In many cases they make no attempt to calculate what might be possible.

Goals formed by ascertaining the ideal long-term solution or vision, and then determining realistic steps toward that ideal, are generally far more inspiring, creative, and motivating. Let me illustrate this very important point with an example. If we set about trying to solve a problem of heavy traffic volume on a strategic route by exploring the reality, we are likely to set goals based solely on relieving existing traffic flow, such as widening a road. This might actually run counter to a more visionary long-term goal, which would be formed by identifying the ideal traffic pattern for the region at some time in the future, and then looking at the stages needed to move in that direction.

So my suggestion is, in most circumstances, to use the sequence suggested above.

More than GROW

I must stress that GROW has little value without the context of **awareness** and **responsibility** and the **intention** and skill to generate them through **active listening** and **powerful questions**. Models are not the truth – by itself GROW is not coaching. Mnemonics abound in the training business. There is SPIN, there are SMART goals, there is GRIT, and there is GROW coaching. These are occasionally presented or misperceived as panaceas to all business ills. They are nothing of the sort: they are only as valuable as the context in which they are used, and the context of GROW is aware-ness and responsibility.

An autocratic boss might charge their employees in the following way:

- My **goal** is to sell 1,000 widgets this month.
- The **reality** is that you did poorly last month with only 400 sold. You are a bunch of lazy so-and-sos. Our principal competitor has a better product, so you have to try harder.
- I have considered all the **options** and we are not going to increase our advertising or repackage the product.
- **What** you **will** do is the following . . .

Any dictator can use the GROW model. This boss has followed GROW to the letter, but they have not asked a single question. They have created no awareness and, although they think they have threatened their employees into taking responsibility, this is not so, because the employees had no choice.

Context and flexibility

If you get anything at all out of this book, let it be awareness and respon-sibility, which are more important than GROW. Having said that, the strongest case for following the GROW sequence with powerful coaching questions is that it is simple, flexible, and it works.

It is, however, subject to recycling. What I mean by this is that you may only be able to define a vague **goal** until you have examined the **reality** in some detail. It will then be necessary to go back and define the **goal** much more precisely before moving forward again. Even a sharply defined initial **goal** may need revising or even replacing with a different goal once the **reality** is clear.

When listing the **options**, it will be necessary to check back to see if each of them would in fact move you toward the desired **goal**. Finally, before the **what** and the **when** are set in concrete, it is crucial to make one last check to see if they meet the goal. If they do, yet self-motivation is low, then the goal, and particularly the sense of ownership of the goal, should again be reviewed.

Move around the GROW sequence according to your intuition. Revisiting each step as necessary and in any sequence ensures that coachees remain energized and motivated and that their goal fits with the goal of the company, while also aligning with their individual purpose and personal values. Follow your own intuition and instinct rather than trying to obey a rule. As you become more familiar with the power of GROW, you will start to feel confident about which element of GROW needs to be explored.

The key to GROW

The key to using GROW successfully is first to spend sufficient time exploring "G" until the coachee sets a goal which is both inspirational and stretching for them, and then to move *flexibly* through the sequence, according to your intuition, including revisiting the goal if needed.

STEP 1: WHAT ARE YOUR GOALS?
- Identifies and clarifies the type of goal through an understanding of ultimate goals, performance goals, and progress goals along the way.
- Provides understanding of principal aims and aspirations.
- Clarifies the desired result from the session.

STEP 2: WHAT IS THE REALITY?
- Assesses the current situation in terms of the action taken so far.
- Clarifies the results and effects of previously taken actions.
- Provides understanding of internal obstacles and blocks currently preventing or limiting progression.

STEP 3: WHAT ARE YOUR OPTIONS?

- Identifies the possibilities and alternatives.
- Outlines and questions a variety of strategies for progression.

STEP 4: WHAT WILL YOU DO?

- Provides understanding of what has been learned and what can be changed to achieve the initial goals.
- Creates a summary and plan of action for implementation of the identified steps.
- Outlines possible future obstacles.
- Considers the continued achievement of the goals, and the support and development that may be required.
- Estimates the certainty of commitment to the agreed actions.
- Highlights how accountability and achievement of the goals will be ensured.

Example questions for each stage of GROW can be found in Question Bag 5 in the Coaching Question Toolkit. In the next four chapters we will take a deeper look at each one of these steps in turn and at the questions that best raise awareness and responsibility within them.

10　G: Goal Setting

When I want to, I perform better than when I have to
I want to for me, I have to for you
Self-motivation is a matter of choice

So much has been written about the importance and the process of goal setting that there is certainly no need for me to repeat it all in a book about coaching. Goal setting could fill a book on its own. However, I believe even those who consider themselves to be goal-setting experts will enjoy this chapter on those aspects of goal setting that are especially important for the coaching process.

The goal for the session

Coaching invariably begins by determining a goal. If the coachee has sought a session, clearly it is they who need to define what they want to get from it. Even if it is the coach who has requested the session to resolve a specific issue that they spell out, the coachee should still be asked whether there is anything else they want from the session.

Questions like:

- What would you like to get out of this time together?
- We have half an hour, where would you like to have got to by then?
- What would be the most helpful thing for you to take away?

would elicit answers like:

- An outline for the month that I can develop.
- A clear idea of and commitment to my next two action steps.
- A decision on which way to jump.
- An understanding of what the principal issues are.
- An agreed budget for the job.

The goal for the issue

Now you come to the goal or goals related to the issue at hand, and here you need to be able to distinguish end goals from performance goals:

- **End goal** The final objective – to become the market leader, to be appointed sales director, to land a certain key account, to win the gold medal – is seldom absolutely within your own control. You cannot know or control what your competitors will do.

- **Performance goal** Identify the performance level that you believe will provide you with a very good chance of achieving the end goal. It is largely within your control and it generally provides a means of measuring progress. Examples of performance goals might be for 95 percent of production to pass quality control first time, to sell 100 widgets next month, or to have run the mile in 4 mins 10 secs by the end of September. Importantly, it is far easier to commit yourself to, and take responsibility for, a performance goal, which is within your control, than an end goal, which is not.

An end goal should wherever possible be supported by a performance goal. The end goal fosters longer-term thinking and may provide the inspiration, while the performance goal defines the specifications, the key results that can be measured.

Performance goals are crucial

The lack of an established performance goal played a major role in a notorious upset for Britain in the 1968 Olympics. Welshman Lyn Davies had won the gold medal in the long jump in 1964 and he, Russian Igor Ter-Ovanesyan, and US champion Ralph Boston were expected to share the medals. Along came a very erratic American, Bob Beamon, who in the very first round jumped some 2 feet beyond the world record. When you consider that the world record had risen by only 6 inches since 1936, this was a truly prodigious feat. Davies, Boston, and Ter-Ovanesyan were all completely demoralized, and although Boston got the bronze and the Russian was fourth, both were 6 inches behind their best. Davies, who was 12 inches behind his best, admits he was only focused on the gold, and that if he had set himself a performance goal of, say, 27 feet or a personal best and kept going for that, he would have won the silver. I wonder how demoralized other male swimmers became 40 years later in China, when Michael Phelps kept accumulating gold medals in every discipline up to his final tally of 11.

From inspiration to action

End and performance goals sometimes need to be topped and tailed by two other components, if not exactly goals (see Figure 10). Take the example of Rebecca Stevens, the first British woman to climb Mount Everest. She gives lectures to businesses and schools on her lofty achievements. You can be certain that after hearing her inspirational talk, many a schoolchild has run home and begged a parent to take them rock climbing or at least to the nearest gym with a climbing wall. "I am going to climb Everest" may be a childlike assertion, but it is also a personal dream, a vision that ignites action. Sometimes you need to remind yourself, or be reminded by a good question, of what inspired you to start or continue to do what you want. You could call that a **dream goal**. After some considerable climbing experience, Stevens reached the skill level from which climbing Everest seemed to be a reasonable end goal; if climbing Everest can ever be considered reasonable! However, she still had a vast amount of work, preparation training, and acclimatization to do. Had she not been willing to invest herself fully in that process, Everest would have remained but a dream. "How much are you willing to invest in the process?" is a question I often ask in the goal-setting stage of coaching for any activity. I call these **process goals** or even work goals.

Ownership of goals

Although company leaders may be free to set their own goals, all too often they pass goals down the line as imperatives not to be questioned. This denies ownership to those who are expected to meet these targets, and their performance is likely to suffer accordingly. Wise directors will strive to maintain a healthy detachment from their own goals when they are

FIGURE 10: *Goal setting – from inspiration to action*

	Desire, inspiration	Intention, commitment
	"What's the bigger picture?"	
DREAM GOAL *purpose and meaning* Desired future or vision The big Why?	Build the "Bank of the Future" that truly serves the diverse communities in which it operates	• I will wisely transform my organization to a modern, innovative bank serving the community by integrating financial technology firms and innovations into our large customer base and relations
	"What are you aiming to achieve?"	
END GOAL *a clear target* Concrete manifestation of dream The big What?	Transform our banking business within the next 5 years using the potential and power of new technology, innovation, and fintech business models, and a coaching leadership style throughout the entire first management level to enable this	• I commit to turn our board-approved vision into reality within 5 years and will transform our bank's success from today's large customer base into the digital economy by developing and providing financial services and technologies
	"What will you deliver?"	
PERFORMANCE GOALS *tangible milestones* Serve the dream and end goals 99% in your control	Build loyalty by delivering a quality customer and employee digital experience in banking	• I will streamline and automate our digital banking operations by the end of 2020 with an integrated finance, risk, and compliance system to reduce cost and complexity, while driving profitable sales of innovative products and services – in line with our board strategy paper

"What actions will you take?"

PROCESS GOALS *SMART steps* The work needed to reach the performance goals Serve ALL the above goals 100% in your control

• I will bring financial processes with automated, real-time analytics, and translate them into forward-looking business insight across the entire organization
   Actions: set up analytics business unit within 6 months; set up analytics management team and responsibility (8 weeks) accordingly; set up a communication strategy (internal & external) (8 weeks)
• I will work closely and regularly with our transformation team to support quick decisions and clear communications to all of our employees that keep the hearts and minds of our people engaged
   Actions: set up a transformation management meeting bi-weekly to be informed about progress; . . .

seeking to motivate their managers, and will always encourage them to set their own challenging goals whenever feasible. But if they don't do this and a job is tightly prescribed, all is not totally lost, for the leader may at least be able to offer employees some choice and ownership of how a job is done, who does what, and when.

COACHING FOR OWNERSHIP

Even if a certain goal is an absolute imperative, it is still possible to coach for ownership. I was discussing firearms training with a county police force. "How would it be possible to have trainees own the absolute, inflexible rules of firearms safety?" they asked. I suggested that instead of presenting them with these rules at the outset, they should have a discussion, using coaching, out of which the trainees would create their own agreed set of safety rules. The chances are that it would closely parallel the institutional ones. Where they were at variance, the reasons for the variation could be coached out of the trainees, with minimal input from the coach. This way the trainees would have a far greater degree of appreciation, understanding, and ownership of the institutional firearms safety rules.

WHOSE GOAL?

The value of choice and responsibility in terms of self-motivation should never be underestimated. For example, if the members of a sales team come up with a goal that is lower than the leader wishes, the leader should consider the consequences very carefully before overriding their figure and imposing their own. They may do better to swallow their pride and accept the team's figure. Insisting on the leader's goal may well have the effect of lowering the performance of the team, even though the leader's target was higher than theirs. They may or may not consider the leader's figure discouragingly unrealistic, but they will certainly be demotivated by their lack of choice. Of course, the leader has one more option if they are sure of their ground, and that is to start with the team's figure and coach them upward by exploring and helping them to dismantle their barriers to achieving more. They then retain responsibility for the figure that is finally agreed.

In the workplace, goals need to be agreed between all the parties involved: the leader who thinks they ought to set them, the sales manager, and the team members who have to do the job. Without agreement, the vital ownership and responsibility of the sales team are lost and their performance will suffer accordingly. As a coaching leader, it is helpful to think that you are side by side, not in front ("pulling") or behind ("pushing") the coachee. In this way, the coachee always retains ownership of the goal.

Some effort may need to be made to ensure that all goals are clearly understood, for all too often inaccurate assumptions may distort some people's perception, even of goals that they have been a party to creating.

Qualities of a good goal

In addition to supporting an end goal, which is not in your control, with performance and process goals, which are, goals need to be SMART:

- Specific
- Measurable
- Agreed
- Realistic
- Timeframed

and also PURE:

- Positively stated
- Understood
- Relevant
- Ethical

and CLEAR:

- Challenging
- Legal
- Environmentally sound
- Appropriate
- Recorded

The point of a goal having most of these qualities is self-evident and needs no further elaboration, but a couple of observations may be helpful.

The SMART framework was created for leaders when setting goals for their teams. Because the targets came from the leader, they had to make sure the goal was clear or "specific," but weren't concerned with how exciting or motivational it was. They also had to be careful not to make the goal too difficult, hence "realistic." If a goal is not **realistic** there is no hope, but if it is not **challenging** there is no motivation. So there is an envelope here into which all goals should fit.

Inspiring goals

It is essential to spend plenty of time at the outset in the "G" stage of GROW, to ensure coachees identify goals that inspire and energize them or which they are passionate or excited about. An inspirational goal which is positively framed will keep the energy levels and motivation high from the start. A goal that is personally framed within the company's goal will make the difference.

When you set goals for yourself you can tend to aim too low, limiting yourself through fear. Encourage coachees to aim high so that they will stretch to achieve the best they can. In a supportive environment, an inspirational goal which is also challenging will result in success, which increases self-belief and confidence and leads to higher performance.

You tend to get what you focus on. If you fear failure, you are focused on failure and that is what you get.

Positive focus

It is very important to state goals in the **positive**. What happens if a goal is stated in the negative, for example "We must not remain at the bottom of the regional sales league"? What is the attention focused on? Being at the bottom of the league, of course. If I say to you "Don't think about a red balloon," what comes to mind? Or if I say to a child "Don't drop that glass, spill the water, make a mistake"? The example I like is from cricket, when a wicket falls and, just as the next batsman passes through the white picket fence, some joker says to him "Don't get out first ball." He has the whole long walk to the crease to think about getting out first ball, and so he does. Negative goals can easily be converted into the positive opposite, for example "We are going for fourth in the league or higher" or "I am going to block the first ball, however tempting it may be to score."

Ethical standards

It may appear preachy to suggest that goals should be **legal**, **ethical**, and **environmentally sound**, but each individual has their own code about these things, and the only way to ensure employees' full alignment is to conform to the highest standards. Younger employees tend to have higher ethical standards than their older leaders, who are often surprised and whose excuse is the usual "we have always done it that way." Besides, the new accent on accountability in business and throughout society, and the consequences of exposure by a whistle-blower or a consumer watchdog, surely outweigh any short-term gain that may tempt the unscrupulous. In *Sporting Excellence*, David Hemery quotes Sir Michael Edwardes as saying:

> *You will not get the TOP people working with you unless you have the highest standards of business integrity. If you value what you get out of corner cutting at £1000, the damage you do in demotivation of good people is minus £20,000.*

Olympic goal

Perhaps the most striking example of good and successful goal setting I know also comes from the Olympics and from swimming, but from a decade before Michael Phelps was born. An American college freshman called John Naber watched Mark Spitz win seven gold medals for swimming in the 1972 Olympics in Munich. There and then, John decided that he would win the gold in the 100 meters backstroke in 1976. Although he had won the National Junior Championship at the time, he was still nearly 5 seconds off the pace required to win the Olympics – a huge amount to make up at that age and over such a short distance.

He decided to make the impossible possible first by setting himself a performance goal of a new world record, and then by dividing his 5-second deficit by the number of hours' training he could muster in four years. He worked out that he had to improve his time by one-fifth of an eye-blink for every hour of training, and he felt that was possible if he worked intelligently as well as hard. It was.

He had improved so much by 1976 that he was made captain of the American swimming team for Montreal, and he won the gold in both the 100 meters and the 200 meters backstroke, the first in world-record time and the second as an Olympic record. Good goal setting! John Naber was motivated by a clearly defined end goal, which he supported by a per- formance goal that was within his control. He underpinned this with a systematic process, and this formed the dais on which he was to stand.

Those who have to win, win a lot.
Those who fear losing, lose a lot.

OLYMPIC PERFORMANCE IN BUSINESS

So how does Olympic performance translate into business? Jorge Paulo Lemann has been a primary figure in Brazil's economic development for more than 40 years. In 1971, Lemann founded Banco de Investimentos Garantia, and he soon recruited Carlos Sicupira and Marcel Telles to join what many regard as the Goldman Sachs of Brazil. As they acquired diverse assets, the trio transformed the Brazilian economy, opening it up to outside investors while creating stability for those at home. Via their private equity firm 3G Capital, they now own or have stakes in huge brands Burger King, Anheuser-Busch InBev, and The Kraft Heinz Company.

They have run their businesses by motivating their people. In her book *Dream Big*, Cristiane Correa explains that they wanted to attract and retain great people who are motivated by more than money. Lemann explains their formula:

> *Create a big dream. Keep it simple, easily understood, and measured. Attract the right people who work well together. Measure results consist- ently. You can create, run, or improve anything with this formula.*
>
> (Harvard Business School, 2009)

In *The 3G Way*, Francisco Homem de Mello summarizes their leadership style as "Dream + People + Culture." They got great people on board and they created a culture in which these people could thrive and share in the rewards of the big dream. This approach took them from investment banking to finance into beer and burgers, from Brazil to Latin America, then Europe and the United States.

So how does it work? First, the big dream is a common dream that is kept alive across the company as a mantra. In the language of the goals pyramid (see Figure 10), if their dream goal had been to transform the Brazilian economy and open up the market in a way that created stability, their end goal might have been to do this by becoming the world's biggest beer company. From the dream and end goals, the company breaks down company-wide yearly goals (performance goals), then process goals in the form of CEO goals, VP goals, director goals, all the way down to goals for the factory employees, who are all aligned by targets derived from the dream goal. And as each dream goal is realized after a few years of fierce focus, the company sets another one, at least as big.

Their approach has been admired by many management commentators and gurus, including Jim Collins, who coined the term Big Hairy Audacious Goals (BHAG), a category into which Lemann, Sicupira, and Telles's dreams fit. After all, as Lemann has observed: "having a big dream brings as much work as having a small dream."

A sample coaching conversation

In the chapters covering practical skills, I will illustrate the points made with the dialogue of a fictional coaching conversation between Sam and his manager, Michelle. Sam is a project manager in a multinational telecoms company. He recently took on the project management of Summit, a cross-company project, which would require him to further develop his people management skills and influence people in the project team who don't report directly to him. Being a doer, Sam has been getting stuck in sorting out the many issues that are coming up in the project, which is leaving him feeling exhausted, overwhelmed, and frustrated with some members of the project team. Let's have a look at how Michelle focuses on goals so that Sam can get himself back on track with a project.

Coach clearly states purpose of conversation and asks coachee what he wants to work on

MICHELLE: I'd like to talk about the Summit project, and in particular I'd like to hear your take on how it's going managing the project team. Is now a good time? (*Sam nods*) What would you like to get from our discussion?

SAM: It'd be good to talk through the issues I've got with some of the individuals who aren't pulling their weight and the fact we don't have adequate resources to meet the current project deadlines.

MICHELLE: OK, sounds like you've got a lot to contend with at the moment. I do want to focus our attention on your people management skills, as you took on this project management role to develop these. However, given what you've just said, I'm wondering what would be most helpful for you to explore or resolve right now.

SAM: Another five people to work on the project would be brilliant, but I bet you'll say there's no budget for that!

MICHELLE: You're right, we don't have budget for more people. I'm hearing that people resource is the biggest thing on your mind currently. What would you say is the most pressing concern?

SAM: To be honest, it's Johann and Catherine, who just aren't delivering. They say they're going to do something and then don't do it. I can't rely on them. Then when I confront them about it, they just get upset or start blaming me. It's a nightmare, and because of them, our first delivery milestone is in jeopardy.

MICHELLE: How are you coping with it all?

SAM: It's stressing me out. I've had enough of their excuses. I don't know how I'll tell the customer that we're going to miss the first delivery milestone.

Shifts focus from the issue/ concern onto a goal that is meaningful for the coachee

MICHELLE: I'm here to support you with this and I'm confident that you will be able to work through it. What would be a good outcome from our discussion on these issues?

SAM: To get Johann and Catherine to step up and do what they're paid to do.

MICHELLE: And what do **you** want?

SAM: To be less stressed and have more time to do the things I'm meant to be doing to get the project back on track.

Gets specific on the desired outcome/goal

MICHELLE: I'm sensing it's important to you that you meet the delivery timescales for the customer. What will it mean to you to deliver this project on time?

SAM: Doing the best job possible and keeping the customer happy is what matters most.

MICHELLE: And taking a step back for a moment to look at the big picture, what's important about that goal for you?

Gets curious about how achieving this performance goal will serve the end/dream goal

SAM: Well, succeeding here will give me the experience and track record I need to apply to join the regional sales team, my ultimate goal.

MICHELLE: Great, so succeeding here will mean you are a step closer to your ultimate goal. Coming back to this project then, what would you say your overall aim is?

SAM: Everyone on the project team pulls together to deliver for the customer, not just a few of us.

MICHELLE: I'm hearing your frustration with some of the team. What do you ideally want your relationship with them to be like?

SAM: I want them to take responsibility for their work and have pride in what they do. I also want them to respect me.

MICHELLE: It sounds like you've got two goals: 1. To get the project back on track and keep the customer happy. 2. To improve your relationship with Johann and Catherine. Would it be helpful to flesh out those two goals?

Summarizes two perform-ance goals and invites coachee to work on process goals next

SAM: Yes, definitely.

Michelle has her own agenda for this discussion with Sam, which she states clearly at the start of the conversation. However, instead of forcing this agenda, she invites Sam to say what he wants to discuss. In the conversation that follows, Michelle acknowledges his concerns and shifts the discussion from problem solving into desired outcomes and goal setting. Notice the different layers of goals within this short dialogue: goals for this conversation – what Sam wants to walk away from the discussion with – as well as his bigger goals – the things that have purpose and meaning to him. This creates the motivation for Sam to keep going despite being overwhelmed, exhausted, and frustrated, and as he determined the ideal outcome and crafted the words for the end goal, he owns the goal and therefore is more committed to achieving it than if Michelle had told him what to do.

GOAL SETTING AND THE PERFORMANCE CURVE

Sam has identified that he is struggling with his relationship to Johann and Catherine. He consistently doesn't get what he wants from them, which points to a lack of communication on his part around the goal, as well as a lack of trust, which they are sensing and responding to by with-holding. Lack of clarity around goals causes so much interference and low performance. Without clear goals, people cannot bring the best of themselves, because there is confusion about what outcome is desired. And if Sam can't be honest with Johann and Catherine about his desire to mend relationships and work toward trust and respect, there isn't much chance that trust will develop on its own.

If we think back to the description of The Performance Curve in Chapter 2, Sam and that part of his team are operating in the lowest performance stage, **impulsive** – things will happen. Notice that Sam seems to be aiming for **dependent** (low–medium performance), because there is a flavor of "if only they would do what I say." Conversely, Michelle is operating in **interdependent** (high performance) – she trusts that by working together with Sam, they will turn this upset into a set-up. Michelle has identified that Sam is struggling with his people leadership skills in this area and is partnering with him to develop these. She is keeping front of mind how achieving this serves Sam's end goal. Through this dialogue, she has become aware of what is happening and this is now her priority, as it will affect the performance of the project as a whole. Through her coaching, Michelle is giving Sam on-the-job leadership development, which is priceless.

From goals, now it is time to take a look at reality.

11   R: What Is Reality?

When the reality is clear, it brings the goals into sharper focus

Having defined various goals, you need to clarify the current situation. It can be argued that goals cannot be established until the current situation is known and understood, and that therefore you should begin with **reality**. I reject this argument, on the basis that a purpose is essential to give value and direction to any discussion. Even if goals can be only loosely defined before the situation is looked at in some detail, this needs to be done first. Then, when the reality is clear, the goals can be brought into sharper focus, or even altered if the situation turns out to be a little different from what was previously thought.

Objectivity

The most important criterion for examining reality is objectivity. Objectivity is subject to major distortions caused by the opinions, judgments, expectations, prejudices, concerns, hopes, and fears of the perceiver. Awareness is perceiving things as they really are; self-awareness is recognizing those internal factors that distort your own perception of reality. Most people think they are objective, but absolute objectivity does not exist. The best you have is a degree of objectivity, but the closer you manage to get to it, the better.

Detachment

To approach reality, then, the potential distortions of both the coach and the coachee must be bypassed. This demands a high degree of detachment on the part of the coach, and the ability to phrase questions in a way that demands factual answers from the coachee. "What were the factors that determined your decision?" will evoke a more accurate response than "Why did you do that?" – which tends to produce what the coachee believes the coach wishes to hear, or a defensive justification.

Description not judgment

The coach should use, and as far as possible encourage the coachee to use, descriptive terminology rather than evaluative terminology. This helps to maintain detachment and objectivity and reduces the counterproductive self-criticism that distorts perception. Figure 11 illustrates the point.

FIGURE 11: *Communication envelope*

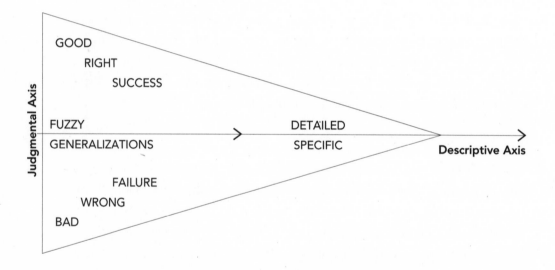

The terminology used in normal conversations, and many leadership interactions, falls generally toward the left-hand end of the envelope. In coaching you try to move to the right. The more specific and descriptive your words and phrases become, the less criticism they tend to carry, and the more productive the coaching will be.

Reality questions, when the coachee applies them to themselves, provide the most straightforward means of self-assessment. The skill of asking powerful reality questions is paramount whatever the application.

Deeper awareness

If a coach only asks questions and receives answers from the normal level of conscious awareness, they may be helping the coachee to structure their thoughts, but they are not probing to new or deeper levels of awareness. When the coachee has to stop to think before responding, maybe raising their eyes to do so, their awareness is being raised. The coachee is having to plumb new depths of their consciousness to retrieve the information. It is as if they are delving into their inner filing cabinet to find the answer. Once found, this new awareness becomes conscious, and the coachee is empowered by it.

You have a measure of choice and control over what you are aware of, but what you are unaware of controls you.

Follow the coachee

Following the interest or chain of thought of the coachee, while at the same time monitoring how that relates to the subject as a whole, is called following the coachee's agenda. It is one of the most basic coaching skills. Only when the coachee is ready to leave each aspect of the issue should the coach raise anything that they deem to have been omitted. If the coachee seems to have wandered far off the track, a question like "In what way does this relate to the goal?" may bring them back or reveal a valid reason. Either way, it allows the coachee to continue to lead the process. This enables them to fully explore the untapped potential within themselves and find their own resources to rise to any given challenge.

Direct communication among peers

In the business context, a leader may need to adjust this approach somewhat. Say a senior leader, Alison, wants to investigate and correct an apparent problem in Peter's department. If she raises the problem at the outset, he is liable to feel threatened and become defensive. If she does not raise it and lets him lead the conversation, will it ever arrive at the matter she wishes to address?

Instead, Alison needs to focus on the goal and ensure that she does not have judgment around what she sees as the problem. This, of course, takes great self-management – you can see why emotional intelligence is the key leadership quality valued above technical knowledge. Alison might start as follows:

ALISON: I would like to put our heads together to address something I am noticing about our two departments. Is that OK with you? (*Peter nods*) What I would love to happen is for the departments to work together seamlessly. What I notice is that sticking points keep occurring. What is your take on this?

In taking a constructive approach, without criticizing, she has managed her own judgment and has created the conditions for her and Peter to work collaboratively to solve this important problem.

When employees begin to see each other as a support rather than a threat, they will be much happier to raise their problems. When this happens, honest diagnosis and dialogue are possible, leading to early resolution. The blame culture that prevails in the majority of businesses works against this, as it causes "false reality syndrome," or "I will tell you what I think you want to hear, or what will keep me out of trouble." Any corrections put in place thereafter will be based on a false reality. The wise coach starts with a more general investigation and follows the conversation of the coachee. The coach might assist the coachee with another, lesser difficulty, thereby establishing credentials as a support rather than a threat. This approach is far more likely to lead in due course to the cause of the problem, instead of the symptom that is what is seen at first. Problems must be addressed at the level beneath that at which they show themselves, if they are to be permanently eliminated.

Use the senses

If coachees are learning a new physical skill, such as operating a tool of their trade, from a railway engine to a tennis racket, the coaching will also be focused on the senses: feel, sound, and sight.

Bodily awareness brings with it automatic self-correction. If this at first seems hard to believe, just close your eyes for a moment and focus your attention internally on your facial muscles. You will probably notice a furrowed brow or a tight jaw. Almost simultaneously with that awareness you are likely to experience a letting go, after which the brow or the jaw will be fully relaxed. The same principle applies to a complex physical movement. If your attention is focused internally on the moving parts, the efficiency-reducing tensions will be felt and automatically released, resulting in improved performance. This is the basis of the new coaching approach to sporting technique and proficiency.

Internal awareness increases bodily efficiency, which in turn results in improved technique. It is technique from the inside out rather than from the outside in. Furthermore, it is technique owned, integrated, and unique to the body concerned, as opposed to someone else's idea of good technique to which you have forced your body to conform. Which is more likely to lead to optimum performance?

> *Trying hard or trying to change causes bodily tension and uncoordinated action, which all too often results in failure.*

Bodily and internal awareness are also relevant if coachees are learning to use a new behavior, such as communicating powerfully so they can improve the effectiveness of their presentations. In this example, have coachees notice their current state as they describe their experience the last time they presented with questions such as:

- What was it like to stand in front of the audience?
- What did you notice about your pace?
- What emotions did you feel as you started to speak?
- On a 1–10 scale, how confident did you feel?
- How was your breathing?
- What thoughts were dominant just before you spoke your first words?
- How were you standing?
- In what way were you being powerful?
- What was your body communicating?

Give them the opportunity to say what they feel – keep asking open questions and listening, and let silence do the heavy lifting.

Assess attitudes and human tendencies

Self-awareness also needs to be brought to bear on your thoughts, attitudes, and human tendencies in the moment, and on those to which you normally have less conscious access. Each of us brings with us, sometimes right from our childhood, long-standing beliefs and opinions that will color our perceptions and our relationships with others. If we fail to acknowledge their existence and to compensate for their effects, they will distort our sense of reality.

Body and mind are interconnected. Most thoughts carry an emotion with them; all emotions are reflected in the body; bodily sensations often trigger thoughts. It follows therefore that concerns, blockages, and inhibitions can be approached through the mind, the body, or the emotions, and clearing one tends to free the others, although not always. Persistent stress, for example, may be reduced by identifying bodily tensions; by evoking awareness of the feelings that fuel overwork; or by uncovering mental attitudes such as perfectionism. It may be necessary to work on all three separately. Here I remind you of Gallwey's theme that the player of the Inner Game improves performance by seeking to remove or reduce the inner obstacles to outer performance.

Limit the depth

It is time for a word of caution. A coach may become aware of probing deeper into a coachee's hidden drives and motives than anticipated. That is the nature of transformational coaching: it addresses cause, not merely symptom. Coaching may be more demanding than papering over the interpersonal cracks in the office with directives, but it is also more rewarding in terms of results. However, if you are inadequately trained in coaching or faint-hearted, stay out. If you suspect that an employee relationship problem has deep-seated origins, then it is better to bring in a professional with the necessary skills. One distinction between coaching and counseling is that coaching is mainly proactive, looking at the future, and counseling is generally reactive, looking at the past.

Reality questions

Reality questions especially need to follow the "watch the ball" guidelines discussed in Chapter 7. Here they are repeated in slightly different terms. They are as follows:

• The demand for an answer is essential to **compel the coachee to think**, to examine, to look, to feel, to be engaged.

• The questions need to demand **high-resolution focus** to obtain the detail of high-quality input.

• The reality answers sought should be **descriptive not judgmental**, to ensure honesty and accuracy.

• The answers must be of sufficient quality and frequency to provide the coach with a **feedback loop**.

It is in the reality phase of coaching that questions should most often be initiated by the interrogatives "what," "when," "where," "who," and "how much." As already discussed, "how" and "why" should be used only sparingly or when no other phrase will suffice. These two words invite analysis and opinion, as well as defensiveness, whereas the interrogatives seek facts. In the reality phase, facts are important and, as in police investigation, analysis before all the facts are in can lead to theory formation and biased data collection thereafter. Coaches will need to be especially alert, listening and watching to pick up all the clues that indicate the direction of questioning to be followed. It must be stressed here that it is the coachee whose awareness is being raised. The coach often does not need to know the whole history of a situation, but merely to be certain that the coachee is clear about it. This is therefore not as time-consuming as it would be were the coach to require all the facts in order to provide the best answer.

One reality question that seldom fails to contribute value is "What action have you taken on this so far?" followed by "What were the effects of that action?" This serves to emphasize the value of action, and the difference between action and thinking about problems. Often people have thought about problems for ages, but only when asked what they have done about them do they realize that they have actually taken no action at all.

In business coaching scenarios, reality includes raising the coachee's awareness of the external reality (organizational strategy, policies and processes, political landscape, behavioral norms, culture, unwritten rules, power dynamics, etc.) as well as the coachee's internal reality (inner thoughts, feelings, beliefs, values, and attitudes). Anyone working in an organization coexists within a system that includes other people and things that may help coachees to achieve their goals, or get in the way. This is perhaps best illustrated by way of an example.

Let's imagine Petra has a goal to successfully implement a new sales process in her organization. When exploring reality, Petra's coach raises her awareness of all the relevant aspects within the outer reality that relate to her goal. This could include things such as understanding the attitude and behaviors of the sales teams that will be affected by the new process; identifying who has power or influence within sales who could block or support implementation; the unwritten rules for processing sales that may affect people using the new process; or the behavioral norms for how this organization deals with process changes. Petra's coach would also raise her awareness of all of the relevant aspects of her inner reality that relate to her goal, such as her motivation, her beliefs about her ability to influence key stakeholders, her confidence in dealing with people who resist, and what success will mean to her.

Early resolution

It is surprising how often the thorough investigation of reality throws up the answer before you even enter the third and fourth stages of coaching. Obvious courses of action that emerge in the reality or even on occasion in the goal stage are often accompanied by a "Eureka!" cry of recognition and an extra impulse to complete the task. The value of this is such that coaches should be willing to dwell sufficiently long in goals and reality and resist the temptation to rush on into options prematurely. So, lest we do just that, let us revisit the coaching conversation between Sam and his leader Michelle.

MICHELLE: One of your goals is to get the project back on track. How far off track is the project currently?

SAM: Well, actually it's only the service delivery element that's way off, as it's not even been started yet. The rest is pretty much on schedule.

MICHELLE: Let's come back to look at the service delivery element in a moment. You said the rest is pretty much on schedule. That's brilliant, well done! What's helped you to keep the rest on track?

SAM: The business analysts have worked really hard and listened carefully to the customer's requirements throughout. The software developers raised issues early, which meant that we were able to resolve problems that would have come up during testing before they became problems.

MICHELLE: How did you contribute to the business analysts and developers working like this?

SAM: I made sure they knew what was expected of them and always had at least two people from each of the teams attend the customer meetings, so they could hear things first hand.

MICHELLE: What else did you do?

SAM: I contracted with the team leaders at the start of the project to agree how we'd monitor progress and individuals' performance.

MICHELLE: What else?

SAM: I raised any concerns I had with the individuals directly and I made sure I recognized people who went the extra mile.

MICHELLE: What's different in the way you've been working with the service delivery people? That's where Johann and Catherine work, right?

SAM: They came into the project team later than everyone else and even though they were invited to project team meetings, they haven't been to any of them.

MICHELLE: What else has been different about how you've been working with them?

SAM: I heard from Bob that they can't be trusted, so I was disappointed when I heard it was them joining the team. I wouldn't have picked them.

MICHELLE: How do you think that has affected the way you interact with them?

Helps coachee to be objective and see things as they are without distortion

Helps coachee to recognize and celebrate what is working well

Raises awareness of coachee's role and contribution, and what he has learned about himself in the process

Expands awareness beyond self to include others (individuals, teams) and the system of which the coachee is part

SAM: I suppose I've been a bit standoffish with them and to be honest, I haven't spent the time with them that I have with others in the team.

MICHELLE: If you were in their shoes, what would you need from the project manager?

SAM: Clear direction and then to be left to get on with it my way, without constant interfering.

MICHELLE: What do you think Johann and Catherine would say about the way you are managing them in this project?

SAM: I'm sure they'd say that I micromanage them.

MICHELLE: What do you sense they need from you as the project manager?

SAM: Autonomy. Trust. To feel like a valued member of the project team.

MICHELLE: What do you need to do to create that?

SAM: Well, I need to contract with the service delivery team leader at the start and spend more time making Johann and Catherine feel a part of the team. I started out all wrong! I am going to go off and do this now.

Michelle uses active listening and powerful questions to help Sam to become more fully aware of the current reality. She starts by raising Sam's awareness about what's working well, to celebrate and highlight his strengths.

Michelle focuses Sam's attention on the external reality. The behavioral norms, culture, and political landscape form the map of an organization. For Sam to be successful in navigating his way through it, he must take an objective look at the lay of the land and the people in it, which Michelle helps him to do by not bringing judgment.

The other aspect to reality is Sam's inner reality, which includes his thoughts, feelings, assumptions, and expectations of himself and his relationship with the external reality of which he is a part.

Notice also that it is only after Sam has shared his thoughts and opinions that Michelle offers her thoughts.

REALITY AND THE PERFORMANCE CURVE

Michelle is raising Sam's awareness of his leadership impact by focusing attention on the effect his people leadership is having on those in the project team. Sam recognizes that he is micromanaging, an indicator of operating from the dependent stage, as also is his lack of trust in others.

This has resulted in low performance, with some members of the project team acting defensively, blaming others, and not taking responsibility. There are indications that Sam is also operating from the independent stage, as he feels that he has to fix things himself and work longer and harder. You may be forgiven for thinking that the prevailing mindset of leading from the independent stage, "I am a high performer," is a healthy one to have. However, notice how Sam puts pressure on himself to fix issues, and work longer and harder himself, and this takes him to the brink of burnout. If Sam were to adopt the prevailing mindset of "we are truly successful together" and operate from the interdependent stage, he would engage the project team members to pre-empt and solve issues themselves, because they feel ownership for high performance and do not accept low standards. It is apparent that Sam has the desire to move toward leading from the interdependent stage. Michelle has, through her powerful questions and active listening, raised Sam's awareness of what it will take for him to lead from there.

12   O: What Options Do You Have?

When you are sure that you have no more ideas, just come up with one more

The purpose of the **options** stage in GROW is not to find the "right" answer, but to create and list as many alternative courses of action as possible. The quantity of options is more important at this stage than the quality and feasibility of each one. The brain-stimulating process of gathering all the options is as valuable as the option list itself, because it gets the creative juices flowing. It is from this broad base of creative possibilities that specific action steps will be selected. If preferences, censorship, ridicule, obstacles, or the need for completeness are expressed during the collection process, potentially valuable contributions will be missed and choices will be limited.

Maximizing choices

Coaches will do all they can to draw these options from coachees or from the team they are coaching. To do this, they need to create an environment in which participants will feel safe enough to express their thoughts and ideas without inhibition or fear of judgment from the coach or others. All contributions, however apparently silly, need to be noted down, usually by the coach, in case they contain a germ of an idea that may leap into significance in the light of later suggestions.

Negative assumptions

One of the factors that most restricts the generation of creative solutions to business and other issues is the implicit assumptions we carry, many of which we are barely conscious of. For example:

- It can't be done.
- It can't be done like that.
- They would never agree to that.
- It's bound to cost too much.
- We can't afford the time.
- The competition must have thought of that.

There are many more. Note that all of them contain a negative or a dismissal. Good coaches would invite their coachees to ask themselves:

- What if there were no obstacles, what would you do then?

If particular interferences came up, they would continue to use "What if . . .?" For example:

- What if you had a large enough budget?
- What if you had more employees?
- What if you knew the answer? What would it be?

By this process, which temporarily sidesteps the censorship of the rational mind, more creative thought is unleashed and perhaps the obstacle is found to be less insurmountable than it seemed. Maybe another team member knows a way round that particular obstacle, so the impossible is made possible by the combined contributions of more than one person.

THE NINE DOT EXERCISE
On our coach training workshops, we sometimes use the well-known nine dot exercise to illustrate graphically the self-limiting assumptions everyone tends to make. For those of you who are not familiar with the exercise, or who have done it but may not remember the answer, take a look at Figure 12.

You may have remembered or realized that the assumption that has to be eliminated is the one that says "You have to stay within the square." However, don't become too smug. Can you do it again with the same rules but using three lines or fewer? What assumptions are you limiting yourself with now?

FIGURE 12: *Nine dot exercise*

Join the nine dots, using four straight lines *only*. Your pen must not leave the page and you may not repeat any line.

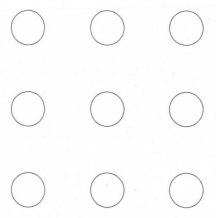

Of course, no one said you had to draw your line through the middle of the dots, but I bet you assumed that. What about two lines, or even one?

No one said you could not tear the page out and roll it into a cone, tear it into three strips, or fold it like a concertina. What this has done is to break another assumption, the one that thought you only had one variable, the position of the lines. But who said you couldn't move the dots? Recognizing all the available variables will expand your thinking and your list of options. Breaking out of these self-limiting assumptions frees you to solve old problems in new ways. The key is to identify the false assumption; the resolution is then much easier to find. (Several nine dot solutions are given in Appendix 3.)

Expanding creativity

When people get too stuck in their familiar perspective or way of thinking, asking a question like "What would you do if you were the leader?" or "Think of the person you most admire as a leader. What would they do?" frees them up to think from their more creative self. You can connect the coachee to their inner strengths by getting them to think of the qualities they admire in their **hero** and ask "How would SuperX do that?"

Or you could invite them to step (even take a physical step) into the mindset of their **subpersonalities** (we all have many – see Chapter 23), especially one they wouldn't usually bring to work, for instance the superbike racer.

Another powerful way of uncovering options is to ask the person to create a **metaphor** for the topic or a situation they are wanting to resolve. Develop that metaphor and stick with it as much as you can; don't try to map it back to reality. See if the resolution shows up in the metaphor world.

When coachees have exhausted their own resources, you can offer to **brainstorm** ideas to expand possible options and inject creativity in a way that reinforces their ability to be creative and resourceful. Offer ideas without being attached to them and encourage coachees to come up with more ideas.

Sorting options

BENEFITS AND COSTS

Once a comprehensive list of options has been generated, the **will** phase of coaching may just be a simple matter of selecting the best of the bunch. However, in more complex issues, as so many in business are, it may be necessary to re-examine the list by noting the benefits and costs of each of the courses of action. This should again be done by coaching, and it is here that some blend of two or more ideas may emerge as the optimum. Here I sometimes invite coachees to note how much they like each option on the list on a 1–10 scale.

INPUT FROM THE COACH

After coachees have exhausted their list of options, the coach can add to this. In order to maintain the development of coachees, however, this comes with health warnings. How can a coach provide input and still not undermine coachees' sense of total ownership? Quite simply by saying "I have a couple of ideas, let me know if you would like to hear them." Coachees might ask the coach to wait while they complete a particular train of thought. Any suggestions provided by the coach should only be accorded the same importance as all the other options.

MAPPING THE OPTIONS

In listing the options, the subconscious hierarchy (the more important things come first) that exists when a vertical column is made can be avoided by writing them randomly on a piece of paper in the way a crossword expert solves an anagram.

Generating options in practice

Let's see how Michelle explores options with Sam.

Expands thinking and creativity with permission to brainstorm and powerful questions "What else?" and "What if?"

MICHELLE: Let's brainstorm a list of things you might do to motivate everyone on the project team. Imagine you had no constraints, what might you do?

SAM: I could give them a pay rise.

MICHELLE: What else?

SAM: I could give them more time off. But these are things that are out of my control.

MICHELLE: What could you do that is within your control?

SAM: I could let their team leaders know what a great job they are doing so they are in line for a bonus and pay rise at the end of the year.

MICHELLE: What else?

SAM: I could say thank you more often.

Going for breadth

MICHELLE: What else?

SAM: I could do something that makes us feel like one big team, but I've no idea what.

MICHELLE: If money and time weren't an issue, what would you do to make everyone feel like one big team?

SAM: I'd co-locate everyone on the project team together in the new building.

MICHELLE: What if you were the CEO of this company? What would you do to motivate everyone on this project team?

SAM: I'd let them know how much I value the work they are doing and how important it is to the company's future.

MICHELLE: If you were Johann or Catherine, what would you do to motivate everyone on the project team?

SAM: Oh, that's a difficult one . . . I think I'd get a new project manager to replace me!

MICHELLE: If you could get a new project manager, what attributes and behaviors would they have that Johann and Catherine would like?

SAM: Patience. Being non-judgmental. They'd help Johann and Catherine to sort out problems themselves. They would discuss rather than confront them on issues.

MICHELLE: If you were the world's leading expert on project management, what would you do to motivate everyone on the project team?

SAM: I'd have monthly progress meetings with every single member of the team to help them reach their potential.

MICHELLE: What else?

SAM: I'd have weekly team meetings that are short and focused so everyone's aware of what's most important this coming week.

MICHELLE: What else?

SAM: I'd introduce a simpler way to track progress of the project for everyone.

MICHELLE: We've looked at a number of options for motivating everyone on the project team: a pay rise, letting their team leaders know what a great job they are doing, saying thank you more, co-locating everyone, regular meetings, simpler project tracking, a new project manager. Which ones do you want to explore some more now?

Summarizes options and invites coachee to consider pros/cons

SAM: Having everyone working together under one roof in the new building would make such a difference.

MICHELLE: Great, just before we do that, I am curious about what you feel right now.

Going for depth

SAM: I don't know, I feel overwhelmed.

MICHELLE: There's an idea I'd like to throw into the pot, if that's OK with you?

SAM: Sure, what is it?

MICHELLE: When I've got loads on and start to feel overwhelmed, I find that going to the gym to exercise more really helps me to work off the stress. What could you do to work off your stress?

SAM: I'm not a fan of the gym, so that won't work for me.

MICHELLE: What would work for you?

SAM: Getting outside either gardening or fishing, or just a walk in the fresh air.

Michelle starts with expanding Sam's thinking about all the possible options that would help him to achieve his goal of motivating people on the project team. The simple yet powerful question "What else?" is useful in generating options beyond the obvious things that Sam was already aware of and moving into new ideas and possibilities. Notice how Michelle playfully invites Sam to explore the seemingly impossible options using "What if?" questions.

Michelle tracks the different ideas and options and summarizes these so that Sam can pick options he'd like to explore in more detail. She's now starting to funnel and move from breadth to depth, raising awareness of the pros, cons, and possibilities for some of the options that most appeal to Sam.

Toward the end of exploring options, Michelle offers Sam an idea she has used herself to address the same issue of being overwhelmed with workload. She does this cleanly, in other words with transparency and without being attached to the idea. When Sam rejects it, Michelle helps him adapt the idea to the broader topic of stress reduction and the ways that work for him.

OPTIONS AND THE PERFORMANCE CURVE

Michelle continues to operate in the interdependent stage as she coaches Sam. The options generated will strengthen the team spirit. And helping Sam identify what will reduce his stress will give him better work–life balance. The coaching approach and ethos demand the coach truly partner with the coachee. This encourages high performance in the coachee through raising awareness and responsibility.

13   W: What Will You Do?

Creating the conditions for continuous learning is the key to performance improvement

The purpose of this final phase of the coaching sequence is to convert a discussion into a decision. It is the construction of an action plan to meet a requirement that has been clearly specified, on ground that has been thoroughly surveyed, and using the widest possible choice of building materials. The "W" in GROW stands for the **will** in "What *will* you do?" to emphasize the principle of will, intention, and responsibility. Without desire or the power of will, there is no real commitment to action. Once you have opened the coachee up to other perspectives and possibilities by asking the goal, reality, and options questions, it is time to tie the new insights down to action so that the new ideas are followed through. This will phase can be split into two stages:

• **Stage 1: Accountability Set-up** – define actions, timeframe, and measures of accomplishment.

• **Stage 2: Follow-up and Feedback** – review how things went and explore feedback for learning.

A recent *McKinsey Quarterly* article by Ewenstein *et al.* stated that many companies, such as GE, the Gap, and Adobe Systems, "want to build objectives that are more fluid and changeable than annual goals, frequent feedback discussions rather than annual or semi-annual ones, forward-looking coaching for development rather than backward-focused rating and ranking." The shift here is to development and continuous learning through a different type of feedback. And this has indeed been our experience – clients like Medtronic, a global leader in medical technology, services, and solutions with 88,000 employees currently, is a trailblazer in using a coaching approach to transform performance conversations. From a partnership that started back in 2008, this approach is now being adopted at the heart of Medtronic's Performance and Career Development process to develop leaders to have a meaningful, coaching-based conversation about performance management and career development that is ongoing. And it is in the will phase that continuous development happens, because it is where people take what they have learned and apply it in their work. We shall return to the Medtronic example, but now let's start the discussion by exploring the setting up of accountability.

STAGE 1: ACCOUNTABILITY SET-UP

Arguably, the most important role of a coach is to hold accountability, which is different from responsibility. Holding accountability means asking coachees to define specifically what they will do and when they will do it, and then trusting them to do just that. The reason accountability is so important is because it has the power to translate a coaching conversation into action. We are individually responsible for our own development. Applying a coaching approach to this vital step means helping someone develop their own appropriate measures of accomplishment and structures of accountability, integrating their purpose, goals, and agenda. This is a key performance management skill, which converts dialogue into concrete decisions and action steps with target dates for completion. It also creates alignment, as a leader who attended one of our internal workshops reported: "My team loved the fact that I would put in the accountability – How will I know? By when? This really helped them to think it through and know we are aligned."

To set up accountability, the key questions to ask are:

- What will you do?
- When?
- How will I know?

Of course, you can add subsets of questions to clarify each of these points and I provide more examples below, but these three principal questions form an effective backbone for this phase. The demands of a managerial autocrat are often met with quiet resignation, resistance, or resentment, however diplomatically they are expressed. As you will see in the example with Michelle and Sam, a coaching style, on the other hand, can bring a surprising degree of toughness into this phase of questioning without causing any bad feelings, since coaches are not imposing their own will, but activating the will of coachees. Coachees always maintain choice and ownership, even if their decision is to take no action, and therefore they will not feel oppressed by hard questions. They might even be amused by the recognition of their own ambivalence. If they do feel pushed, it suggests that coaches are unconsciously revealing that they think coachees *should* take a particular action. These requests must be communicated directly rather than coached.

Let's explore the following example will questions, which are applicable to the majority of coaching situations, from the perspective of what makes them powerful questions.

• **What will you do?** This question is quite distinct from "What could you do?" or "What are you thinking of doing?" or "Which of these do you prefer?" None of these implies a firm decision. Once a coach has asked this question in a clear, firm voice, indicating that it is decision time, they may follow it up with a question like "Which of these alternatives are you going to act on?" In most coaching issues the action plan will incorporate more than one of the options or parts of the options combined.

The options have been only loosely defined. Now is the time for the coach to ask questions to clarify the detail of the chosen options. By far the most important of these will be:

• **When will you do it?** This is the toughest of all the questions. We all have big ideas of what we would like to do or are going to do, but it is only when we give it a timeframe that it takes on a level of reality. And sometime next year is insufficient too. If something is going to happen, the timing needs to be highly specific.

If a single action is required, the answer sought might be "At 10 a.m. next Tuesday, the 12th." Often both a starting time and date and a finishing date will be required. If the action to be followed is a repetitive one, then the intervals need to be specified: "We will meet at 9 a.m. on the first Wednesday of every month." It is up to the coach to tie the coachee down to exact timings. The coachee may wriggle, but a good coach will not let them off the hook.

- **How will this action serve your goal?** Now that you have an action and a timeframe, it is important before you proceed any further to check that this is leading in the direction of both the goal of the session and the long-term goal. Without checking back, the coachee may find that they have wandered a long way off track. If this has happened, it is important not to rush to change the action, but to check if in fact it is the goal that needs to be modified in the light of what has come up since it was defined.

- **What obstacles might you meet along the way?** It is important to prepare for and pre-empt any circumstances that could arise that would inhibit completion of the action. Disruptive external scenarios might be looming, but internal ones could also occur, such as the faint-heartedness of the coachee. Some people experience a shrinking commitment and just can't wait for an obstacle to appear and provide them with an excuse for non-completion. This can be pre-empted by the coaching process.

- **How will I know? Who needs to know?** All too frequently in business, plans are changed and the people who should be told promptly hear this only later and at second hand, something that is very bad for employee relations. Coaches need to satisfy themselves that all the appropriate people are listed and that a plan is made for them to be informed.

- **What support do you need?** This is possibly related to the previous question, but support can come in many different forms. It could mean an arrangement to bring in outside people, skills, or resources, or it could be as simple as informing a colleague of your intention and asking them to remind you or keep you on target. Merely sharing your intended action with another person often has the effect of ensuring that you do it.

• **How and when are you going to get that support?** It is no good wanting some support but not taking the steps necessary to get it. Here the coach needs to persist until the coachee's actions are clear and certain.

• **What other considerations do you have?** This is a necessary catch-all question so that the coachee cannot claim that the coach omitted something. It is the coachee's responsibility to ensure that nothing is left out.

• **How committed are you to this action, on a scale of 1–10?** This is not rating the certainty of the outcome actually happening. It is a rating of the coachee's intention to carry out their part of the job. Completion of the task may depend on the agreement or the action of others, and that cannot be rated.

• **What prevents it from being a 10?** Check the coachee's motivation, and persist by asking a question such as: "If you have rated yourself at less than 8, how can you reduce the size of the task or lengthen the timescale to enable you to raise the rating to 8 or above?" If the rating is still below 8, suggest the coachee cross out the action step, as they are unlikely to take it. This is not to sabotage completion, as it might appear, but it is our experience that those who rate their commitment at less than 8 are not committed to those actions and seldom follow through. However, when faced with having to admit failure, the coachee may all of a sudden find the necessary motivation.

COMMITMENT

Most of us are familiar with the items that keep recurring on our to-do lists, be it at work or just the odd jobs around the home. Our list becomes so crumpled and scribbled on that eventually we rewrite it, and those same few items keep getting copied over. In time we begin to feel appropriately guilty, but still nothing happens. "How is it that I never complete this?" we moan at ourselves. Our uncompleted job list is evidence of our failure. Well, why feel bad about it? If you aren't going to do something, cross it off your list. And if you want to be a success for ever more, don't put anything on your list that you don't intend to do!

Remember that coaching aims to build and maintain the self-belief of the coachee. You must therefore coach people to success for their own sake as well as for their company's.

WRITTEN RECORD

It is important that both the coach and the coachee have a clear and accurate written record of the action steps and timeframe agreed. Decide which one of you will write down notes and then share them so you are on the same page. The coachee is the person who owns the action, so if the coach takes notes the coachee must read and confirm that it is a true record, that it constitutes their plan, that they fully understand it, and that they intend to carry it out. This is when I as coach usually offer myself as further support and reassure the coachee of my accessibility should they need me. Sometimes I offer to initiate the contact myself after a suitable interval, just to see how things are going. All this serves to help the coachee know that not only do they have challenge (in the session), they also have support (after the session). It is my intention that the coachee leave the session feeling good about themselves and inspired to take action. If they do, the goal will be achieved.

For the coach, making sure each party is clear on what will happen next and making agreements about when and how it would help to check in along the way are key to accountability.

ACCOUNTABILITY SET-UP IN PRACTICE

Let us put all this into action and look at how Michelle handles this important first stage of the will phase of GROW with Sam.

Once options have been fully explored, moves to exploring will

MICHELLE: We've explored a number of possible things you could do to motivate your team and get the project back on track. What are the things you want to move forward with?

SAM: Definitely the way I deal with issues that come up so I feel less stressed and, hopefully, others will too.

MICHELLE: So, what are you going to do about dealing with issues?

SAM: Deal calmly and confidently with issues when they arise and discuss them with people and help them to sort issues out themselves.

MICHELLE: When will you start?

SAM: Now.

MICHELLE: What will you do to ensure you feel less stressed and more able to have productive conversations?

Makes questions specific and exact

SAM: I will take three deep breaths and then listen non-judgmentally to understand the other person's point of view before forming my opinion. I will also make sure my questions are formulated in terms of what's working and not working, versus whose fault the problem is.

MICHELLE: What might get in the way of you remaining calm and confident and discussing rather than confronting?

SAM: If there are too many issues happening at once.

MICHELLE: What would help with that?

SAM: A bit of fresh air to clear my head.

MICHELLE: What specifically will you do the next time there are too many issues and you need to clear your head?

SAM: I'll go for a 15-minute walk in the park outside.

MICHELLE: What else do you want to do to motivate the project team and get things back on track?

SAM: I think I will explore the possibility of moving the project team to the new building.

MICHELLE: What exactly will you do to explore this possibility?

Helps to identify and access different resources

SAM: I'll need to find out who's responsible for premises and what the process is for getting approval.

MICHELLE: I know the person in charge, would you like me to put you in touch with them?

SAM: Yes, please.

MICHELLE: What else can I do to support you with this?

SAM: Could you find out what criteria they use for moving to the new building?

MICHELLE: Yes, I can ask about that. Let's turn our attention to Johann and Catherine. What do you want to do there?

SAM: It'll be a good opportunity to make peace with them.

Pre-empts and plans to deal with potential obstacles

MICHELLE: What specifically will you do differently the next time you speak with them?

SAM: I will be patient and calm.

MICHELLE: What will help you be patient and calm in an actual meeting?

SAM: I need to make sure I have time to be fully present in my meetings and start the meeting off by asking for others' assessments of what the issues are and how they might be resolved. I will then recap what I have heard and ask non-judgmental questions to get a clear picture of reality.

MICHELLE: Sounds great. And what else?

SAM: I will acknowledge the fact that we've got off to a bad start, and I will let them know how important they are to the project.

MICHELLE: What will you do about making it easy for them and others to raise issues easily?

SAM: I'm not sure. I'll need to give that some more thought.

MICHELLE: When will you do that thinking?

SAM: On the train this evening.

Sets up accountability, question: How will I know?

MICHELLE: How will you hold yourself accountable for doing that?

SAM: I will take notes of my reflections and share them with you in the morning.

MICHELLE: What I believe about you is that you are ready to let go of the stress of doing it all yourself and have the potential to bring out the best in your team and enjoy what you do.

SAM: Thanks!

Checks in on commitment

MICHELLE: Let's just check back to the goals you set at the start of our conversation. You said you wanted to feel that you can get things back on track, and you wanted some ideas on how to motivate the project team and forge healthy relationships with Johann and Catherine. Where are you with these?

SAM: I'm feeling much more confident and optimistic that I can get things back on track. In fact, I feel I am back on track and things aren't as bad as I thought. I've got some solid actions too that I'm sure will motivate the whole team, including Johann and Catherine.

MICHELLE: It looks like you've made a note of all your actions. Do you want to recap them now?

Makes sure a written note is taken

SAM: No, I'm confident I've got everything noted down and I'm eager to get on with things.

MICHELLE: On a 1–10 scale, how committed are you to take all of the actions you've agreed?

Checks commitment level

SAM: A 9.

MICHELLE: What would make it a 10?

SAM: To know the project team members are in alignment with all of this. I think I'll have a chat with some of them now.

The nature of Michelle's questions changes, moving from open and expansive questions that mainly start with what, to precise questions that move Sam into action and include when and how questions.

Michelle holds Sam's feet to the fire, challenging his commitment and not leaving any stone unturned. For example, when Sam says he needs to give some more thought to making it easy for people to raise issues, Michelle prompts him to say when he will do this thinking. This is all in service of Sam's stated agenda, and is not an opportunity for Michelle to tell Sam what she thinks he must do!

She demonstrates that she is a partner to Sam in this, offering her support, providing access to resources, offering ideas to help Sam achieve his goals, and expressing confidence in his potential through the use of acknowledgment.

Michelle checks back to Sam's original goal to ensure that his actions are aligned with this, and does one final check on how committed Sam is to the actions he's agreed using a simple 1–10 scale. You can feel Sam's commitment to taking action, because he's come up with the actions that will move him toward goals that have meaning and purpose to him personally, as well as serving the project team and the project's customers.

This example is typical of a coaching leadership style in action and it serves to illustrate the majority of the coaching principles.

STAGE 2: FOLLOW-UP AND FEEDBACK

It is at this stage that any gaps in expectations surface and learning and alignment happen. It is crucial that feedback pathways are created if people are to learn, develop, and improve performance. By partnering for feedback and using a coaching style, all of these happen. Feedback becomes the opportunity to activate the natural learning system that lies within each person.

CHECKING IN, NOT CHECKING UP

When following up on actions, one of three things will have happened:

- The coachee succeeded (or partly succeeded).
- They did not succeed.
- They did not do it.

Question Bag 6 provides a list of questions you can use in each case. It is key to bear in mind here that you are checking in (as opposed to checking up on the coachee) about what has happened at an agreed later point in time. This keeps communication channels open and maintains alignment. Building a partnering relationship founded on trust with your coachee will help them to feel they can approach you for help to get back on track. If you are coaching members of your team, establishing trust between you will encourage them to tell you before the deadline if something changes or they are deviating from what was agreed.

The purpose of reviewing someone's actions and progress is development. Developing people on the job has been shown to be the most effective form of learning – the often cited 70:20:10 model for learning and development indicates that for successful and effective leaders, most learning (70 percent) happens through experience on the job, while 20 percent comes from learning from others and only 10 percent from "formal" learning such as instructional training and coursework.

Using coaching to help people rise to challenges and solve day-to-day problems fits into this most effective form of learning. And it is easy to understand why: it is putting learning into practice immediately, so, in line with adult learning theory, people are learning by doing. It is follow-up that increases learning and awareness, identifies possible blocks, and offers further support or challenge to meet goals. Blame or criticism has no place here and will undo all your good work. This is not to say that you cannot be candid.

EXPLORING FEEDBACK

How do you turn feedback into a learning and development opportunity? To complete the will phase, you must follow up and see what went well and what could be done differently next time by exploring feedback perspectives rather than giving feedback. This means coach and coachee sharing information-rich feedback from the environment, rather than the coach delivering their opinion to the coachee, as we shall now explore.

Let's first look at the five levels of feedback that are in common use. They are illustrated below in order from A, the least helpful, to E, the most productive and the only one of the five that promotes major learning and performance benefits. The other four at best produce minimal short-term improvement, and at worst cause further decline in performance and self-esteem. A to D are widely used in business circles and at first glance might seem reasonable – that is, until or unless they are examined with care.

A. Coach's exclamation: *"You are useless."*
This is a **personalized criticism** that devastates self-esteem and confidence and is bound to make future performance even worse. It contains nothing helpful.

B. Coach's exclamation: *"This report is useless."*
This **judgmental comment** directed at the report, not at the person, also damages the coachee's self-esteem, though less badly, but it still provides **no information** on which they can act to improve the report.

C. Coach's intervention: *"The content of your report was clear and concise, but the layout and presentation were too down-market for its target readership."*
This avoids criticism and provides the coachee with **some information** on which to act, but in insufficient detail and it generates **no ownership**.

D. Coach's intervention: *"How do you feel about the report?"*
The coachee now has ownership, but is likely to give a non-response such as "Fine," or to make a **value judgment** of the work such as "Great" or "Lousy," rather than a more useful description.

E. Coach's interventions: *"What are you most pleased with?" "If you could do it again, what would you do differently?" "What are you learning?"*
In response to a series of questions such as these delivered in a non-judgmental manner, the coachee gives a **detailed description** of the report and the thinking behind it.

So why does the form of feedback illustrated in E dramatically accelerate learning and improve performance? Only E meets all the best coaching criteria. In order to answer the coach's questions in E, the coachee is compelled to engage their brain and get involved. They have to recollect and formulate their thoughts before they can articulate their responses. This is awareness. It helps them to learn how to evaluate their own work and thereby become more self-reliant. In this way they "own" their performance and their assessment of it. This is responsibility. When these two factors are optimized, learning occurs. Conversely, if a coach just gives their own opinion, the actual engagement of the coachee's brain is likely to be minimal; there is no ownership and no means for coaches to measure what has been assimilated.

The use of descriptive rather than judgmental terminology, either by the coachee, as seen in E, or by the coach, as in C, avoids evoking the coachee's defensiveness. Defensiveness must be avoided, because when it is present, the truth/reality becomes smothered in inaccurate excuses and justifications, which both coachee and coach may believe and which are no basis for performance improvement. However, in intervention C, as well as in A and B, the coach retains ownership of both the evaluation and the correction and the relationship is one of dependency, so learning for the future is correspondingly minimized. Interventions A–D all fall short of the ideal; nevertheless, they are the ones most frequently used in business.

THE GROW FEEDBACK FRAMEWORK

I have talked about using GROW to structure a coaching conversation. Feedback is actually a coaching conversation all of its own. Therefore, within will, I am sharing a routemap for having successful feedback conversations which is called the GROW Feedback Framework. In order to make feedback a learning opportunity, the key questions to ask are:

- What happened?
- What did you learn?
- How will you use this in the future?

TABLE 4: *GROW Feedback Framework – tips*

The golden rule at each step is that the coachee shares first and the coach gives their perspective second.			
1. Set Intention	**2. Recognize**	**3. Improve**	**4. Learn**
• Goal questions set the intention and context for the feedback discussion. They focus attention and raise energy. • Setting context and goals up front lays the foundation for a productive conversation.	• Focusing on what the coachee did well will raise energy and awareness of strengths, thereby building confidence, and accelerating learning. • If performance is low, this step is still vital. Once they have finished, highlight what you thought they did well. Acknowledge their effort, even if the goal hasn't been fully achieved. • Remember: No negative judgment or criticism.	• Non-judgment is key to a safe learning environment that inspires creativity, and creates engagement. • Giving the coachee time to reflect on what they would like to change before you add any of your own suggestions will build self-reliance and responsibility.	• Checking in on learning and what will be different builds a partnering relationship that reinforces confidence and expectation. • Link to overall development goals where relevant. • Agree specific actions. Check you are both clear on priorities, timeline, and commitment.
Ask: "What do you/we want to get out of this?" Add: "I want . . ."	Ask: "What is going/ went well?" Add: "I like/liked . . ."	Ask: "What could be done differently?" Add: "How about . . .?"	Ask: "What is the learning and what will you/we do differently?" Add: "I am learning . . ."; "I will do . . ."
G	R	O	W

Let's look at these questions in the context of GROW (Figure 13) and see what a whole feedback conversation would look like when using a coaching style to accelerate learning and improve performance. Follow the golden rule and tips set out in Table 4, and dip into Question Bag 7 to help you explore different phases in more depth.

FIGURE 13: *GROW Feedback Framework*

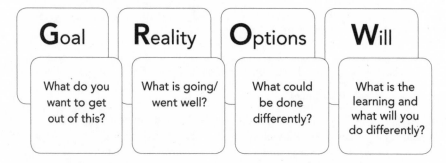

GOLDEN RULE FOR EACH STEP: coachee shares first, coach adds their perspective second.

Goal	**R**eality	**O**ptions	**W**ill
What do you want to get out of this?	What is going/went well?	What could be done differently?	What is the learning and what will you do differently?

FEEDBACK AND EMPLOYEE ENGAGEMENT

The quality of feedback is one of the areas measured in employee engagement surveys and this is what our client MasterCard asked us to focus on – people want to work in an environment where there is high-quality feedback. When Ajaypal Singh Banga became CEO of MasterCard, he set the business the remit of "competing to win." Using information gathered from its 6,700 global employees in an annual employee engagement survey, the Learning and Development team identified that a key area for development that would support this remit was improving feedback. They approached Performance Consultants to help them create a performance feedback culture.

We tailored a program for MasterCard's 1,500 global leaders called Coaching for Impact, which featured the GROW Feedback Framework. The types of items in an employee survey around feedback are:

- "I receive regular feedback."
- "I receive feedback that helps me improve my performance."

Thinking about these two items, you can see how a coaching style and the GROW Feedback Framework ensure more regular feedback and also quality feedback. One year later, when the next employee engagement survey was done, all the global leaders had been through the program and the results of the survey showed an improvement across the board, with a noticeable jump in the area of feedback.

LEARNING FOR ALL

And, make no mistake, not only is this development for the coachee, it is development for the coaching leader too. This is an opportunity for leaders to get curious and learn what they can do differently next time to create high performance. After all, as I have discussed, leadership mindset and behavior are the biggest factors influencing performance, and they are 100 percent within the leader's control.

REVIEWING IN PRACTICE

Let's see this in a practical example and find out what happens a few weeks later when Michelle follows up on accountability with Sam. You will see her use questions from Question Bag 6 as she checks in on how some things are progressing, as well as following up and reviewing.

MICHELLE: I'd like to follow up with you on the actions you agreed to take. I recall you were feeling somewhat overwhelmed with project Summit. How's it been going these past few weeks?

Clearly states the purpose

SAM: Better. But I'm still having problems with Johann and Catherine.

MICHELLE: OK, sounds like that's one for us to talk through. You said you're feeling better. What's making it better?

Starts by focusing on what's working well

SAM: I had a really good team meeting using the new structure we talked about and everyone's keen to have a monthly one-to-one chat.

MICHELLE: That's great. What else?

SAM: I've spoken with the facilities guy you put me in touch with and he's going to consider my request to move the team to the new building – the great news is that the cost implications are very low. I will need you to approve the request when it gets to that stage. Are you still OK with that?

MICHELLE: Absolutely. How about the process for raising issues and mutual accountability? You were planning to make some changes there, weren't you?

SAM: I'm in discussion with some of the project team members on that one. I'm putting together a subteam led by Kim to review the process and come up with a new one. Jenny is facilitating our team meeting next week to discuss accountability and create some rules of engagement.

Celebrates success

MICHELLE: That sounds like a brilliant step forward! I was wondering how you were getting on with not doing it all yourself. You were going to experiment with adopting a new attitude. How's that going?

SAM: Surprisingly well. Seeing issues as opportunities for people to step up and grow is helping me to get back to focusing on people.

MICHELLE: What's it like for you to get back to focusing on people?

SAM: Really good, in the main. I've been spending more of my time chatting things through with the project team and I guess I've been coaching them.

MICHELLE: What are you noticing about the impact that's having on the team?

SAM: Everyone seems happier so far, and there's less tension. I wish the same were true with Johann and Catherine.

MICHELLE: Yes, you said that you're still having problems there. Is now a good time for us to chat that one through?

SAM: Definitely. I think we're reaching the stage where we need to escalate this further. They're still not doing what they're meant to and seem to be ignoring all my emails.

Remains non-judgmental and inquires about what's happened or what's not happened without making out the coachee is wrong

MICHELLE: How have you been interacting with them?

SAM: I've been really careful with the wording of my emails so that I don't put anything that they could take the wrong way, and at the same time I've tried to be firm so that they will get on with things.

MICHELLE: It sounds like you've not had the chance to speak to them yet then.

SAM: No, I have emailed them several times, but they are not replying.

MICHELLE: Hmmm . . . seems like they are showing some real resistance. What else have you tried?

SAM: I've tried resending the emails, but still nothing.

MICHELLE: I'm sensing that there's something more going on here. What's your take on this?

SAM: I think they're deliberately out to prove a point and I'm not going to stoop to their level. It's about time they started to earn the huge salary they get paid for doing nothing.

MICHELLE: I'm noticing your language is different when you're talking about them and I'm hearing your frustration. What are you noticing?

SAM: I'm angry alright. It's ridiculous that they think they can get away with this.

MICHELLE: Are you willing to hear some feedback that might be hard to hear?

SAM: Yes.

MICHELLE: It sounds as though your approach is combative – I'm hearing us versus them. How do you see it? Is that a fair statement?

SAM: Well, they've not exactly made any effort to be part of the team.

MICHELLE: What have you done to make them feel part of the team?

SAM: I've invited them to project team meetings and they don't show up.

MICHELLE: We had a conversation about this last time we spoke, and I recall you were going to make peace with them by acknowledging things got off to a bad start, and you were planning to let them know how important they are to the project and that you'd like a clean start with building trust and respect. What happened with that?

SAM: It hasn't happened.

MICHELLE: Ah, OK. How come it hasn't happened?

SAM: As I've already said, they aren't replying to my emails.

MICHELLE: It seems like we're going round in circles on this one, Sam. I'm concerned that you're using email as a way to communicate with people you're in conflict with, especially when your intention is to make them feel like they are an integral part of the team. I feel you may be putting off having what could be a difficult conversation with Johann and Catherine. What's going on for you?

SAM: I am not looking forward to the conversation, but it's not my fault if they don't reply to my emails.

MICHELLE: You're right that you can't make them reply to your emails. However, I wonder what you could do differently to get the conversation started?

Says what she's sensing then lets coachee respond with what's true for him

Points to language the coachee is using to raise awareness, reflects back emotions

Reflects back with non-judgment, checks if coachee agrees

Positively confronts the coachee with the fact he did not take agreed actions

Senses resistance and names it so it's on the table and can be discussed

SAM: I suppose I could pick up the phone and call them. But they'd probably see it's me and not answer the phone.

Partners with coachee to develop structures and/ or measures of success

MICHELLE: If you were to approach this with the attitude you've been experimenting with – an opportunity for people to step up and grow, including yourself – how would you go about interacting with Johann and Catherine?

SAM: I'd take a deep breath and walk over to their desks and take them for a coffee, so we could have a proper chat.

MICHELLE: Sounds like a good start. What else would you do?

SAM: I'd probably go for a walk outside before then, so that I have a clear head and feel calm.

MICHELLE: OK, what else?

SAM: I'd probably write down the key points I want to cover so that I don't forget them. In fact, I will do all of that.

MICHELLE: How will you remember to see this as an opportunity for you all to step up and grow?

SAM: I think that I'll put that sentence on the top of my notes.

MICHELLE: When will you have this conversation, Sam?

SAM: Next week.

Makes requests to help coachee break through his resistance

Championing

MICHELLE: I would like to see you make this a priority and bring the conversation forward into this week, Sam. I can see how this has been affecting you and I know that you want to get this sorted. You've had success with approaching issues as an opportunity to grow, so I am confident that you will be able to make peace with them and make them feel like integral members of the project team. What are you thinking now?

SAM: I think it is a priority and I will tackle it now.

MICHELLE: Do you want to tackle it or resolve it?

SAM: Resolve it once and for all.

Sets up new accountability, checks what the coachee is learning

MICHELLE: What specifically will you do, Sam, and when?

SAM: I will walk over to the new building with two bars of chocolate as a peace offering and invite them for coffee.

MICHELLE: What exactly will you say and what are you learning?

SAM: I will start by saying sorry that I've been hounding them with emails, and say that I want to put our heads together to figure out how we can have relationships built on trust and respect, and so they can make the contributions to the team that I know will benefit everyone. I am learning that I needn't feel that it's me against them, that we are all on the same side.

MICHELLE: Sounds like a good start. Let me know where you are with this before you go home this evening, Sam. I appreciate you being willing to get this sorted sooner, it demonstrates real strength of character.

Further acknowledgment to build confidence and self-belief

Notice how Michelle asks powerful questions to have Sam reflect on what's happened, what the impact has been, what he's learned, and what he will do differently. Although Michelle probably had to bite her tongue a few times to stop herself from telling Sam to go and speak to Johann and Catherine, she coached Sam to his own conclusion with this, so he is much more likely to follow through.

Michelle didn't skirt around the resistance that Sam was exhibiting and simply named it and without judgment invited him to say what was going on for him. This enabled the conversation to move forward and unveiled Sam's reluctance to have what he saw as a difficult conversation, so Michelle helped him to come up with a new plan of action that he was more comfortable with, and made a request for prompt execution of the plan, before setting up new accountability.

As with this example, if coaching is integrated in the leadership style it won't feel like a "coaching session." The uninitiated might not even recognize it as coaching, they would simply think one person was being particularly helpful and considerate of the other, and was obviously a good listener. Structured or informal, the fundamental principles of raising awareness and building responsibility within the coachee remain the key to the coaching approach.

WILL AND THE PERFORMANCE CURVE

When Michelle moves into the final step of this coaching, her aim is to motivate Sam to take action that will move him closer to his goal. This moves the conversation from good ideas to commitment to taking action that will serve a higher purpose. In connecting Sam back to what's motivating for him in delivering this project, Michelle is enabling him to move toward leading the project team in the interdependent stage, where Sam's potential to enable and inspire great teamwork can be released. Michelle recognizes that it's vital for leaders to keep the balance within themselves so they don't revert to any of the earlier stages, so she is proactive in pointing Sam toward self-management to preserve balance. Finally, she demonstrates that she's in it together with him, letting him know that she has his back and that she believes in him.

Creating learning

To revisit the example of Medtronic, by teaching leaders how to have an ongoing performance conversation in a coaching style, a whole new approach to performance management is created. Gone is the traditional approach of delivering a message to an employee that they are broken and need to be fixed. Instead, the coach and coachee partner to explore what is going well and where the opportunities for growth are. The focus is on learning. When applying a coaching ethos to accountability, you are focused on creating learning, choice, and self-motivation by looking for what's working well and reaffirming this, and where necessary supporting the coachee to change direction or do something differently. Setting and following up on accountability keep people connected to their inspiring dream goal and make what can seem like a dull process goal more compelling (see Chapter 10). Accountability thus moves light years away from its unpopular footing in traditional command-and-control culture to become a critical instrument for high performance through the overarching principle of coaching – to raise awareness and responsibility.

14 Coaching for Meaning and Purpose

The point is not to become a leader. The point is to become yourself, and to use yourself completely – all your gifts and skills and energies – to make your vision manifest. You must withhold nothing.
Warren Bennis

Now that we have looked at the GROW sequence from start to finish and started to get to grips with practicing the fundamentals of coaching, it is a good time to add the crucial depth and look at how coaching helps you to connect with meaning and purpose in your life. I highly recommend that you choose to travel this road, for this is where the real gold lies. Although finding meaning and purpose might sound daunting, your journey is totally within your control.

I mentioned in Chapter 1 that self-actualizers seek meaning and purpose, and very often find it by contributing to others, to their community, or to society at large. More and more people are demonstrating that they care as much about fairness and the plight of others as they do about themselves. These emerging altruistic tendencies are also causing them to question corporate ethics and values as well as the profit motive. How successfully and sustainably the human race responds to external challenges is directly linked to how connected we are with ourselves. It is no coincidence that Google chose to call its Leadership Institute "Search Inside Yourself," nor that leadership pioneer Warren Bennis said that it is not about becoming a leader but becoming yourself.

Both the coaching leader and the professional coach are looking to unlock potential to maximize performance – leaders the potential of their teams, and coaches the potential of coachees. A look at current business reality will illustrate why this is so urgently needed.

The war for talent

The summarizing heading of a *Financial Times* article reads: "A reconnection with core values: Greed is not good in the new age of business: Workers are more than the sum of their parts: Spirituality in business: Stephen Overell joins the search for the ultimate competitive advantage, and finds that companies are trying to offer staff meaning and purpose." High salaries alone are not enough to secure top talent.

Ken Costa, then vice-chairman of banking group UBS Warburg, says: "You can see the frustration. It demonstrates itself in uncertainty and a lack of fulfilment and ultimately leads people to leave an organization. More are leaving to work in the voluntary sector . . . In the last round of graduate recruitment we did, a surprising amount of people asked 'what are your policies regarding social responsibility'. That has never happened before."

Can businesses experience the same kind of crisis of meaning that many individuals are currently undergoing? I suggest that they can and they do. And could it be more widespread still? Could the corporate world, or the world itself, be approaching a collective crisis of meaning? There are many telltale signs. Economic and political indicators are no longer providing clear signals of what is happening. The environment, the unstable economic and political landscape, and declining corporate ethics are posing immediate, unprecedented challenges to business, but business is not responding, paralyzed by its old paradigms and by the need for immediate crisis management. In the view of many people, a greater crisis is here now, and denial of it is rife.

AN ECONOMY THAT SERVES PEOPLE

Many people believe that a major shift in the attitude and role of business is inevitable and in fact is already under way, driven in large measure by public demand. People are signifying that they will no longer tolerate being in service to the economy; instead, they are demanding that the economy be made to serve people. Will this come about by a series of managed course corrections as businesses learn to accept their responsibility, their true meaning and purpose, or will they continue their blinkered pursuit of wealth at any price, until they run into barricades manned by ordinary people with higher demands and aspirations?

A company with meaningful vision will not just be keeping pace with the public mood, but will be ahead of it, particularly because it realizes that it has a responsibility to society.

THE CHANGING ROLE OF BUSINESS

And we are beginning to witness the changing role of business. John Browne, the ex-CEO of British Petroleum, wrote in his recent book, *Connect*:

> *In an era of unremitting transparency, the world requires much more from the private sector . . . There is an enormous prize for companies which choose to meet these new demands with respect, authenticity and openness, making society's needs part of their business model.*

Claude Smadja of the World Economic Forum wrote:

> *Private companies must assert a much wider and stronger sense of corporate social responsibility. And we must listen to the responsible voices of a new "civil society" . . . The rise of NGOs also reflects increased public disenchantment with all institutions – governments, corporations, international organizations, media.*

Michael Hirsh of *Newsweek* commented that the debate is less about privatizing the public sector than the converse, "publicizing" the private sector.

THE NEXT WAVE OF EVOLUTION

Globalization and instant, frequent communication around the world are blurring the space and time distinctions between "us" and "them." Thus both external forces and our inner development are conspiring to break down barriers and persuade us to accept and embrace the common destiny that all people share – and share responsibility for. At last, this is Maslow's final level that relates to a mindset of interdependence: "we are all in it together."

OUTER REALITY REFLECTS INNER REALITY

Shifts are occurring in our outer reality that correspond to our increasing awareness of our inner reality. Global investment in what are called ethical funds is increasing fast; sexism and racism, previously endemic in many workplaces, are now widely condemned; and corporate social responsibility and triple-bottom-line reporting are increasingly being adopted.

The drive for these changes is coming from ordinary people who want more say in how they are treated at work and by business. However, climate change is also sending all of us, and business in particular, some harsh messages about our values, behaviors, and responsibilities in the global context. In addition, the potential consequences of the intensive farming of animals, of biofuels, and of genetic modification of crops are forcing a serious re-evaluation of agricultural methods that is way beyond the province of mere "nature lovers." What will the next beachhead be? It will probably be in the environmental arena, but we don't know where it will come from, as nature's system controls are breaking down and we are now past the point at which the reactions are predictable. The next point is the one of no return. The greatest concern is that it appears far more serious than is suggested by short-term and wholly inadequate political and corporate responses.

MEANING AND PURPOSE IN ORGANIZATIONS

With all this going on, it is not surprising that the issue of meaning and purpose is being raised more and more often by people we work with in organizations, stemming from the desire to escape from what many see as the meaningless corporate world. A coach often hears a coachee lament this and talk about changing jobs, but beware the seduction of changing forms and structures – it is consciousness that must change.

Meaning and purpose: The difference

In Chapter 6, I stated that through heightening our awareness, we can discover and connect more deeply with our purpose. Meaning and purpose are spoken of as being joined at the hip, but they are not identical and they need to be distinguished. **Meaning** is the significance we ascribe to an event or an action in hindsight, while **purpose** is our intent to embark on a course of action. Meaning is mainly psychological, whereas purpose is a spiritual concept. To be more precise, we should specify either meaning, or purpose, or both. Let's look at this in relation to two areas:

- Finding your meaning and purpose in life.
- Finding meaning and purpose in situations that arise on a daily basis.

Uncovering your meaning and purpose

One of the mantras of Performance Consultants which is central to coaching is to "meet people where they are." Once you have met someone where they are, you can partner with them to go as far as they would like to go. This is full partnership, and it respects the unfolding of awareness on the journey of the evolution of consciousness. Here is an activity that you can do now to explore your meaning and purpose.

ACTIVITY:

Explore Your Meaning and Purpose

Sit down somewhere quiet with some colored pens and a piece of blank white paper. Jot down your responses to the questions below. If images come to mind, draw them. The key here is not to think too hard or to try to get things right – see what comes to mind and use whichever color takes your liking for each answer.

- What's your dream?
- What do you yearn for?
- What difference would you love to make in the world?
- What's important about that to you?
- Deep down, what do you really want from your life?
- Imagine you are 80 years old and you are looking back at your life. What are the highlights? Write or draw what comes to mind.

From your answers to these questions, you will start to get a sense of your meaning and purpose. This exploration will begin to create a breadcrumb trail – a trail that you can follow to find your meaning and purpose in life. As more details of the picture come to you, add them to the piece of paper. Take your first step on this journey and ask that part of you that is your unlimited potential to create this with you.

FROM VICTIM TO CREATOR

The biggest step to finding meaning and purpose is to realize that, ultimately, your current reality is your opportunity. It means stepping from being a victim of fate into being a creator of destiny. Coaching empowers the coachee to take responsibility for their current situation, choose how to relate to it, and take action to create or change things and ultimately create something more meaningful.

Try this activity.

ACTIVITY: *Rise to the* *Challenge*	Think of a challenge that you are currently facing and answer the following questions: • Imagine that challenge contains the perfect gift that you need now in order to grow, what is that gift? • What are you grateful for? • Who will you become in order to rise to that challenge?

Such an activity can be an extremely challenging slant on situations that arise in your life. However, questions like these will enable you to fully step out of being a victim of fate into being a creator of destiny, which will help create meaning and purpose in every moment of your life.

Carl Jung said: "What you resist persists." If you don't want the same challenges to rise again and again in work, life, and love, I encourage you to turn to face the challenges that come into your life.

Uncovering meaning and purpose in the workplace

Let's link this back to the work we have done up to now in the previous chapters. In the coaching dialogues starting in Chapter 10, we followed Michelle and Sam as they worked together on project Summit. What if Michelle were to delve more into meaning and purpose with Sam? What would that look like?

Here are some questions that she might ask:

- Sam, I notice you allow Johann and Catherine to trigger you into reactive behavior. What do you notice about that?
- If you knew, what would you say is the source of that trigger in you?
- How would you respond to this if you could choose?
- What would enable you to choose a different response?
- What's important for you about choosing a different response?
- What impact would this have on your life?

In fact, if we take this lens, project Summit is the platform through which Sam is fulfilling his potential; what he needs to do is recognize this and discover the intrinsic meaning and purpose therein. Of course, his attention does need to be pointed in this direction, and who Sam is yearning to become is part of his career development. This could happen through Michelle having sat down with him at the beginning of their work together to explore his vision for what he wants to achieve, through his leadership, at work, and in his life. A note of caution here, however: as a coach or as a leader adopting a coaching style, it makes sense that you should have already explored your own meaning and purpose and started to create your own destiny before leading your coachee into this advanced space. Another key tenet of coaching is not to ask a question of your coachee that you wouldn't be willing to answer – or haven't already answered – yourself.

It is beyond the scope of the book to teach advanced coaching skills, so I will leave this here for the moment, but a professional coach or a leader who has done advanced coach training would be able to facilitate this exploration.

PART IV

Specific Applications of Coaching

15   Formal 1:1 Coaching Sessions

87% of employers surveyed offer one-to-one coaching
ICF and Human Capital Institute

It is time to dedicate a chapter entirely to formal 1:1 coaching sessions conducted by internal or external coaches. Setting up formal coaching sessions, dedicated periods of time in which 1:1 coaching will occur, requires a structure to be in place at the outset. Whether you're an internal or external coach conducting formal coaching sessions in organizations, here are some guidelines to help you get the best from your coaching.

Time periods for formal coaching

Formal coaching, commonly called 1:1 coaching or executive coaching, works best if it takes place over a period of six months. By spacing the sessions out over months, the coachee benefits from plenty of practice of new habits and ways of doing things with you, their coach, as a champion and support. Also, since coaching is an ongoing partnering relationship focusing on development and sustainable behavioral change, this requires time. Six months of coaching is recommended for the coachee to obtain real benefit, and that is what this chapter focuses on.

There is a shorter alternative known as "laser coaching," which takes the form of three 60-minute virtual coaching sessions and focuses on a specific challenge that the coachee faces. Often organizations will buy such sessions in bulk and offer them as a resource for their employees.

Number of coaching hours

The first step to any coaching engagement is for the coach to find out from the purchaser of the coaching what they are looking for. This is most easily done in number of coaching hours and the preferred format. There may be a different cost for face-to-face compared to virtual coaching, which will affect budget. Bear in mind that the ideal initial period of coaching is six months, and can always be extended.

Format and length

Once the number of coaching hours has been agreed, the second step is to agree with the coachee the most suitable format and also the length of the sessions. There are three main options, but again, the format and length of coaching vary according to where in the world the coaching is happening. For example, in India, where one can spend three hours getting from one side of Bangalore to the other, coaching is mostly virtual. In contrast, in the Middle East, coaching sessions are most often face to face and can last up to three hours. At Performance Consultants, every coaching engagement ends with a 1:1 evaluation of 60 minutes (how to conduct an evaluation is covered in Chapter 19).

These are the options:

• **Face-to-face coaching** e.g., 6 sessions of 120 minutes each, once a month for 6 months.

• **Telephone or virtual coaching** e.g., 12 sessions of 60 minutes each, every other week for 6 months.

• **Mixed format**, e.g., a face-to-face session of 60 minutes, plus 12 telephone coaching sessions of 45 minutes each, approximately every other week, completed by another face-to-face session of 60 minutes.

Figure 14 illustrates a typical mixed-format coaching engagement. The next few sections provide more detail on the individual sessions and other considerations.

FIGURE 14: *A typical "mixed-format" coaching engagement*

		Week 1	Optional 360° with stakeholders	Week 2–24	Optional 360° with stakeholders	
Session	Chemistry Meeting	Foundation Session		Periodic Coaching Sessions		Evaluation Session
Format	Face to face or virtual	Face to face		Face to face and virtual mix		Virtual
Length	Approx. 30 mins	1 hour		Twelve 45 mins virtual session approx. every 2 weeks One 60 mins face to face		60 mins, within 1 month of final session
	12 hours of mixed-format coaching over 6 months					

Chemistry meeting

The chemistry meeting is where you meet the coachee for the first time and is usually free of charge. It is an opportunity for both you and your coachee to check that you feel you are a good match to work together. It is customary to let each other know after the chemistry meeting if, on reflection, you feel you are a good fit or not. If not, don't worry – sometimes the chemistry is just not there.

Confidentiality

Once you and your coachee have decided to work together, it is important to set up a partnership and establish confidentiality. Confidentiality is key to any coaching relationship, and the boundaries need to be defined at the outset. Imagine being your coachee, who is going to discuss deep and personal issues. Without confidentiality, coachees, particularly in organizations, will be unwilling to share sensitive information that could be important to the coaching, and this will very likely limit its positive impact. Figure 15 shows how keeping confidentiality means that the coachee's leader or sponsor will not get to know everything that is discussed in the coaching – the ovals represent what are sometimes referred to as "Chinese walls."

FIGURE 15: *Confidentiality is key to the coaching relationship*

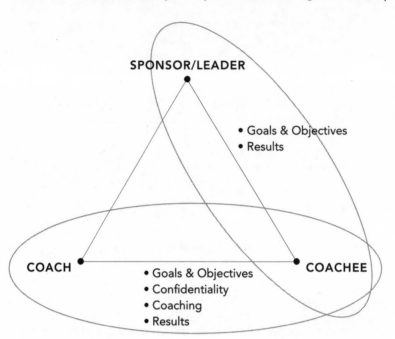

As the coach, you need to be clear about who has engaged you, their relationship to the coachee, and who you are accountable to regarding the coaching. For example, you might have been engaged by:

- A leader to work with a team member.
- An individual who engages you through the HR department.
- HR to work with a leader in the business.

The sponsor who has the budget for the coaching and who is paying your invoices may or may not be the same person as the coachee's leader. In Figure 15, the term sponsor has been used for the individual who has budget responsibility. The sponsor, and possibly your coachee's leader, may want to see both the goals and objectives of the coaching and the results. It is important that you co-design with your coachee how these people are involved in the coaching and that the coachee communicates this to them.

Communicating goals and objectives at the start of the relationship and results at the end are great opportunities for you to empower the relationship your coachee has with the organization. It creates alignment between the coachee and the organization. This is a crucial part of coaching and could be one of the reasons it is taking place. For this reason, communication with the coachee's leader, the sponsor, or others in the organization should always go through the coachee, so that at all times you are empowering the relationship of your coachee with the organization.

Here are two areas to think about to ensure that confidentiality is maintained and that you are empowering coachees:

• Help coachees to have conversations with their leader or sponsor that will help them own their goals and objectives.

• Where coachees are not fully committed to their goals and objectives, explore what is blocking them and help them find the resources within themselves to have authentic conversations with their leader. These conversations will usually bring them into alignment.

In some instances it may be appropriate to have a three-way goal-setting and evaluation conversation. However, your focus should always be on empowering and supporting the coachee, while maintaining confidentiality, rather than strengthening your own relationship with the organization.

Foundation session

A successful foundation session will set up a successful coaching engagement. As the name implies, the foundation session is dedicated to creating the basis of the coaching relationship with your coachee, and it is important that you spend enough time doing this. This is more than just hearing what the coachee wants, it is where you get to set out your needs and expectations so that together you can design a successful coaching relationship.

There are a number of areas that it is useful to cover in this session; although I outline these in the checklist, I do not recommend you conduct formal 1:1 coaching without having undergone certified coach training.

Checklist for Foundation Session

Format and logistics – format (virtual, face to face, or a mix); length; frequency; location (also important for virtual sessions).

Agreements – get clear on permissions and share assumptions; ask how much support and challenge the coachee wants from you; agree accountabilities.

"Train" the coachee – what is coaching (not mentoring, consulting, or counseling); coach and coachee have a shared responsibility for coaching relationship; coachee needs to participate fully.

Goals – set inspiring and energizing goals (short term and long term); if relevant refer to recent appraisal; agree how you will both work with goals.

Potted history – in advance, ask coachee to prepare a summary of pivotal moments in their life to date (not whole life story); work together to identify patterns of behavior and belief systems.

Power sources or values – values discovery; strengths discovery; metaphors that inspire the coachee; mindsets and limiting beliefs.

Between sessions

Don't forget that the real work happens between sessions, when the coachee consciously tries out different ways of doing things and puts the learning into practice in life and work. This is one of the reasons that accountability, checking in, and follow-up are key.

It is important to keep a record of desired outcomes, actions, and timelines committed to and check back in at subsequent sessions to follow up on those actions (see Chapters 13 and 19 for more on record keeping).

Subsequent sessions

For the most part, the structure of the remaining coaching sessions will be something like this:

- Checking in and following up from last session.
- Setting the session goals.
- Coaching.
- Setting accountability.

360° feedback

A 360° feedback session can be a very useful before-and-after benchmark for coaching. This is where you send a survey to or interview the coachee's leader, direct reports, and peers to gain a 360° view on the impact of the coaching on the coachee. A simple 360° survey is available for download at www.coachingperformance.com. At the outset of the coaching relationship, this gives you a baseline or starting point to explore areas of development to focus on in the coaching. Then doing it again at the end of the coaching enables you to see the extent of the coachee's development. If you have a long-term coaching engagement, for example for 12 months, you could do 360° feedback halfway through as well.

Evaluation

Measuring the impact of a coaching engagement on the individual and in the wider context of the organization, and obtaining a figure for the ROI requires a chapter to itself and is covered in Chapter 19.

16 Coaching for Team Performance

Coaching develops the identity and creativity of teams to reach their potential

For teams to establish a coaching culture, a mindset of openness and curiosity needs to be fostered and skills in coaching conversations need to be developed. The team leader is in the best position of authority and influence to promote such a mindset and skills, so I will focus in this chapter on how team leaders can be coaches. The coach needs to approach the team with full attention, curiosity, trust in the team's resourcefulness, and openness to exploring different ways of achieving the task. What is more, in order to fully mobilize the potential of the team as a whole, the coach needs to understand the following:

- A team is its own entity, with intelligence we can tap in to.
- Coaching can mobilize the team's intelligence and potential by revealing, rather than overstepping or correcting, the dynamics present in the team.
- The aim of coaching is to create collective awareness, and generate co-responsibility and alignment within the team.

Understanding how a team develops is important in terms of being able to coach it to reach its potential and to understand which level of performance it has reached on The Performance Curve. Therefore, I will start by exploring the theory of how teams develop. Research by the ICF and the Human Capital Institute shows that coaching leads to improved team functioning and teamwork skills. Later in this chapter I will shed light on the nuances of coaching teams as opposed to individuals, and how to tap successfully into the unique identity and collective intelligence of a team. First, the chapter offers some background theory on the personality, characteristics, dynamics, and evolution of teams to help explain how best to enhance a team's performance during different stages of its development.

Teams are the essential working blocks of an organization. They perform tasks that are interconnected and too time-consuming for an individual or too complex or difficult for a group of individuals working in parallel. The team's ability to perform does not depend only on the individual talents and skills of team members, but on the way those members work together, and on the degree to which they share objectives, values, purpose, and responsibility. There is great interdependency in high-performing teams. In fact, without interdependency, you could say that a team is just a group. A task can only be successfully performed if synergy and cooperation are present. As such, teams and their power and potential are greater than the sum of their parts. They have an identity of their own that is different from all the individual identities within them.

Real teams (1) have clear boundaries; (2) are interdependent for some common purpose; and (3) have at least some stability of membership, which gives members time and opportunity to learn how to work together well. (Hackman *et al.*)

Stages of team development

Part of the role of a coach is to get to know the identity of the team they are coaching, and to help the team create or strengthen that identity and realize its potential. In a way, getting to know a team is like getting to know a person. It is useful to know at which stage of its "life" it is in, as there are some general rules about different stages of development that are applicable to all teams. At the same time, every team is unique and has its own personality, talents, and strengths. Teams of more than 15 or 20 members are likely to be made up of subteams, but whether it is a first team or a sub-sub-subteam, certain characteristics remain the same.

In the same way that individuals cannot jump from childhood into adulthood, teams cannot become mature overnight. Individuals have to develop through infancy, childhood, and adolescence, and teams need time to develop fully into the interdependent stage of The Performance Curve.

It is important to remember this and view it as a natural and necessary process which can be assisted with coaching.

I use a simple four-stage model of team development that is easy to understand – Inclusion, Assertion, Cooperation, Co-creation. The first three stages follow William Schutz's Firo-B theory of interpersonal behavior and are readily recognized in most sports and workplace teams. More complex and sophisticated models exist, but they are of less practical use, in my experience. Schutz was one of the forerunners of "encounter group" therapy, based at the Esalen Institute in Big Sur, California, along with other legends like Abraham Maslow, Fritz Perls, and Carl Rogers, the fathers of humanistic psychology. I was at Esalen at the time in 1970 and I participated in many Firo-B groups.

Group therapy participants find it hard to expose their emotional vulnerabilities until they can feel safe with the other participants, so it is incumbent on the group therapist to create that safe environment as fast as possible. Coaches can help achieve the same by understanding the principles of team development. Let's look at each of the stages in turn.

INCLUSION

The first stage is called **inclusion**, since it is here that people determine if they are, and if they feel they are, a team member. Anxiety and introversion are common, but they may be disguised by the compensatory opposite behavior in some people. The need for acceptance and the fear of rejection are both strong.

When faced with a new social environment, your brain is busy trying to keep you safe, so you are invested in being accepted by the team. Team members may not be very mentally productive in this phase, since their focus will be on their own emotional needs and concerns.

If there is a designated leader, the members will look to them for acceptance and guidance. They want to conform; they seek to comply. The tone and the example that the leader sets at this stage are important, because it will quickly become the team's accepted norm. For example, if a leader displays openness and honesty and discloses feelings or even a weakness, others will tend to follow suit and a good relating practice will be established. It is a time of tentativeness, and a good leader will attempt to address and satisfy individual concerns so that the group as a whole can move forward.

Fortunately, for many people this phase does not last too long, although for a few it may take weeks or months to feel part of the team. Those who had a childhood in which they developed a strong sense of personal security – and those who rise to leadership positions tend to be this type – would do well to be tolerant and supportive of those who were not so lucky.

ASSERTION

Once the majority of team members feel included, another dynamic emerges, that of individual **assertion**. Schutz described this stage as the need for control. It is a time of expressing power and of extending boundaries. Animals do this: they mark out their territory, and woe betide any opponent who dares to enter. It is the phase in which the pecking order gets worked out. The polite business term for it is the establishment of roles and functions, but the words are often nicer than the actions. Competition within the team is hot, which may lead to exceptional individual performance, although sometimes at the expense of others. It is a phase in which people try out and discover their strengths, and the team may make up in productivity what it lacks in cohesiveness.

This is an important and valuable development stage, but it can be tough for the leader. There will be challenges to the leadership. Team members have to find out that they can disagree with the leader before they will be willing to agree. They need to exercise their will internally, in order to hone it for team application externally. A good group leader will offer, and encourage team members to take, responsibilities and thereby satisfy their assertion needs. It is important that the leader allows the challenges, but unfortunately many leaders are threatened by them, and assert their own authority in order to control the process. It requires a balancing act.

As I have said, a team in this stage can be quite productive, which may shield the recognition of yet greater potential. In fact, the majority of business or sports teams seldom advance beyond the assertion stage, by and large because that is about as far as Western industrial society has collectively reached. To go beyond this is therefore to go above the norm, but that is not as difficult to achieve as is generally thought – with coaching.

COOPERATION

Schutz's third and ideal team stage was the affection stage, but some business people balk at too much mention of affection, so I call it **co-operation**. I do not wish to imply that such a team would be all sweetness and light, nevertheless. In fact, one danger of the cooperation stage is that an overemphasis on the team develops, which becomes too comfortable and does not allow for any dissent. The most productive teams will be highly cooperative, but will retain a degree of dynamic tension. A coach preserves this sensitively.

If a team is in the cooperation stage and one of its members has a bad day, for example, the others will rally round and support. If it is in the assertion stage, the others may quietly celebrate the fall of a competitor. If it is in the inclusion stage, few will know or care. On the other hand, if a team is in the cooperation stage and a team member has a personal triumph, the rest will join in the celebration. If the team is in the assertion stage, the rest may become jealous. And if the team is in the inclusion stage, the others could even feel threatened.

CO-CREATION

Our experience of working with teams shows that there is a fourth stage to the development of teams that goes beyond cooperation. It is the stage of **co-creation**, of transformation, and of personal and organizational evolution. A team operating at this stage is aware that it is greater than the sum of its parts, and that the team is the space where the organization's potential can be harnessed.

In each of the stages it is important to create awareness of the team dynamics at play and identify what is needed to reach greater performance. A coach who creates a safe space for team members to express their fears, discomfort, and needs will foster the team's resilience, self-care, strength, and co-responsibility. By making the team aware of what stage it is at, the coach invites the team to take responsibility for the development process and to self-adjust.

Maslow's Hierarchy of Needs and The Performance Curve

Just as for personal evolution, teams need to go through some development in order to reach the cooperation and co-creation stages, and this is where coaching can help. It is not necessarily a linear process, but rather a succession of progress, stagnation, a leap, regression, and development.

In Chapter 1 we looked at Maslow's Hierarchy of Needs. The level of group development runs parallel to Maslow's top needs in individual development. A team of **self-actualizing** individuals would quickly attain the dizzy heights of co-creation and outstanding results in the interdependent stage. A team of those seeking **self-esteem** would perform very well individually, but would be inclined to "do their own thing," fitting into the independent stage. People seeking **esteem from others** would compete strongly against each other, producing some great performances – and some losers. A team of individuals seeking to **belong** would be compliant and irritatingly helpful, more in words than deeds, and would map to the dependent stage.

TABLE 5: *Stages of team development*

Team development stage	Culture	Characteristics	Maslow's Hierarchy of Needs
CO-CREATION (performing)	Interdependent	Energy directed to shared values and the world outside.	Self-actualizing
COOPERATION (norming)	Independent	Energy directed outward to common goals.	Self-esteem Esteem from others
ASSERTION (storming)		Energy focused on internal competition.	
INCLUSION (forming)	Dependent	Energy turned inward within team members.	Belonging

Table 5 maps Maslow's Hierarchy of Needs and, in parentheses, Bruce Tuckman's set of labels, forming–storming–norming–performing, to the developmental sequence and three stages of The Performance Curve. It also highlights some of the main distinguishing characteristics during each stage of team development. Of course, the divisions between these stages are permeable and overlapping, and the position and state of the team are subject to fluctuation when there is any turnover in team members.

Coaching teams for high performance

It could be said that it is even more difficult today to get the best out of a team, for the following reasons:

- Global mobility brings diversity to teams which requires greater flexibility of mindset.
- People no longer work in settled groupings but are continually forming and reforming teams.
- Teams can be project based, functional, matrix based, operational, virtual, self-organized.
- Some teams are spread across geographical boundaries, making contact more infrequent and more problematic, or entirely virtual in nature.
- The timescales within which teams are expected to join, form, and perform to meet a business challenge are shorter than ever before.
- The business challenges themselves have increased in complexity.

Coaching has a very important role to play in helping people to work well together. It can help people establish whether and when they need to be in a team.

Coaching also has a fundamental role in helping with team leadership. It is said that leaders only have two functions: first to get the job done, and second to develop their people. All too often, leaders are too busy doing the first to get around to the second. Equally, the first and second sometimes can seem conflicted. The urge to get the job done well has created the "audit culture" – we started believing that we can be in full control of our output (be it individual, team, or organizational output) by quantifying and measuring everything. Yet development is always about potential, about the future, the vision, innovation, creativity, and growth. Stuck with the tension between getting the job done and developing our people, organizations tried to separate them by separating management and leadership. To quote Alma Harris:

> *Leadership is about learning together and constructing meaning and knowledge collectively and collaboratively ... It means generating ideas together; seeking to reflect upon and make sense of work in the light of shared beliefs and new information; and creating actions that grow out of these new understandings.*

Management became about the operational, getting the job done, about the process and the present. Leadership, on the other hand, had its focus on development, vision, and the future. However, in today's fast and complex world, the lines between management and leadership are blurred, especially when it comes to day-to-day business.

A coaching approach allows for the tension between management and leadership to be embraced and leveraged. Coaching can support teams to navigate between a management culture and the pull toward "playing safe," and a leadership culture and the pull toward "taking risks." It allows for an environment where learning, innovation, and raising awareness, as well as action and accountability, can be pursued simultaneously.

Project performance

A coaching approach is always applicable when working with a team, as it helps to tap into the collective intelligence. A place where a lot of team leaders find it easy to start using this approach is at the beginning of a new project, as well as during the review of a finished task. Having coaching conversations at those stages of a project cycle creates an environment where the team can think together, learn together, and tap into their resourcefulness. This in turn will lead to performance at much higher levels than if every team member merely got on with their part of the task after a short briefing about their role.

What might these conversations look like? Let's imagine that a business team is tackling a new project. Some key questions a coach can have in mind are:

- How do I raise this team's awareness of their own resourcefulness in light of this particular project? (The focus is on the team as a whole, as opposed to on each member individually.)
- How do I invite them to take ownership and responsibility for the project as a whole? (Again, not just individually in their roles, but as a team.)
- How can this team be a net that holds this project strongly yet flexibly?

Approaching the conversation through this collective lens, the coaching can then follow the GROW model. Here are some sample questions. The list is endless, and it will be defined by the particular context.

GOAL
- What is our goal?
- What is important about this goal?
- If this project/task were a success, what would the outcome look like?
- What would be different for us/our customers/our stakeholders?
- If we worked together in the best possible way, what would that look like?

REALITY
- What strengths do we have as a team that can help us accomplish this task?
- What challenges might we encounter as a team? (Both external and internal)
- On a scale of 1–10, how ready are we to tackle this task?
- What help do we need?

OPTIONS

- How can we get more prepared for the task? (Brainstorm possible ways)
- Who can be our allies in accomplishing this task? (Make a list)
- What can we do? (Brainstorm actions)

WILL

- What will we do as a team? (Create team actions)
- What will we do individually? (Individual actions and accountability)

While for ease of use these questions are listed in GROW order, as with all coaching the process is rarely linear.

Facilitating coaching conversations

The process of facilitating a team coaching conversation can vary. The coach might ask questions and get the team members in pairs or trios to discuss their responses to **goals** and **reality** with each other, and then report on their conclusions to the whole group. They might mix people with different functions for this process to stimulate new ideas. They might themselves participate in one of the pairs or trios. The resources and ideas of the whole team are employed to brainstorm the **options**, and an agreed action plan is reached and driven forward by the combined **will** of the group.

Another instance where a coaching conversation can be implemented easily and naturally is in reviewing the team's past performance on a task. If the focus is on team learning, then the conversation will follow the GROW Feedback Framework but focus again on the team as an entity:

- What did we do well as a team?
- What team strengths showed up while we carried out this project?
- What was difficult for us as a team?
- What did we learn?
- What will we do differently next time?

As we have explored before, notice how this process simultaneously creates self-directed feedback and feed-forward loops. It is very thorough, it brings out detail, it ensures clarity and understanding, and it draws on all team members' resources. The process also promotes ownership and commitment, and builds self-belief and self-motivation.

Coaching by example

The only way of genuinely promoting a desired change is by modeling it, first through attitude, since attitude will color all of our actions, and then by interactions with others.

The team leader needs to be clear about their own willingness to invest time and energy in developing their team, with a view to fostering long-term quality relationships and performance. They need to create a culture where the whole team views relationships as something worth time and investment. If leaders only pay lip service to team-building principles, they will get no more than they pay for. Dedication to a team process pays off.

If team leaders wish to establish openness and honesty in the team, then they need to be open and honest from the outset. If they want team members to trust them and each other, they must demonstrate trust and trustworthiness.

However, the team leader is not the only one creating this culture, and they need to involve the team in the conversation and co-create with them. The leader has that delicate yet powerful role of both initiating and facilitating, of leading but not imposing, of accepting what is while seeing clearly what can be and what is possible for the team.

Coaching and team development

The four team development stages form an excellent basis for the application of coaching in teams. If the leader understands that teams perform at their best when they reach the co-creation stage, they will use coaching with the team as a whole and with individual members to generate upward progress through the stages. For example, if the agreed goal is to lift the team into the cooperation stage and the reality is that it is now somewhere between the inclusion and assertion stages, what options does it have and what will its members do? The process of coaching itself is modeling transformation, leveraging the collective wisdom to enable the next level of team development.

DEALING WITH UNCERTAINTY

Teams need to be agile, creative, and innovative in order to perform. Most people experience change, real or anticipated, as a stressful factor and are challenged by the speed and scope of change. The brain does not like uncertainty and, when operating in an environment we cannot predict or control as much as we would like, we tend to operate in survival mode. The direct consequence of stress in the workplace is that we become less collaborative, less creative, and less efficient. A coach has a crucial role to play in reminding team members what is under their control and what strengths they possess to help the team succeed.

Practical ways to foster a coaching culture in teams

Each team, like each family or partnership, is different. While there are general principles and practices that are true for increasing positivity and productivity in all relationships, I do not quite agree with Tolstoy, who said "Happy families are all alike; every unhappy family is unhappy in its own way." Each team is an ecosystem of its own, and it has to discover its own way of being through curiosity, commitment, and creativity. What works for one team might not work for another, and the dynamics of the team require continuous attention, exploration, and care to get the best out of it.

The list of options that follows has been compiled from suggestions by participants on our team development workshops. Each of these options can be considered by the team using a coaching approach: the discussion may be facilitated by the team leader, but what happens should be decided on by team members themselves.

Agree a set of ground rules or operating principles acceptable to all team members and to which all have contributed

These ground rules should be subject to regular checking as to whether they are being adhered to and whether they need to be changed or updated. All parties should also agree the procedure if the agreements are overlooked or broken – not as a punitive measure, but as a way for a member or the team to take responsibility to repair their relationships. By consciously creating working agreements up front, and redesigning them as often as necessary, the team will build strong relationships, collaboration, and high performance. (Many of the suggestions that follow could be included as ground rules.)

Educate leaders and teams on the key communication skills and dynamics needed for a team to thrive

While each team is unique, there are some guiding principles and practices that can help improve communication as well as the team's well-being and effectiveness. Making these practices transparent and educating people on how to use them will enable them to create the interactions and results they want. Team members also need to understand that while each of them has an impact on the well-being of the team, the dynamics of the team influence their own well-being too. Moreover, even though each team member has an impact on the culture of the organization, the team has the power, through its development, to transform the organization as a whole.

Discuss and agree a set of common goals for the team

This should be done within the team regardless of whether the organization has defined the team's goal at the outset. There is always room for modification and for deciding how the task should be carried out. Each team member should be invited to contribute as well as to add any personal goals that might be embraced within the overall team goal.

Hold team discussions on individual and collective meaning and purpose as perceived by team members

This is both broader and deeper than exploring goals. Meaning and purpose are what drive people, and a lack of them leads to lethargy, depression, and poor health. Throwing more light or awareness on something so pervasive that we are barely conscious of it will increase the purposefulness and the quality of life at work and at home.

Set aside time on a regular basis, usually in conjunction with a scheduled task meeting, for team development work

During this time agreements are reviewed, appreciations and gripes are expressed, and personal sharing may be included so that openness and trust are built. After experiencing a few such meetings facilitated by the coach, a high-performing team will be able to do this work on its own.

Put support systems in place to deal, in confidence if requested, with individual troubles or concerns as they arise

If process meetings cannot be held frequently for geographical or other reasons, a buddy system might be instituted whereby each member of the team has another member as a buddy to whom they can talk with if necessary. This way minor issues can be resolved promptly and valuable process meeting time is not wasted.

Canvass team members' views about the desirability of arranging structured social time together

Some teams perform better if they strengthen relationships through shared experience of non-work activities. If a regular event is planned for the team, the preference of an individual not to attend because of prior commitments or to respect the need for more family time should be acknowledged. That team member, on the other hand, needs to be prepared for some feeling of separateness as a consequence of that choice.

Develop a common interest outside work

Some teams have found that a group activity such as a sport or a common interest outside of work that is shared by all members can be an excellent bonding opportunity. I recall one team who "adopted" a child in a developing country and, with a small monthly contribution each, paid for her schooling. This team felt that she had contributed even more to their lives than they had to hers.

Learn a new skill together

Some teams have agreed to learn a new skill such as a language, or to attend a work-related course together, or even to undertake training in coaching! This might be in healthy competition with other regional teams, for example, in the same organization.

The decision to adopt one or more of these options must be made democratically, but it also must be specific and recorded, in ways recommended in Chapter 13. Remember that the basis of coaching to improve team performance is not imposing, but increasing individual and collective awareness and responsibility.

As The Performance Curve shows, it takes will and focus from a coaching leader and a good deal of emotional intelligence to create the conditions and foster the mindset and culture needed for teams to become and remain high performing. Team coaching provides the space where learning, adjusting, and real-time development are possible.

17   Coaching for Lean Performance

Together, Lean and coaching create a virtuous circle of unparalleled performance improvement

The Lean manufacturing system has been adopted in many industries to improve process performance through eliminating waste, reducing inconsistencies, and smoothing out workloads. Developed by the Toyota Motor Company in the second half of the twentieth century, it is now being used in a wider business context.

Organizations and teams which use Lean principles can create the ideal conditions for a true learning environment and maximum performance if they also bring in a coaching style of leadership. This is because achieving continuous improvement through learning, which is the essence of Lean, requires people to make continuous steps out of the "comfort zone" where they regularly operate and into their "learning zone," which brings them closer to their potential. Coaching challenges people to stretch into this area, and supports them in learning and developing to create new behaviors and standards, rather than just "getting through" the experience before returning to their comfort zone. Caroline Healy, senior learning and development manager at Medtronic, says that bringing a coaching approach puts "empathy, heart, and purpose right at the center of Lean, and gives practitioners a turbo boost to improve performance. By equipping them with coaching skills that perfectly complement what they are already doing, both Lean practitioners and their teams feel more empowered, more engaged and able to do more with less."

Some organizations struggle to fully embed Lean practice, possibly because they miss the necessity of engaging their people in the process through practicing a coaching approach. This chapter illustrates the compatibility of coaching and Lean by outlining the elements of most successful Lean systems and relating them to coaching.

From dependence to interdependence

In production terms, Lean systems which are operating well are the manifestation of a high-performance, interdependent, learning culture. They demonstrate the value of understanding each of the steps in a process, and the impact each step has on the next, as well as what the next step's current needs are. If we were to translate that into a team of people, imagine if every individual understood how their actions affect others in the team, and was able to communicate their needs to each of the others in order to achieve a successful outcome together.

Why is it, then, that many organizations that choose to implement Lean find it difficult to sustain the benefits after the first flush of cost saving or efficiency improvement has been achieved? One possibility is that so much effort is put into implementing the technical processes of Lean, and so little attention is given to the human element. In the same way that just using GROW in itself isn't coaching (any dictator can use GROW), simply following a series of steps set out in a Lean intervention won't bring sustainable process improvement – if people aren't engaged and involved, it is more than likely that the leader is using a directive style, which simply reinforces a culture of dependency and undermines the Lean process.

Indeed, the importance of the relationships established between leaders and their teams is an integral part of arguably the most successful Lean culture, the Toyota Production System (TPS), in which respect for people and team working are key principles. This is where applying coaching skills and principles can support the impact of Lean processes and lead to true interdependence and, of course, high performance.

Start with the goal in mind

On setting out to develop a Lean culture, the starting point is to identify the overall challenge the team wants to strive for. Common examples of challenges that organizations might aim for include to eliminate all waste, to reduce costs, and to improve customer satisfaction. Compare these to the end goals and dream goals discussed in Chapter 10, which provide a consistent direction to head for in the coaching process.

Identifying overall challenges in this way then helps to connect to shorter-term targets and activities (performance goals and process goals), which in turn allow the team to focus efforts and efficiently work toward what it wants to achieve. In Lean practice, the habit of having frequent improvement conversations creates a focus on the shorter term, always with an awareness of the overall challenge to keep them as relevant as possible. Having a clear sense of direction means people can become much more intentional in their actions – and working with intention in your actions is more likely to bring you closer to what you are working toward.

Good enough never is

Kaizen, or "good enough never is," is a well-known principle within Lean cultures. The belief that no process is ever perfect opens up the possibilities of continuous innovation and evolution to move toward the challenge through incremental improvement and occasional breakthroughs.

The fact that all of us possess much more potential than we usually demonstrate is so important to enable us to hold a coaching mindset, and actively look for the potential that does exist. Coaches can help coachees to access this resource to achieve continuous performance improvement.

High-quality awareness is the key

Finding out the true current situation (reality) is critical in both Lean and coaching. In Lean systems, this means going to where the work happens, and making things as visible as possible so that problems aren't hidden. In coaching, it means working from the coachee's perspective and not basing decisions on assumptions or habits.

Lean can be a great way of applying scientific thinking and learning to situations – identifying what is *actually* happening through focused attention and measurement, rather than stopping at what you expect or assume is happening. Using powerful questions to probe in greater detail and challenge assumptions is where learning starts, in both Lean and coaching. In practice this is about raising high levels of awareness – the starting point of improving performance, from which you can generate responsibility and self-belief.

Plan–Do–Check–Act

It is no surprise that a system of continuous improvement such as Lean has continued to develop as a way of managing performance. It is important to check regularly and frequently that what you are doing is still working and, when you identify opportunities to improve, to make adjustments to ways of working.

In Lean, the practice of incremental improvement comes from the Plan–Do–Check–Act (PDCA) cycle:

- **Plan** – what is the goal for this process, what will change as a result of this next improvement?

- **Do** – implement the changes identified.

- **Check** – evaluate the results against the plan.

- **Act** – what will be standardized now into the new process?

FIGURE 16: *Coaching and the Plan–Do–Check–Act cycle*

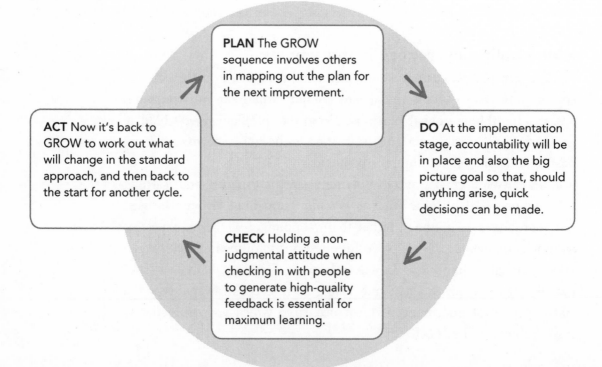

PLAN The GROW sequence involves others in mapping out the plan for the next improvement.

DO At the implementation stage, accountability will be in place and also the big picture goal so that, should anything arise, quick decisions can be made.

ACT Now it's back to GROW to work out what will change in the standard approach, and then back to the start for another cycle.

CHECK Holding a non-judgmental attitude when checking in with people to generate high-quality feedback is essential for maximum learning.

A benefit of following this cycle is that it leads to a continuous focus on performance improvement – it builds on the kaizen approach that there are always opportunities to build on what has already been achieved.

Holding a coaching mindset and using coaching processes naturally support each stage of this cycle – and create more time for coaching. This virtuous circle is illustrated in Figure 16.

The learning zone and the human element

Perhaps the deciding factor in how a coaching style will maximize the benefits of following a Lean methodology is how it balances the levels of support and challenge. When Lean works well, the process requires people to experiment, to try different approaches. Often they will be successful, and sometimes they will fail. In both cases, it is the learning from the experiment that is important.

Whenever an individual, team, or organization wants to change, an element of learning will be required. This requires each person to step out of their comfort zone into their learning zone. You might recall a time when you were part of a team or organization that operated in a dependency culture, with lots of rules about what people should or shouldn't do. What would taking the first step toward working more independently have required? How would some leaders have reacted to allowing others to make decisions, letting go of their "expert" role?

If you think back to the example of Fred in Chapter 5, the learning zone can sometimes be an uncomfortable and scary place to spend time. By definition, it's partly unknown – you're never 100 percent certain of what you'll encounter and you're anxious about failing.

Coaching processes on their own will have limited impact if coachees don't feel able to step into the learning zone, or if they fear the consequences of making a mistake. The role of the coach therefore is to help each individual, team, and organization to navigate between the comfort zone and the learning zone by balancing the levels of support and challenge people need to take steps into the unknown – by helping them manage their fears and anxieties.

A coaching approach

Let's look at how a leader using a coaching approach might tackle a situation where a problem in the process has arisen. Jim, the supervisor of a team of machine operators, is meeting with his manager, Alice.

Plan stage of PDCA

ALICE: Hi, Jim, what's on your mind today?

JIM: We've been having a problem with surplus units – the team in stores have told me that they're running out of space for our line.

Identifies the goal(s)

ALICE: Well, we've got 10 minutes now, what would you like to have by the end of this conversation?

JIM: I'd appreciate having an idea of what I could change to fix the situation.

ALICE: OK, I get that fixing this problem is a priority to you right now. Before we get down to the specifics, if you did fix this, how else would that help?

JIM: It's just about being as efficient as we can – I'm never sure from one week to the next what the workload's likely to be, so planning the employee rotas and overtime is a nightmare.

The bigger "challenge"

ALICE: What's the longer-term picture you'd like to paint?

JIM: Well, consistency I suppose.

ALICE: Consistency?

JIM: Yes, having a more predictable flow of work – we seem to constantly be playing catch-up or slow-down. I guess it's hard for the team too, as they never know when I'll be asking them for overtime or knocking back their requests to work extra, because I don't know. It's affecting the quality too – when we're rushing I can see that more units are being returned.

Next target condition

ALICE: What else are you noticing?

JIM: Well, at some point it's got to be hitting the company. I'm sure things aren't as efficient as they could be, and at the end of the day we keep getting reminded that that's what we're aiming for – maximum efficiency.

ALICE: Yes, that's definitely the vision long term. What step would you like to aim for in relation to this immediate problem to improve efficiency?

JIM: Managing a steady production rate to meet demand would be a great start.

Establishes reality

ALICE: What's the situation right now?

JIM: We've got a large surplus.

ALICE: How many units?

JIM: As at last night it was 20, which is way too high – the aim is to have a maximum of 2.

ALICE: OK, what have you already tried?

JIM: Mainly it's about adjusting the production rate – I've told two of the agency employees we won't need them for the rest of the week, and I'm letting a couple of the team leave early tonight.

ALICE: What effect do you expect that will have on the situation?

JIM: At current rates, we'll remove the surplus by the end of this week.

ALICE: How often is this happening?

JIM: It feels like every month at the moment, either having to ask people to work overtime or slowing things down.

ALICE: What else do you need to help fix this in the longer term?

Possible next steps

JIM: What I need is access to information about future demand – what orders are in the pipeline.

ALICE: Where would you find that information?

JIM: Well, the sales team – they are agreeing the deals with customers, so they should have details about quantity and deadlines etc.

ALICE: What's stopping you getting that from them?

JIM: Nothing, really.

ALICE: So, what are you going to do next?

Agrees actions

JIM: I'll speak with Mark, the manager there.

ALICE: What are you going to say to him?

JIM: That I'd like more notice about sales.

ALICE: Specifically, how much notice do you want?

Challenges to be as specific as possible on action

JIM: As much as possible.

ALICE: I understand, but that is pretty hard to measure. What about putting a timeframe on it so we can assess how it's working?

JIM: Well, if I had two weeks' notice for new orders that would certainly help.

ALICE: OK, two weeks, and what about the amendments to orders you mentioned earlier?

JIM: Oh yes, where we have regular, repeat orders that's fine, as I know how many are required each week. It's when something changes and I'm not aware of that until the last minute that there's a problem.

ALICE: So what do you need in those cases?

JIM: If it's a small change, probably only a week, but for something larger I'd like two weeks' notice again.

ALICE: What do you mean exactly by small and large?

JIM: Well, less than 10 percent of the normal order is small, anything over that large.

ALICE: That's clearer. So what's your request going to be for Mark?

JIM: Two weeks' notice for new orders and changes over 10 percent to regular ones, and one week for changes below 10 percent to regular ones.

ALICE: And how would you know that it was working?

JIM: Ideally, we would have no overtime and still meet demand.

ALICE: What about stock levels?

JIM: Well yes, we'd stay within the maximum of two.

ALICE: OK, it sounds like speaking with Mark is your first step. When do you want to do that?

JIM: I should be able to manage that this week.

ALICE: This week? When exactly this week?

JIM: I'm seeing Mark later this afternoon about a customer query anyway, so I'll do it then.

ALICE: So when would be a good time for us to check in to see what happened?

JIM: I can let you know about the conversation with Mark after the meeting. I guess it will take a couple of weeks before we can see how it's affecting our workflow.

ALICE: OK, let's catch up by the end of the day, and then we can agree on the next catch-up.

FOLLOWING UP

The benefit of helping Jim get very clear about accountability is that there is a clear alignment of expectation and goals. Alice will want to check in with him, not from a position of judgment, but rather to establish his learning from the initial action, and later as part of the "check" stage of the PDCA improvement cycle. Checking in and following up are ways of creating a learning culture by supporting people as they step into their learning zone.

Let's look at the initial check-in.

ALICE: Jim, I wanted to check in with you about the conversation with Mark you were planning. Do you have a couple of minutes now?

Do stage of PDCA

JIM: Yes, no problem. It went well, thanks.

ALICE: What happened?

What happened?

JIM: I told him about the problems we've been having with keeping surplus stock down, and he agreed that it needed to be addressed.

ALICE: What did you agree about next steps?

JIM: I told him it would help if I had more notice about orders, and asked if he could help with that. He said that would be OK, and he's going to let me have orders covering a rolling four-week basis.

ALICE: Four weeks? That's longer than you needed, isn't it?

JIM: Well, it is, but they produce that information anyway, so this way they won't have to create any new reports. I'll just use the nearest two weeks' orders for my planning.

ALICE: When will that start?

JIM: The end of this week, which is great.

ALICE: You do seem happy about that. I'm glad it's working out, and great to see the progress you've made. It will be interesting to measure the impact now on the situation. What have you learned so far?

What's the learning?

JIM: That people are happy to help when we explain the situation.

ALICE: That's good. What else are you learning?

JIM: That there might be other areas which we could improve through working more closely with other departments.

ALICE: Such as?

JIM: Well, I haven't had a detailed conversation with the stores team about the situation, but I'm sure they could add some more insight.

ALICE: So what would the next step be with that?

What's next?

JIM: Would it be possible to set up a three-way meeting – us, sales, and stores?

ALICE: I'm sure that would be possible. Would it help if you and I met again to talk about that in more detail – maybe at our next 1:1?

JIM: Yes, that sounds like a good idea.

ALICE: Could I leave you with a question to think about ahead of that meeting?

JIM: Sure, go ahead.

Sows seeds for more inter-dependent working

ALICE: Thanks, Jim. I'd like to hear your thoughts on what could be possible if every department understood what they could do to make life easier for each of the other ones?

JIM: Right, that's a great question and it's going to take some thinking about! I'll let you know at our 1:1 next week.

CHECK AND ACT STAGES OF PDCA

Over the next four to eight weeks, Alice would be working closely with Jim to establish what was happening regarding surplus stock levels in order to evaluate the impact of the change they have implemented. It's likely that further changes would be identified along the way via regular follow-ups and feedback conversations (such as the three-way meeting identified in the second conversation). Each change would create a "mini" PDCA cycle using the follow-up conversations, the purpose of which is to encourage experimentation and greater awareness of the situation.

So after eight weeks a thorough evaluation could be conducted, and an agreement reached about what permanent changes to processes and systems will be made. The GROW sequence could be used as a structure for the conversation, as well as highlighting the next improvement to focus on – and so the cycle would start all over again. This is one illustration of the huge opportunities there are for users of Lean to gain from taking a more coaching-like approach in their interventions.

18   Coaching for Safety Performance

Coaching creates a culture of interdependence and high safety performance

As mentioned in Chapter 2, teaching a coaching approach in a safety environment radically improves safety performance – at the HRO Linde, for instance, performance improved by 73 percent. The reasons for this are clear: studies show that a culture of interdependence has the highest safety performance. Through coaching, leaders and supervisors can create this kind of culture and engage and empower all team members directly in safety performance. As well as creating a safe environment in general, particular safety situations in which the coaching approach can be applied include workplace inspections, safety dialogues, incident investigations, toolbox talks, and risk assessment.

Coaching creates interdependence

Let's think about two different approaches to learning: instruction, which fosters a dependent culture, and coaching, which fosters an interdependent culture.

It's fair to say that both can result in an improvement in performance, but they go about it in very different ways, and the performance of the latter far exceeds that of the former. Why is this? Instruction can be quite limiting, because it's usually around learning somebody else's way of doing something, rather than your own way. As a result, it leads to dependency on the other person. For example, there could be a lot of information to try to retain in a short period. So the next time you have to repeat that task, you may need to find the trainer again to remind you of some of the information.

Coaching, on the other hand, uses a process of exploration. It helps you find your own best way of achieving that particular job. That allows you to explore potential and possibilities, rather than being fixed on an idea that there is just one way of doing a task. In the process, coaching grows self-belief: as you find your own way and recognize your own progress, so your self-belief can grow. It's also a more enjoyable way of learning, which means that in terms of being able to replicate performance, it should be easier to do.

There's a famous story about a presidential visit to NASA in the early 1960s when America was preparing to send people into space. President John F. Kennedy was walking down a corridor where a janitor happened to be working. The President stopped to have a chat with him and asked, "What are you doing here?" "Well, Mr. President," he replied, "I'm helping to put a man on the moon." That is a great example of somebody who understands that, however small their contribution might be, without that contribution it would be more difficult to achieve the overall aim. Having sight of the impact of what each person does on other people is a real key factor in teams that work interdependently.

In a safety environment, imagine a team that is heavily dependent on the leader. Probably there would be a long list of dos and don'ts, of rules around safety, and the leader would spend a lot of time enforcing those rules, making sure that people were following them, were avoiding making mistakes. The team members might not really understand why the rules were there, but they would comply if the leader was looking over their shoulder. If the leader was not looking over their shoulder, however, they would be more likely to cut corners. The risk, of course, would be that then accidents are much more likely to happen. And when those accidents do happen, the reaction in a dependent environment is more likely to be one of blame and judgment and punishment, where very little learning can take place. So the likelihood of those accidents being repeated greatly increases.

There are several things that distinguish a team that is working interdependently from teams that are working at the other stages of The Performance Curve:

- An interdependent team recognizes the value and potential of working collaboratively, its members are much more likely to set ambitious goals. They see that more is possible.
- The activity that is taking place is much more likely to be focused.

- There is more fun, because working together with people is usually more fun than working independently or in an isolated fashion.
- Lots of feedback occurs, not just in one direction but in all directions, inside the immediate team and also outside it, because that creates learning.
- There is a high level of trust and openness.
- Team members are happy to have challenging conversations if that surfaces issues to enable greater performance.
- There is mutual accountability, so people are more likely to be catching colleagues doing things right and giving them feedback, as well as catching them doing things wrong and feeding back on that as well.
- There's a greater awareness of how the team is doing and knowing how other team members are. So they're much more likely to recognize when a challenge or some support is required.
- There's a continuous emphasis on review and learning to enable improved performance on an ongoing basis.

Creating interdependence in practice

Let's look at how coaching might work to create a culture of interdependence in a safety context.

If someone in the workplace is putting themselves or their colleagues in danger, you would of course immediately instruct them to stop and tell them to do it in a safer way. This would usually result in a safer situation at that moment. However, if a worker doesn't understand "how" what they were doing was so dangerous, or think about other, safer alternatives, the next time they are faced with that situation, they may repeat the mistake – and you might not be there to stop them.

We can explore this in more detail by looking at two contrasting approaches dealing with an incident involving a forklift-truck driver.

HOW NOT TO DO IT

MANAGER: I don't believe what I'm seeing here. You're speeding out of this . . . I mean, speeding! You have your forks lifted way way too high.

DRIVER: Yeah, but I'm just trying to . . .

MANAGER: This thing is going to tip over.

DRIVER: Look, there's nobody around.

MANAGER: Don't you think I saw you when you jumped out of the cab? This is unsafe, this is seriously unsafe. You're jumping out of the cab. Where's your three-point contact?

DRIVER: I'm just trying to get the job done.

MANAGER: In fact, I don't think I even saw you wearing a seatbelt. Were you wearing a seatbelt?

DRIVER: But there's nobody around.

MANAGER: Where's your visibility? You've come out forwards. Don't we reverse coming out of a . . .

DRIVER: I need to get going, I have work . . .

MANAGER: You can't get going anywhere right now, this is not going to go away. We need to have a chat about this. I think you don't quite understand. Suppose I hadn't been walking through here? Is this how you normally drive?

DRIVER: But there was nobody around. It wasn't really a problem, was it?

MANAGER: I don't want to hear your excuses. This afternoon we need to have a sit-down chat, because this is serious. This is probably going on all the time if I'm not around.

DRIVER: I'm just trying to get the work done, please.

MANAGER: Of course you're trying to get the work done, but not in an unsafe way. It does not happen like this. We'll talk this afternoon, end of story.

You can clearly see how the manager's behavior creates a dependent culture. Now let's look at how it can be done with a coaching approach.

HOW TO DO IT

Stops unsafe behavior immediately

MANAGER: I've stopped you because I'm concerned about the way I saw you coming out of the store. What are you noticing about your driving?

DRIVER: I had my forks up high.

MANAGER: A little bit high, yes. What else?

Asks open questions to check awareness

DRIVER: I was driving forwards.

MANAGER: Yes, and . . .

DRIVER: My speed was maybe a little too high.

MANAGER: Alright! So driving forwards, bit speedy, forks a little bit high . . .

Prompts for further awareness and allows time to think and respond

DRIVER: I'm just rushing to get the job done.

MANAGER: Just rushing, I can see that.

DRIVER: I'm just coming out of the store and I'm going up to the loading bay.

MANAGER: Did you unclip your seatbelt when you jumped out of the cab?

Asks closed questions to establish specific behavior

DRIVER: No, I wasn't wearing my seatbelt.

MANAGER: Remember the three-point contact . . . 1, 2, 3.

DRIVER: It all goes with rushing to get the job done.

Allows time to think, which highlights potential interferences to safe performance

MANAGER: It all goes with rushing . . . You're an experienced driver, you've been with us a while. Tell me what happens when you go at that speed, forwards with a heavy load, forks lifted. What could happen?

Recognizes the driver's strengths and checks for understanding of risks

DRIVER: The forklift could tip over and the load could get spilled.

MANAGER: The load could get spilled. That could be the material cost – and the human cost? How can we make sure this doesn't happen again?

Asks open questions to seek future change in approach to avoid repeat

DRIVER: I must make sure I drive the truck the way I was taught, coming out of the store in reverse if my vision is obscured, reducing my speed. I must slow down.

MANAGER: I'm hearing you say "I must" do this. Can we make that "I will" do this?

Checks for personal responsibility – independence (I will) rather than dependence (I must)

DRIVER: I will make sure from this point forward to have the forks at the correct traveling height, at the correct speed. I will make sure of that.

Checks for understanding of what safe driving looks like – does not tell

MANAGER: You will make sure of that happening. So every time you come out of the store, what will I know is happening for you to be driving safely?

DRIVER: I will do it correctly, how I've been trained.

MANAGER: Right. So you're coming out in reverse, you've got the forks down, and you're at the right speed.

DRIVER: Yes.

The second example illustrates some of the key coaching practices explored in previous chapters in action. For instance:

• Non-judgment – the behaviors observed may fall below the standards required, but this can be explored in partnership to create a learning culture.

• Looking for learning – there is always learning to bring out, whether the actions observed are above, at, or below expectations.

• A coaching mindset – see the person as capable, resourceful, and full of potential.

• Curiosity – get curious about the challenges the person is experiencing, and what is needed to overcome these.

• Look for potential as well as interferences – it's more effective to build on strengths, and where a person is already most engaged, than to focus on weaknesses.

A coaching conversation will create a learning culture by raising awareness of why what the person was doing was so dangerous and, more importantly, foster ownership of how the activity could be completed more safely in the future.

In this way, the level of learning will increase, the leader's confidence and trust will rise, and the probability of long-term change in behavior will be greater. Taking an instructional approach may successfully react to a situation and treat the symptoms of unsafe actions, but coaching is more likely to lead to a cure.

PART V

Realizing the Potential of Coaching

19 Measuring the Benefits and ROI of Coaching

Measuring the financial impacts justifies future investment. Once you can demonstrate the tangible impacts, it's a different ball-game.
Alan Barton, Director, Arup

What are the benefits of coaching to the leader and the led, the coach and the coachee? What are the benefits to an organization of adopting a coaching culture, and how do you measure the return on investment (ROI) as a result of coaching? Measuring the impact of coaching is the holy grail, and I will cover that later, but first let me list some of the benefits of coaching in an organization.

IMPROVED PERFORMANCE AND PRODUCTIVITY
This kind of improvement must be number one, and people would not do coaching if it did not work in this way. Coaching brings out the best in individuals and in teams, something that merely instructing does not even aspire to do, and therefore will never be able to achieve.

IMPROVED CAREER DEVELOPMENT
Developing people does not mean just sending them on a short course once or twice a year. Developing people on the job creates a learning culture at the same time as increasing enjoyment and retention. The way you lead will either develop people or hold them back – it's up to you.

IMPROVED RELATIONSHIPS AND ENGAGEMENT
Respecting and valuing individuals improves relationships, increases engagement, and boosts the success that will accompany coaching. The very act of asking people a question values them and their answer. If you only tell, there is no exchange and thus no value is added anywhere. You might as well be talking to a load of bricks. I once asked a particularly silent but promising junior tennis player what he thought was good about

his forehand. He smiled and said, "I don't know. Nobody has ever asked me my opinion before." That said it all to me.

IMPROVED JOB SATISFACTION AND RETENTION

The atmosphere at work will change for the better because of increased enjoyment derived from a more collaborative approach. People using a coaching leadership style report that their own job satisfaction has increased, along with the satisfaction and retention of their team members.

MORE TIME FOR THE LEADER

Team members who are coached welcome responsibility and do not have to be chased or watched. Leaders report feeling a weight being lifted from their shoulders, less stress, and having more time to step back and think strategically, rather than getting sucked into day-to-day operations.

INCREASED INNOVATION

Leaders say that coaching and a coaching environment encourage creative suggestions from all members of a team, and therefore increase innovation without the fear of ridicule or premature dismissal. One creative idea often sparks others.

BETTER USE OF PEOPLE AND KNOWLEDGE

Leaders very often have no idea what hidden resources are available to them until they start coaching. Coaching will equip them with the mindset and skills to tap into the strengths and qualities of their people. In this way, they will uncover many previously undeclared talents in their team, as well as solutions to practical problems which can only be found by those who have in-depth knowledge as a result of carrying out a task regularly, or being directly in touch with a particular stakeholder group.

PEOPLE WHO WILL GO THE EXTRA MILE

In an atmosphere in which people are valued, they are invariably willing to push the boat out when or even before being called on to do so. In far too many organizations, where people are not valued they only do what they are told, and as little as possible at that.

GREATER AGILITY AND ADAPTABILITY

The coaching mindset is all about change, being responsive and responsible. In future the demand for flexibility will increase, not decrease, as a direct result of increased competition in the market, technological innovation, instant global communication, economic uncertainty, and social instability. Only the flexible and resilient will flourish.

HIGH-PERFORMANCE CULTURE

Coaching principles underpin the leadership style of the high-performance culture to which so many business leaders and organizations aspire. More importantly, they enable leaders to bring their people on the journey alongside them, rather than telling and expecting them simply to follow.

LIFE SKILL

Coaching is both an attitude and a behavior, with multiple applications both in and out of work. It is more and more in demand, so that even those who are looking to change their job soon are going to find it an invaluable skill wherever they go. Leaders express profound gratitude that their organization is investing in life skills which have a positive impact on their whole lives. The use of coaching skills with difficult teenagers has been reported to be particularly successful.

Coaching for Performance ROI

So how can these benefits be measured? There are very few people or organizations globally who are able to do this, and I believe this is holding back the coaching industry. Coaching will remain a black box unless the behavior change and the ensuing benefits, including those to the bottom line, are tracked.

Over 10 years ago, Performance Consultants developed an evaluation methodology called Coaching for Performance ROI to measure the impact of behavior changes on the bottom line. When we share it with clients, we repeatedly hear a collective sigh of relief, because they haven't seen anything like it before. We are consistently able to show an average ROI for coaching engagements and leadership development of 800 percent. Part of our mission is to professionalize the coaching industry – to create the excellence and standards for coaching in organizations. To this end, we are making our methodology available – you can download the templates for this evaluation tool from the website, www.coachingperformance.com.

The methodology is based on adult learning theory; doing this evaluation with your coachees will help them to be more conscious and therefore own and sustain their development more fully. The methodology is entirely facilitative and respectful of confidentiality, and is fully in line with the principles of coaching.

We can take a look at an evaluation example from a young operations manager who had responsibility for a team of 180 people. Let's call him Ken. When he started the coaching, his long-term goal was to become a director in three years. He had not told his boss that this was his goal, but through the coaching he and his boss were able to align their views on his career development. I have already discussed how important goals alignment is for individual engagement and company success.

At the beginning of the coaching, Ken's boss evaluated him at 1 out of 10 on his route to becoming a director. Three months later, when this evaluation was done, his boss evaluated him at 9 out of 10. The exponential jump in performance is evident in these figures. The fact that he achieved his goal within six months shows that 1:1 coaching is a fast-track, tailor-made, leadership development program. The Coaching for Performance ROI opens the lid of the black box and allows a look inside, enabling sponsors of the coaching to see the impact of the investment on the organization.

In order to measure the benefits of coaching, it is critical to record three things, as described in Chapter 13:

- **Goals and objectives** – goals that the coachee owns.

- **Ongoing actions** – both coachee and coach need to record information to refer back to regarding action taken.

- **Notes on what happened** – both coachee and coach should record information about progress made, for future reference, including any feedback from peers that happens along the way.

The recording of actions and progress needs to be done in a shared document. If things are not written down, they cannot be captured and referred back to. Too many coaches are lazy about this. However, if you are working in a business environment where you are being paid well for your coaching services, you need to hone your administration skills around record keeping, lest all your great coaching, not to mention your coachee's great work, is left unacknowledged, because neither of you is clear on where you came from and what progress has been made.

Here are the goals that Ken set:

GOALS AND OBJECTIVES: 6 MONTHS

- Shift to working on the business (60% of time) more than in the business.
- Improve delegation.
- The restructuring to be in place.
- To have recruited one senior leader.
- To have direct reports down to five.
- Develop own leadership style.
- Develop direct reports.

GOALS AND OBJECTIVES: LONG TERM

- To be a director by 35.

Note that there is a mix of behavioral goals as well as organizational or technical goals. In this example, an evaluation was done after three months to ascertain whether the coaching was of benefit and would be continued.

Let's look first at the qualitative impact of the coaching – the changes in behavior and attitude and the impact those changes have had. It is an opportunity to explore the subjective behavioral impact, for example on the coachee's leaders, team members, and peers through the eyes of the coachee. Table 6 is an excerpt of this part of the report. You can see that the first two areas of work correspond to the first two goals above.

TABLE 6: *Coaching review – qualitative*

Area of work	Skill level at start and currently practiced	Behavioral change	Impact on the business
Becoming more strategic Working on the business/in the business	Was 1, now 7	Spend some time each day trying to look at the whole business, thinking about future ideas, and trying to look at current problems in the light of a wider concept.	Spotted some potential problem areas. Also, looking slightly more forward, made some contacts for the future. Spending time on employee development of management team.
Delegation Ability to delegate work	Was 3, now 8	Am delegating instead of getting involved with everything myself. I hand projects and tasks to my team on a daily basis.	Enthusiasm and development of team have increased significantly. Productivity has improved. Cost savings identified and then fed back to me. More time spent on new project initiatives.

Key

Area of work: The concept worked on and a short description.

Skill level at start and currently practiced: Scale of 1–10, with 10 being the ideal level at which you would like to practice this concept in your work.

Behavioral change: Changes in attitudes and behaviors that you have noticed.

Impact on the business: Intangible or tangible impact on the business that the changes in attitudes and behaviors have had.

Now it is time to move to the next level down and, where possible, trace the quantitative impact to the bottom line in order to get an ROI. Of course, it must be stressed that estimating an ROI is an art, not a science, and we have found that this fact needs to be particularly underlined when the coachee is precision minded, say an engineer. Table 7 follows the same two areas of work.

TABLE 7: *Coaching review – quantitative*

Area of work	Monetary impact	Note of calculation method	Confidence level	Return over 3 months
Becoming more strategic Working on the business/in the business	Identification of issue of marketing problem – saving of £6,400 per month.	Reduction in costs by £1,600 per week.	100	£6,400 x 3 x 100% = £19,200
	Distribution redesign resulting in a £5,000–10,000 saving.	Redesign to save money – had time to review and suggest a new solution.	60	£7,500 x 60% = £4,500
Delegation Ability to delegate work	Identification by team member of potential logistics savings – £1,000–2,000 per month.	Reduction in costs by average of £1,500 per month.	60	£1,500 x 60% = £900
		Total return		**£24,600**

Key

Area of work: The concept worked on and a short description.

Monetary impact: Where applicable, a quantification of the business impacts identified using your own calculation methods.

Confidence level: Your % confidence level in your monetary impact estimate.

Once the qualitative impacts have been gathered, the next step is to calculate an ROI for the coaching using this formula:

$$\frac{\text{Sum (\underline{Monetary Value x Confidence Level}) x 100}}{\text{Cost of Coaching}}$$

The table is an excerpt from the full report. Estimates are corroborated by a third party or complementary survey data where possible. The total ROI estimated by the coachee was in fact £78,000 over the three months. Once the evaluation has been done with the coachee, in order to respect confidentiality it is the coachee who shares this report with the organization. We find that coachees are only too pleased to be able to demonstrate the work they have been doing and the impact on the business. In fact, as a result of this evaluation, Ken went on to become a director three months later, which was three years ahead of schedule.

Another part of our mission at Performance Consultants is to change the way investments in human capital are thought about – to ensure that investments in people development cease to be seen as a cost-center activity, and are viewed instead as revenue-generating activities that are integral to strategy. I urge all who are conducting formal coaching sessions in organizations to use the Coaching for Performance ROI. Together, we can help organizations to see that they are sitting on great untapped reservoirs of potential – their people.

Measuring cultures and performance

Chapter 2 introduced The Performance Curve. In a similar way to the Coaching for Performance ROI, the Performance Curve Survey measures the impact of coaching on the whole organizational culture. Drawing on established knowledge in the field of industrial psychology, it measures the collective prevailing mindset of the culture and the conditions for performance that the mindset creates, mapping a culture to a single point on The Performance Curve.

Chapter 6 talked about awareness and responsibility being fundamental to the coaching process. Like an individual, once an organization is clear where its culture is predominantly operating from, it is clear what behaviors need to shift in order to improve performance. The Performance Curve Survey is designed to create awareness and collective responsibility to act. It is the responsibility of both organizations and individuals working in them to create the conditions for high performance.

The results of the survey state which of four performance stages the organization is operating in and the immediate next focus to improve performance. And in fact the survey does not only apply to organizations – it can be taken by a team or even a curious individual. You can take the survey at www.coachingperformance.com.

20 How to Effect Cultural Change

Could the only thing limiting you be the size of your vision and your own self-limiting beliefs?

An interdependent, high-performance culture of the kind that coaching for performance can produce will provide the best chance of adapting to and flourishing in the face of the unsettling waves of change that businesses are facing. These businesses will adopt a supportive, people-oriented culture, one in which coaching is commonplace, downward, with peers, and even upward. In this way people's needs are acknowledged and they are helped by coaching to clarify their direction for themselves, while at the same time the coaching leader learns a great deal about their wishes and hopes. If leaders truly listen to their people, act on what they learn, and enable their team to take responsibility for themselves and others, people will be happier, they will perform better, and employee turnover will plummet. On the other hand, if leaders only pay lip service to coaching, they will have raised expectations only to dash them again, and will have made things worse than they were before.

In addition to this change in leadership style being demanded, in today's environment companies are likely to be called on to live up to the principles and ethics they so boldly claim in their mission statements. If they don't, they may be taken to task by their people and their customers. Both are liable to vote with their feet. Companies providing products and services that make a genuine contribution to society offer meaningful employment by their very nature. Those whose products and services are questionable or downright harmful are most likely to fall foul of people who seek meaning and purpose at work.

On this scale, few companies are wholly black and few wholly white. The majority are a shade of gray. The wiser ones can and do compensate for any perceived failings in various ways, for example by contributing to the local community or lending employees to social projects.

Coaching is therefore both the destination – the future high-performance culture – and a key ingredient in how to get there. A values-based future cannot be prescribed by some outside authority. Performance will always be at its best when employees, shareholders, directors, and even customers share the same values, but before that can happen, people need to be encouraged to identify what their own values are.

So where do you start in bringing about cultural change – with the people or with the organization? The answer must be both. Imposing democracy and demanding cooperation are unacceptable contradictions. Here are a few guidelines:

- If you redesign the company structure too radically or too quickly, you are liable to get too far ahead of your people.
- If you impose a redesign on your people, they are likely to object, even if it is intended to be entirely for their benefit.
- Executives and senior leaders must, from the very beginning, set an example and model the ideal attitudes and behaviors authentically and well.
- People cannot be forced to change, they need the opportunity to *choose* how to change.
- You must help people develop themselves and, through coaching, experiment with some of the attitudes and behaviors you expect in the new organization.
- Without a collective vision with which people are engaged, change cannot succeed, but without vision at the top it will not even start.
- You must be prepared to make changes across the entire living system of the organization. Widescale behavioral change will not be sustained without congruent processes, organizational and reward structures, and so on.

The living system

Changing an organization's culture requires an emotionally intelligent approach that seeks congruence and balance across all elements of the organizational "living system." This includes *both* the "harder," technical elements such as processes, systems, and structure, *and* the "softer," people,

FIGURE 17: *The living system*

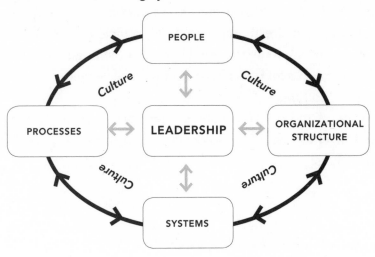

Leadership is at the heart of the living system

social, and behavioral elements, with leadership at the heart of the system (see Figure 17). Only by addressing all these elements can the organization be transformed.

Organizations often make the mistake of focusing on one element or the other, which I define as taking a transactional (and unsuccessful) approach. They may fall into one of two camps. Either the organization misses the fact that cultural change is required at all and tries to improve performance by introducing a new system or moving boxes around on the organizational chart. Without also focusing on the new behaviors and environment required to operate such a new system, the required shift in performance does not materialize. Or, on the other hand, the organization identifies that the culture needs to change, so focuses on behavior and people, without also adapting systems and processes to support and reward the required new behaviors or to provide a congruent context in which they can flourish. The former approach to transactional change may be outsourced to a business improvement function, while the latter is often outsourced to the human resources function.

If you as a coach are working with the leadership team of a company that wants to transform itself to improve performance, the first step is to help them become clear about what they require from the change and what it involves. You also need to ensure that they are fully committed to seeing it through. This is likely to require an investment of time that board members are often reluctant to make because of short-term pressures. However, lasting and effective change is only a pipe dream without the commitment and championing of the board. The willingness to see change through is vital to avoid people becoming disillusioned if all the grand plans come to nothing.

Achieving clarity on the fundamentals of what they want to achieve can be facilitated by encouraging the leadership team to ask themselves the following questions:

WHY?
- Why are we making this change?
- What are the internal and external drivers?

WHAT?
- What are we changing into?
- What needs to change and what needs to remain?

HOW?
- How will we design and deliver the change?
- Who will do what?

Once they understand and accept where they are now, you can partner with them to design an approach that addresses the relevant changes across the entire living system of their organization.

On the people and behavioral side, a leadership development program can be helpful to develop the leadership skills, behaviors, and mindsets required for the organization to operate as a high-performance culture. The next chapter turns the attention to the foundation of leadership, since both coaching and leadership have crucial roles to play in achieving lasting change.

21   The Qualities of Leadership

Leaders for the future need to have values and vision and to be authentic and agile, aligned and on purpose

Leaders of the future should be obliged to embark on their own journey of personal development to earn the title of leader, in my opinion. We live in a world that seeks, even expects, instant gratification, but leadership qualities come neither quickly nor cheaply.

This chapter emphasizes the essential qualities that are likely to be common to all responsible leaders, and ones that are especially relevant to the current times. The first is values, by which I mean personal not company values.

Values

It is widely believed, especially by religious people, that values stem from religion and that without religion we would have no values. This idea is false, for there are plenty of people who have no religious conditioning in their background and may be agnostic, if not atheistic, but still display exemplary values. The deeper reality is that our true values reside within us, and at the deepest level those values are universal.

In the lower stratum of personal development, which is unfortunately where much of humanity is at present, people are only vaguely in touch with their inner values, although those values may suddenly come to the surface in response to a crisis. The rest of the time they are buried in layers of parental, social, and cultural conditioning.

The extent of corporate crime and just plain greed is confirmation that many of those in power lack sufficient maturity or psychological development to be aware of their deeper inner values, let alone lead lives guided by them. This is made worse by a business ethos that, if it does not oblige people to focus on the financial rather than the social or environmental scorecard, encourages them to play the game that the rest are playing. Shareholders, the institutional ones in particular, expect and demand financial returns, not those measured in human terms.

That is the old game, the old mentality, which is no longer sustainable or acceptable to a growing number of more mature and values-driven people. These are the leaders of the future, the only ones we can afford to accept or vote for if we care about the survival of our children and grandchildren.

A well-trained professional coach will be able to use a number of exercises to penetrate beyond the conscious mind to enable aspiring leaders to access their values and other vital qualities. A coaching exploration of past activities and passions will reveal a pattern that can then be further honed in precision and broadened in scope. I can perhaps best illustrate this from my own experience.

A PERSONAL EXAMPLE

I actively embarked on my own journey of personal development in 1970, when I went to study leading-edge psychology in California. I learned that I first had to escape from the worst of my parental, social, and cultural conditioning before I could begin to discover myself and my values, and to explore deeper social issues with greater clarity than I had ever experienced before. My concern then shifted away from myself toward others, and I was not happy with what I now saw in the world that I had ignored before.

I began by evangelizing about personal development without much success; few people had heard of it. Then I got involved with anti-Vietnam war activism and moved on to concern about inequity and deprivation anywhere, and before long I was being drawn into many issues. By this time I was clearly values driven, but I was far too scattered. With the help of a therapist, since coaching did not exist then, I discovered that the issues over which I was able to have some influence and the ones I was most passionate about were all related to justice. I cared about many other things, and was always supportive of others who were dealing with them, but it became clear that social justice was my path. I explored my subconscious to see if this was a therapeutic issue, in the sense that I had, at some time in my distant past, suffered or caused some injustice and was trying to redeem myself. There was nothing there, so I began to accept that my purpose was to promote justice whenever possible.

Over time, it became obvious that this was also too general and I needed to be more specific, so again, with the help of a coach by this time, I looked at the characteristics of all those things I had become most frustrated by and most committed to changing. I discovered that the form of injustice I abhorred most was the abuse of power all the way from the micro to the macro, from child abuse to large companies' abuse of their employees, customers, and suppliers. This gave me real clarity about how and why I was attracted to coaching and leadership in big corporations. More macro still and most abhorrent of all to me is the abuse of small countries by superpowers and their power elite, their leaders.

I hope that this brief personal revelation illustrates the type of steps that can be taken if you choose first to become values driven and then to zero in on those values, which in turn can guide you to reset the sails of your lifeboat.

VALUES-DRIVEN LEADERS

So we need leaders who are values driven – that means collective values, not selfish values – and who are specific about their values so they can put them to best use for the most suitable issues. If a corporate executive suddenly has a wake-up call, a heart murmur for example or a growing feeling of purposelessness, they might want to explore their values with a coach. The question may well arise of whether their personal values are sufficiently aligned with the corporate values; by that I mean the ones the company lives, not the ones it shouts about. If they are not, the executive is faced with some tough choices: to quit, to take responsibility to change the existing corporate values to be more aligned with universal higher values, or, if they are less senior, to find how they can still express their own values within the corporation to the benefit of all.

Richard Barrett, who used to work in HR for the World Bank, has devised what he calls corporate transformation tools, based on a model similar to Maslow's, to measure the values of everyone in a corporation. All employees have to do is spend 15 minutes online to select from a template, customized for the specific company, a set of values that they hold, another set that represent how they see the existing corporate values, and a third set indicating the values they would like the corporation to have. The results give each person their own values sheet, together with a compilation of how employees see the company and how they would like it to be. The differences between the two show precisely where work needs to be done.

Smaller slices can also be extracted to show the values present by department, pay grade, gender, age, function, and so on, so that strengths and weaknesses in selected areas can be identified. The process provides much more valuable information than I can describe here, including a special section on leadership, but it is all available in Richard's books (see Bibliography). It is an outstanding system that I commend to all corporate coaches and human resource professionals, for use when the board, or the finance director in particular, does not think internal policies and processes need to change. The findings are clear, stark, revealing, and persuasive in most cases.

However, if the directors, who are the ones who usually draw up corporate mission and values statements, find that they want to go one way and the employees call for another, they have a dilemma. Trying to force employees to change their deeper values to align with the prescribed ones is likely to be disastrous – and ineffectual. The directors will need to consider how they can better align the corporate values with those of their employees. That is indeed a switch of responsibility. In practice, an articulation that meets everyone's needs can usually be found or negotiated.

PRINCIPLES

Not only do leaders need to be values driven, they also need to be able to translate those values into principles that will act as a guide for people working in the organization. Whole-system thinking relates strongly to principles, in the sense that any and every action may lead to unexpected consequences in areas that appear unconnected. Since such eventualities are often totally unpredictable, doing the best under the circumstances means that every action a person takes needs to be in the context of the organization's guiding principles. This in turn is in line with the leader's purpose, if they have traveled far enough along the journey of personal growth.

Let's look at an example of this. As John McFarlane, former chief executive of ANZ Bank, says in the Foreword to this book, "leadership within extraordinary companies is based on principles." Here is what ANZ currently says about its values on its website:

At ANZ, our values are about "doing the right things well".

Our values are a shared understanding of what we stand for as an organisation – they describe the things we are not willing to compromise on in any situation – with our customers, our shareholders, the community and each other.

Living our ANZ values helps us to achieve better business outcomes. Together with our Code of Conduct and Ethics, our values guide our behaviors and help us make decisions in our day-to-day work.

Our values are:

Integrity	Do what is right
Collaboration	Connect and work as one for our customers and shareholders
Accountability	Own your actions, make it happen
Respect	Value every voice, bring the customer's view to ANZ
Excellence	Be your best, help people progress, be business minded

---

What we can see here is that the values have been articulated as principles. The point about principles is that they guide actions and behaviors, leaving enough agility for one-off situations to be dealt with in a way that rules cannot. As discussed in Chapter 2, principles are the center of gravity of an interdependent, high-performance culture.

Vision

The second essential quality that leaders must have is broad and deep vision. Because of increasing competition and uncertainty, business leaders can easily become fixated on the bottom line. It is as if they are blinded by watching the numbers and are unable to raise their eyes to look beyond their computer screen, let alone out of the window to the world outside. How many leaders consider the impact of their decisions on future generations? Does that decision reflect and perpetuate old ways and therefore more environmental degradation or social injustice, or does it change things for good?

It is a no-brainer to say that leaders should have long-term vision, if only in the financial sense, but in the world of the revolving door at the top and a big bonus each time they pass "Go," leaders are often chosen for their ability to deliver an immediate financial result, not for their vision. Long-term vision has been downgraded and devalued as a leadership quality, with potentially far worse consequences.

Vision in the past was largely narrow and focused, despite the fact that innovation and breakthroughs invariably come from a different or broader perspective on an issue. Today's world is so interconnected and communication so instant that whole-system thinking is already necessary, and it will be essential tomorrow. This emerges automatically as a product of the further reaches of personal growth.

So what is vision as a leadership quality? It can be broken down into two parts. The first is the ability to "envision" and dream; that is, to create a clear and bold image of how the leader wants things to be in the long term without the impediment of conventional limits. This includes depth in terms of a lengthy timescale and breadth in terms of a whole-systems mindset, making connections beyond boundaries. The second part of vision is the ability to communicate this image in such a way as to inspire others – to be "visionary." It is through the communication of vision and the resulting inspiration that followership is created, for what is a leader without followers?

Authenticity

The next essential leadership quality is authenticity: when a person is who they really are, and is not afraid to be so in front of others. To achieve authenticity is an endless journey. It is about freeing yourself from parental, social, and cultural conditioning, and also the false beliefs and assumptions you have accumulated along the way. It is also about freeing yourself from fear: fear of failure, fear of being different, fear of looking stupid, fear of what others might think, fear of being rejected, and many more egocentric fears.

The subpersonality model, described more fully in Chapter 23, can be very useful for coaches addressing authenticity issues. One stage further in personal growth is to learn, with the help of an experienced coach, to step back and become a dispassionate observer. This is a similar role to the conductor of an orchestra, who can call up any instrument or group of instruments and manage the whole symphony, but without playing a note. This is what we might describe as a state of self-mastery, and it brings with it a great deal of personal power and self-belief.

In psychosynthesis terms (again, more in Chapter 23), this place is known as the "I," sometimes described as who we really are or our authentic self. Roberto Assagioli's definition of the "I" was a place inside of pure consciousness (awareness) and pure will (responsibility). This is the ideal state for a true leader to be in most of the time. It is a very powerful, fearless, authentic, consistent state that few people attain without being deeply invested in their own development. It equates with the top level of leadership, described in Jim Collins's book *Good to Great*, the principal qualities of that level being personal humility (self-awareness) and professional will (collective responsibility).

Every time a coach helps coachees to meet a small challenge, by being more aware and responsible for it, at the same time this is helping them to become more familiar with expressing the qualities of their "I"; in other words to draw closer to living from their "I" more regularly, or to be more authentic more of the time.

This sort of transformation does not occur overnight or in a couple of coaching sessions. It is the product of commitment and persistence, and perhaps the odd "dark night of the soul," but this is a small price to pay for the benefits of being your "I" or who you really are much of the time. That is the place from which to lead others. It is absolute authenticity, and it stands alongside the best of values and vision.

Agility

Another vital leadership quality is agility. The ability to be flexible, to change, to innovate, and to give up beloved programs and goals is essential given the uncertain circumstances and speed of change in today's world. The willingness to change direction quickly when new conditions so demand may well become a survival necessity in the future. I must stress that this is not about reinventing yourself at the level of your personal values or your authentic "I" self.

Agility is the product of two areas of personal growth work, to which I have already referred at some length. They are ridding yourself of the straitjacket of parental, social, and cultural conditioning and old beliefs and assumptions, and of eliminating fear, particularly the fear of the unknown that prevents you from being open to change. The unknown encompasses many things, like uncharted waters, unforeseen reactions from others, and unexpected consequences in whole systems.

The term agility conjures up images of youthfulness and physicality. It is a widely held belief, and to some extent a reality, that we become less agile as we get older. Every muscle or joint in our body needs to be exercised if it is to remain pliable, and the same is true of our mind. As we get older, usually starting at about age 30, we fall into countless small habit patterns. The same holiday location, the same wine, the same shopping day, the same clothes, the same walks or route to work, the same order in the same restaurant, the same phrases, the same reactions – these are all examples and causes of ossification. Try this agility homework.

ACTIVITY: *Exercise Your Agility*	For one week at first – watch out, it may later become a habit – each day try to avoid repetition in every little thing you do, from the smallest to the greatest. List all the things you still did habitually and change them the following week. Greet people with the truth rather than a gratuitous platitude, ask taxi drivers about their interests, visit people in an old people's home, pick up rubbish in the hedgerow, talk to the busking musician or the street beggar and give £5 instead of 50p. Think of a food you would never order, and eat it anyway.

Just do something different – try it. In this way you are exercising your mental agility and probably your body as well. You will find out that you can survive when you do things differently. After all, habits are the safe repetition of fear-avoidance behavior. Breaking habits gives access to new avenues, makes life more interesting, opens the door to new discoveries, introduces new friends, makes you a far more interesting person, and may even give you tears of joy.

Some people may find it easier to experiment with such changes outside the workplace at first, but just the same principles can be applied at work too.

Alignment

Alignment in business is usually assumed to mean the alignment necessary between the members of the board or of a work team for the achievement of a goal or an agreed way of working. This type of alignment is indeed important, but even more important is the inner or psychological alignment within leaders themselves, without which the more common, outer form of workplace alignment is hard to achieve. So what is inner alignment?

It is, of course, alignment and collaboration between our subpersonalities. If business leaders experience an inner conflict over a major decision, the consequences can be far-reaching. For example, one option might result in personal gain for the decision makers, as can be the case in an acquisition or a demutualization. Another option might offer the leaders less personal benefit but provide better long-term benefits for the business and its customers; a third option might be healthier for the community, for society, and for the environment.

Until leaders clearly resolve the inner conflict, they will not be fully committed even to the option they choose. That choice will depend on what they value most, or simply on their values. When different parts of yourself, or your subpersonalities, hold differing values, decision making becomes an internal battle of values for dominance. Since what you value changes, or rather expands, as you develop psychologically, this inner conflict is a natural consequence of your maturation process.

When team members have different objectives, the team will not be nearly as efficient or effective as it would be if these objectives were aligned. However, the news is not all bad. Different views in a team can engender a healthy debate and a well-considered result that embraces several perspectives. Nevertheless, once the debate is over, everyone needs to be committed to the agreed decision. So it is with individuals, or should I say within individuals. Anyone who aspires to be a leader needs to develop inner alignment. If that does not happen, others will experience them as somewhat schizophrenic and they will not know where they stand – they will not know who they are dealing with.

Sometimes the cause and extent of a leader's lack of alignment will not be consciously identifiable by the leader or by others; to other people they will just seem inconsistent, unreliable, untrustworthy, or inauthentic. You do not have to look far among the current crop of corporate and political leaders to see how apparent and widespread that problem is. It is not surprising really, because we all have this problem to a greater or lesser degree. It is a part of the human condition, though it could be mitigated considerably in the parenting, education, and skill training process, were it more widely recognized and accepted.

Leaders for the future

So leaders for the future need to have values and vision and to be authentic and agile and internally aligned. Add awareness and responsibility to the mix, self-belief, and a good measure of emotional intelligence, and it's a powerful recipe. All these ingredients are organic, home grown, and carbon neutral, for nothing is imported. In fact, they are already just where you are and waiting to be harvested.

22 The Ladder to Mastery

You do not have to know how to do something to be able to do it. You learned to walk, run, ride a bike, and catch a ball without instructions

Much of this book so far has been about learning. The learning of physical skills in sport has provided a number of examples illustrating the coaching process. But the widespread use of instructional methods of teaching in sport, at work, and at school is an indication of how poor general understanding remains about how people really learn. Part of the problem is that instructors, teachers, and leaders are concerned more about short-term gain, passing the exam, or getting the job done now than they are about learning or about the quality of performance. This is going to have to change, because results are simply not good enough to meet our needs or to surpass the competition. We have to find a better way.

It is a common misconception that good leaders are born, not made, or that a coaching style is the preserve of people who possess certain natural traits. However, our ways of communicating are learned from our parent or other early influences. If coaching skills were not acquired in childhood, there is no doubt that anyone can consciously learn them later in life and, with plenty of practice, develop a coaching style. In time, this coaching behavior will become unconscious.

Participants on our coaching programs are struck by how obvious and commonsensical the principles of coaching are, by their irrefutable logic – once we can escape from the tyranny of old, redundant thinking patterns that we have never thought to doubt or question. Many find helpful a way of looking at learning that is widely accepted in business training circles. It postulates four stages of learning:

- **Unconscious incompetence** = low performance, no differentiation or understanding.

- **Conscious incompetence** = low performance, recognition of flaws, and weak areas.

- **Conscious competence** = improved performance, conscious, somewhat contrived effort.

- **Unconscious competence** = natural, integrated, automatic higher performance.

FIGURE 18: *The learning ladder*

The learning ladder (Figure 18) generally takes you through each of these segments in turn. As one piece of learning becomes fully integrated, and if you are endeavoring to continue to improve, you embark on the next climb of the ladder.

Do you always have to follow these four stages, or are there exceptions or accelerations? A child learns to walk and talk, throw and catch, run and ride a bicycle by passing fairly directly from **unconscious incompetence** to **unconscious competence**. Later, when a teenager learns to drive a car, the four stages are clearly identifiable, with the driving instructor's input applied in the **conscious incompetence** and **conscious competence** stages. After the driving test, learning continues in **conscious competence** and evolves into **unconscious competence** as the act of driving becomes more integrated. Soon you are able to drive relatively automatically while concentrating on your thoughts, on a conversation, or on the sounds of the radio. Your driving skill continues to improve slowly by experience.

Learning can also be accelerated by consciously setting out up the ladder again. This can be done in two ways, either by employing an advanced driving instructor to take you through stages 2 and 3, or by a process of self-coaching. The first way assumes that you are incapable of determining what you are doing wrong and what you should do differently in future. You give responsibility for improvements in your driving to another person.

With the second method you retain that responsibility, shutting off the radio and your extraneous thoughts so you can observe or become aware of different aspects of your driving. If you do this consciously, non-judgmentally, and honestly, those areas of your driving that need improvement will reveal themselves. It might be harsh gear changes, misjudgment of speed and distance on occasion, or tension in the arms and shoulders causing premature tiredness. You are now in the phase of **conscious incompetence**, and you are likely to enter the next phase by making a conscious effort to operate the clutch more smoothly and watch the rev counter, or keep an eye on the speedometer and always leave a set distance between your vehicle and the one in front. Eventually and by conscious repetition, the improvements become a habit and **unconscious competence** commences.

There is, however, a very important variation on this theme of self-coaching that is far more effective. Instead of making the effort to change certain flawed aspects of driving that have been identified in **conscious incompetence**, you can achieve better results with less effort.

NOT TRYING

Identify the quality you would like to bring in, say smoothness in gear changes, and, rather than trying to change gear smoothly, simply continue to observe how smooth your gear changes are. In order to quantify this to give yourself a more precise feedback measurement, you might create a 1–10 smoothness scale, with 10 representing a gear change that you could not feel at all. You would drive as normal, but simply rate the smoothness to yourself after each gear change. With no increase of effort the numbers will begin to rise, and in a surprisingly short time they are likely to hover between 9 and 10.

Unconscious competence slips in, monitoring of the scale falls away, and you maintain smooth gear changes even when driving conditions become extreme or you are driving an unfamiliar vehicle. If any lapse does occur, a mere mile or two of **conscious competence** monitoring and rating will restore the smoothness. This effort-free learning or performance improvement is surprisingly fast and delivers a higher-quality result.

In process terms, this is a leap from **conscious incompetence** directly into **unconscious competence** without going through the phase of **conscious competence**. The driving instructor will keep you wallowing in **conscious incompetence** and **conscious competence**, at great expense of time and money. However, they provide the consciousness, such as it is, by their criticisms and their instructions, neither of which you as the learner own. The more critical and dictatorial they are, the more your ownership is undermined.

There is a world of difference between continuously trying to do something right and continuously monitoring what you are doing non-judgmentally. It is the latter, the input–feedback loop, that results in quality learning and performance improvement – this is allowing rather than forcing. It is the stressful former that is the least effective and the most used in common practice.

Learning and enjoyment

Many businesses are beginning to recognize that they need to become learning organizations if they are going to stimulate and motivate their employees and if they are going to cope with the demand for almost continual change. **Performance**, **learning**, and **enjoyment** are inextricably intertwined. All three are enhanced by high awareness levels, a fundamental objective of coaching, but it is possible to focus primarily on the development of one of them quite successfully, though only for a while. When one of the three is neglected, sooner or later the other two will suffer. Performance cannot be sustained where there is no learning or where there is no enjoyment.

Were I to devote an entire chapter to enjoyment in a book primarily focused on work, it might cause a raised eyebrow or two. It is a subject that deserves its own chapter, but I will restrain myself! Enjoyment is experienced in many different ways by different people, but I will attempt to boil it down to its essence, in a couple of paragraphs.

The AT&T example in Chapter 7 shows that enjoyment is vital for accuracy. We can also learn much about the impact of learning and enjoyment from Nobel prize-winning psychologist Daniel Kahneman and his colleague Amos Tversky, who upended traditional economics in the late 1960s. Organizations focused on learning and innovation would do well to take a leaf out of their book. In his Nobel prize biographical, Kahneman wrote that learning and enjoyment were key to the world-changing discoveries they made:

> *The experience was magical. I had enjoyed collaborative work before, but this was something different. Amos was often described by people who knew him as the smartest person they knew. He was also very funny, with an endless supply of jokes appropriate to every nuance of a situation. In his presence, I became funny as well, and the result was that we could spend hours of solid work in continuous mirth . . . Amos and I shared the wonder of together owning a goose that could lay golden eggs – a joint mind that was better than our separate minds. The statistical record confirms that our joint work was superior, or at least more influential, than the work we did individually.*

Kahneman confirmed: "Our enjoyment of the process gave us unlimited patience, and we wrote as if the precise choice of every word were a matter of great moment."

As we see here, enjoyment can come from experiencing a fuller expression of your potential. Each time you experience yourself stretching to somewhere you have never been before – in exertion, in courage, in activity, in fluidity, in dexterity, in effectiveness – you reach new heights in your senses, accentuated by the flow of adrenalin. Coaching works directly on the senses, particularly where physical activities are concerned. Therefore, coaching by its very nature enhances enjoyment. In practice, the distinction between performance, learning, and enjoyment becomes blurred, and at the limit of this merger lies what is often described as the peak experience. Far be it from me to be promoting peak experiences at work, but there is a serious side to this: the need to understand the way coaching works, particularly advanced coaching, which is what the next chapter considers.

23   Advanced Coaching

Much of the psychological dysfunction in the world stems from frustration about the lack of meaning and purpose in our lives

Too much workplace coaching is transactional, limited to cognitive psychology, or else constrained within the principles of humanistic psychology, which maintain that awareness itself is largely curative. The Inner Game, however, reflects a transpersonal psychology which emphasizes the principle of will, intention, or responsibility. It is on this philosophy of awareness *and* responsibility that coaching is built. Many years ago I was drawn to the depth and inclusiveness of psychosynthesis, a whole-system perspective of psychology, and it has informed my coaching work ever since. We call this transformational coaching to distinguish it from that which is transactional.

Psychosynthesis was conceived by Roberto Assagioli in 1911. He had been a student of Freud and was the first Freudian psychoanalyst in Italy. Like Jung, his friend and fellow student, he rebelled against Freud's limited pathological and animalistic vision of humanity. Both suggested that humans possess a higher nature, and Assagioli asserted that much of the psychological dysfunction in the world stems from frustration or even desperation about the lack of meaning and purpose in our lives.

Psychosynthesis offers a number of maps and models, the strands of which weave a very useful cradle for in-depth coaching. One of these is a simplified model of human development that, like all models, is not the truth, merely a representation that enables a conversation to take place with a coach or within your own mind. This kind of advanced coaching will invite the coachee to reframe life as a developmental journey, to see the creative potential within each problem, to view obstacles as stepping stones, and to imagine that we all have a purpose in life, with challenges and obstacles to overcome in order to fulfill that purpose. The coach's questions will seek coachees' recognition of the positive potential in the issue and the actions they choose to take. It is this that is the culmination of The Performance Curve, because it is looking both inward and outward, linking the individual and the organization to society and the planet.

Two dimensions of growth

FIGURE 19: *Two dimensions of growth*

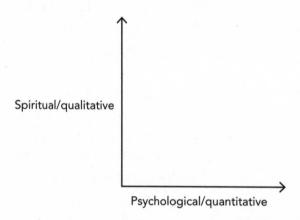

You can trace your experience of your own life track or that of others on a two-dimensional graphic model (Figure 19), of which the horizontal axis represents material success and psychological integration, and the vertical axis represents values or spiritual aspiration. Here is an example of two very different types of people to illustrate the two axes.

A businessperson may be focused on personal achievement and success in the material world and may have become a well-integrated person, a good parent, and a respected member of society, without ever having asked themselves a meaningful question about life. The businessperson might regard the opposite type as lazy, disorganized, a sponger, a dilettante.

The opposite type of person leads a contemplative and ascetic life, but seems ill equipped to cope with the realities and essentials of the everyday world. Their home, their finances, and even their personality may be in a bit of a mess. These people live a monastic life of study or art, and readily give gentle assistance to others. They see the businessperson's pursuits as pointless, ego driven, and often destructive to themselves and to others.

FIGURE 20: *Achieving balance*

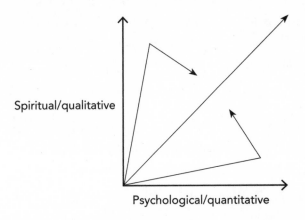

There can be little argument that Western culture has focused its energies on moving along the horizontal axis of Figure 20, and that people have done this with enthusiasm and to good effect. Western influence and economic imperatives have long been a pervasive global force but, in both East and West, there are many who journey up the vertical axis. The further we progress along either path to the exclusion of the other, the more we depart from the ideal or balanced path between the two, and the tension thereby created increases.

FIGURE 21: *A crisis of meaning*

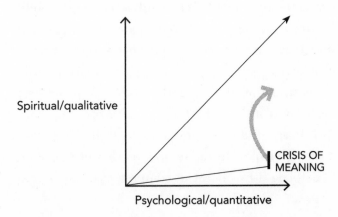

If social pressures, business imperatives, or blind determination to achieve override the tension that is attempting to pull us back on track, we are liable eventually to run into a wake-up wall. This wall is known as the crisis of meaning (Figure 21). When we hit the crisis wall, we tend to bounce back in shock into temporary confusion and even performance regression for a while, but at the same time we are likely eventually to be pulled upward toward the ideal to discover a more balanced path. We may become more introspective, paint or write poetry, and want to spend more quality time with our children.

KNOWLEDGE

The horizontal axis can also be equated to knowledge. The crisis of meaning occurs when our accumulation of knowledge far exceeds the tempering effect of our values. In the crisis we experience a breakdown of the false sense of security provided by the illusion of power and certainty that great knowledge gives us.

Wisdom lies beyond knowledge and is deeper. It provides foresight, it is often paradoxical, and it offers a different order of security that a person emerging from the crisis is then able to experience. The 45° line in the graphs could thus be said to represent wisdom, lying between the extremes of what we might describe as indiscriminately exploited knowledge on one side and ungrounded spiritual fanaticism on the other. Vertical excess can also lead people to a crisis, known as the crisis of duality, the split between their idealistic vision and the harsh realities of mundane life. They are brought down to earth with a bump, and may find themselves compromising their values to get a proper job.

I have omitted one element from these psychosynthesis graphs, a point of light that lies beyond the 45° arrowhead. It represents our higher self or soul, which could be seen as the source of our purpose and of wisdom. It exerts a gentle pull on us to "get back on track," one that is easily overridden by our more earthbound desires and ambitions. In the past such a notion could easily be dismissed by rational scientific minds as fanciful speculation. However, recent advances in neurobiology have revealed what is called the "God spot" in the temporal lobes of the brain that, to quote Danah Zohar, could be "a crucial component of our larger spiritual intelligence."

Business rightly recognizes that many systems in the world are shifting from prescription to choice. A coaching leadership style does the same. People want and will continue to expect more personal choice in the future. Of course, a crisis is not a prerequisite for psycho-spiritual development. Some people travel far along their journey with neither a crisis nor a coach. Others progress with less dramatic consequences through a series of mini-crises and the direction changes are not as acute.

Subpersonalities

There are times when I look over the various parts of my character with perplexity. I recognize that I am made up of several persons and that the person that at the moment has the upper hand will inevitably give place to another. (W. Somerset Maugham)

This model of advanced coaching works with what are called subpersonalities, different aspects of ourselves that may have different characteristics and objectives. For example, have you ever woken up some bright, sunny morning and thought "Wow, why don't I get up and go for a walk on the beach?" and within an instant you hear another inner voice countering "No, relax, stay in bed; it's so warm and comfortable here"? Who is talking to whom? These are two of your subpersonalities and you have many more, including the one that listened to both sides of the dialogue.

We all know people who put on business attire, admire themselves in a mirror, and walk, shoulders back and upright, to the office. Is that how they walk and talk when they are out with their mates, or visiting their grandmother, or with their kids? Probably not. We all adopt certain characteristics, or even personalities, in different circumstances depending on how we see ourselves or want to be seen. Many subpersonalities stem from our childhood when we subconsciously, in part anyway, used a strategy to get what we wanted from a parent. "Can I have another chocolate please – oh pleeeese!" with the high voice, the bowed head, and the poor-me stance to match. If that strategy does not work, we try another until we succeed, then we refine it. We find it works with other people too, and into our adulthood, and not only for chocolate. Most subpersonalities have a need and many have a gift too – for example, the Hero is likely to be courageous, a useful gift if someone needs to be saved.

COACHING FOR AN INNER CONFLICT

When a coachee has an inner conflict of some sort, you can ask "What part of you wants to do that?" and then "What other characteristics does that part have? What does the other part want?" The purpose of these coaching questions is to help coachees to recognize and understand more about their drives and their inner conflicts as a prelude to resolving them. When coachees are comfortable with you, you should be able to ask them to list some names (Chocoholic, Hero, Victim, and so on) for their sub-personalities. Many coaching questions evolve from that point:

- Which one of these do you find most disruptive?
- Under what circumstances does this one show up?
- Give me an example of a recent time.
- What did it want at that time?
- Did it get it? And if so, how do you think the other person felt?
- What would be another way of getting what you want in those circumstances?

Coachees' self-awareness is being increased by this process to the point at which they can begin to make choices about how they present themselves, instead of going into a certain subpersonality automatically because of the circumstances. Their self-responsibility is being strengthened and they are moving toward a greater sense of self-mastery. When two subpersonalities are in conflict with one another (e.g., walking on the beach) – and that will often be a repetitive pattern – it is possible to invite the coachee to conduct an imaginary conversation between the two parts and even have them negotiate (e.g., walk three times a week and stay in bed on four days).

WHO ARE YOU?

One way of describing our subpersonalities is to recognize that we "iden-tify" with certain descriptions, roles, and even objects. If you ask a stranger "Who are you?" they will usually give you their name. But if people are gathering to help or gawp at an accident, a police officer or a relative might ask someone pushing through the crowd "Who are you?" In this circumstance the person may say "I am a doctor," since that is more relevant than their name. Under various circumstances people will see and describe themselves as a businessperson, an Arsenal supporter, an accountant, a racing driver, a feminist, an American, a parent, a schoolteacher, an academic; you name it. None of those things is really who they are, but they are the part of themselves that they are identified with at that moment or under those circumstances.

Some people get severely stuck in one subpersonality, thereby denying their own access to other parts of themselves that may be more interesting, creative, humorous, appropriate, and so on. Some even get identified with objects, like their clothes or their car; they don't just *have* them, they *become* them. It is important that people get to discover who they are behind these temporary and superficial identifications.

A person can be likened to a team in which the different members have different qualities and different wishes and expectations. It is important to get the team to be open with each other, talk about their needs and differences, and start to collaborate and even support each other in order to meet their individual aspirations. Coaching can help people to become much more integrated and consistent in themselves and with other people. You will notice that this process is a matter of raising self-awareness and then self-responsibility.

In the workplace, and indeed at home too, a great deal of conflict comes from one subpersonality of one person locking horns with one subpersonality of another, and that becomes all consuming. Once they are aware that it is only a part of one person in conflict with a part of the other, the energy in the conflict is defused, both can start to manage their subpersonalities and can adopt a different one with each other, and they may even find themselves in agreement about things they previously fought over.

Subpersonalities can be used in many ways and they appear in many forms. Even teams can be viewed as having subpersonalities. Another useful analogy is that the subpersonalities are members of a symphony orchestra: each plays a different instrument, but they can be grouped together. When they tune up before the concert, each makes their own sound and the uncoordinated noise if heard outside is far from pleasant. Then, however, the conductor appears, and in an instant the orchestra is playing in harmony.

SELF-MASTERY

This raises the next question: "Can I become the conductor of my own orchestra?" The answer is yes, by disidentifying or stepping back from your subpersonalities and becoming the observer of the process. I hasten to add that this is quite deep stuff and it does not happen overnight, but being the conductor of your own orchestra is a very calm and powerful state that is called self-mastery. In psychosynthesis terms the conductor is known as the "I" and it is described as a center of pure consciousness and pure will. This equates precisely with awareness and responsibility, so you can now see that the core purpose of coaching is building the qualities and the presence of the "I." It is no coincidence that this also equates with the qualities of the leaders in the highest level of leadership identified by Collins in *Good to Great*: humility, an inevitable partner of self-awareness, and will or passion.

So what is the sequence that needs to be followed to reach alignment?

• Step one is the recognition that you have subpersonalities at all, identifying your most active ones and when they take you over. This requires honest self-reflection of a kind that would benefit greatly from the assistance of a coach.

• Step two is the willingness to acknowledge to another person or people that conflicting subpersonalities exist, and to discover when they show up and take you over, what they want, how they limit you, and how they may serve you.

• Step three is to get them to cooperate with one another, and this is where inner alignment starts. For example, going back to the earlier story about different voices advocating going for a morning run or staying in bed, the two voices could, in a role-play exercise, negotiate a compromise such as two early runs a week in exchange for three guilt-free lie-ins.

• Step four, the final stage is true synthesis or collaboration to the same end for the good of the whole. While this kind of developmental process can be undertaken at home through self-reflection, meditation, and visualization, the processes themselves need prior experience or training. It is probably best done with the help of an advanced coach, and there are additional benefits of doing it in a training group designed for this express purpose.

I have described the advanced coaching realm here for the understanding of aspiring coaches. I strongly advise all interested coaches and leaders formally train in advanced coaching skills, because practice in a safe environment and getting feedback are crucial to learning. There is no one right way to do anything, but what follows is a detailed description of the use of one form of advanced coaching that you could, at first at least, follow quite closely.

Structured daydreaming or visualization

Many advanced coaching methods seek to reach beneath the rational, logical, and limited mind into the subconscious, which is a whole system. For example, as in Chapter 3, guided imagery can be used in structured daydreaming or visualization to have coachees imagine themselves on a journey up a mountain, an archetypal symbol for growth; suggest to them that they meet certain things on the way, from gifts to obstacles, from an animal to a wise old teacher; and ask them to imagine what happens when this occurs. The events that occur, the obstacles they find, and the beings they meet on the way are all symbols of something in the coachee's mind that is uncovered during the subsequent coaching.

Do the following activity to explore this. Of course, for coaches, this is something you can also do with your coachees. I recommend saying it unprepared and spontaneously when you are confident enough, as it will sound more authentic.

When coachees have finished this visualization and after a breather, I coach them on the experience, focusing mainly on what the obstacle symbolized to them and what qualities they deployed to overcome it. What was the animal and what were their feelings about it? What was the conversation with the animal, and what did that symbolize? Next, what was the gift, who was it from, and what does it mean? And finally, who was the wise old person, what were the questions, what were the

ACTIVITY:
Structured Vizualization

Practice this visualization script with a colleague, coachee, or someone at home, and ask someone you feel comfortable with to read it to you.

- Just sit quietly and comfortably for a moment and take a few deep breaths.
- Now see yourself in a field surrounded by nature at the foot of a mountain.
- Begin to slowly walk toward the mountain, and start up the first gentle slope.
- As you go it begins to get steeper and more rugged.
- You are now in a group of trees and there are rocks around you.
- All of a sudden you come upon an apparently insurmountable obstacle.
- You want to continue and you figure out how to overcome it.
- It may be a struggle, but eventually you make it and continue on your way.
- Unexpectedly you meet an animal and, more unexpectedly still, it speaks to you.
- Are you afraid? What does it say? Is it afraid? What do you say?
- It is time to continue your climb and you say goodbye.
- You come to the edge of the treeline and the clear mountain opens before you.
- There on the path is a gift that you know is for you. You pick it up and take it with you.
- Now you are approaching the top of the mountain and the view is magnificent.
- As you come round a piece of rock, there is a wise old person sitting there.
- They greet you and indicate that they were expecting you.
- They invite you to ask them three questions and they will give you the answers.

ACTIVITY:

Structured
Vizualization
(cont.)

- You ask the questions that come to your mind one at a time and receive their answers.
- You let the answers sink in and they bid you farewell, and you begin to retrace your steps.
- The journey down the mountain is leisurely, but it does not take very long.
- Soon you find yourself back in the field where you started.
- When you are ready, slowly come back to the room and open your eyes.

Now take a pen and paper and make notes of everything you remember, including the conversation with the animal, the questions you asked, and the answers you received from the wise old person.

answers received, and, importantly, what did they reveal? There are, of course, many other aspects of the experience that might arise and need to be explored, but this gives you the gist.

In terms of timing of the visualization, the mountain climb should be slow and deliberate, with enough time between each sentence, maybe around 20 seconds, and the whole journey up and down taking, say, 15 minutes. The debriefing will be as long as a piece of string.

I hope this gives you enough of an idea about this sort of process to allow you to experiment with it. It is very important that you develop your own authentic style with this type of work.

Finding out more

A professional coach who has attained ICF Professional Coach Certification or similar will be able to use all of these tools seamlessly. For leaders, who are not usually looking to become a professional coach, I do highly recommend a leadership coach training that teaches advanced coaching, as it will not only broaden your range of skills but, crucially, foster your own development. Advanced coaching skills will be more and more in demand as time and society progress.

APPENDIX 1:
Glossary of Coaching Terms

ACCOUNTABILITY The coach TRUSTS the coachee and holds them account-able for progress in their thinking, learning, or ACTIONS in relation to their AGENDA and goals, through structures and measures co-designed and agreed from the start, and without blame or judgment. The coach assists coachees in creating accountability structures for themselves with the mindset of "we are each responsible for our own development." Questions to set up account-ability include: "What will you do?," "By when?," and "How will I know?" *See also* CHECKING IN ON PROGRESS

ACKNOWLEDGMENT The coach senses and articulates a deep knowledge of the "self" within the coachee taking the action, developing the awareness, or having the desire. *See also* APPRECIATION

ACTIONS *see* ACCOUNTABILITY, BRAINSTORMING, CELEBRATING, DESIGNING ACTIONS, REVIEWING ACTIONS

ACTIVE LISTENING The coach listens to understand the essence of what the coachee is communicating in words, silence, tone of voice, body language, emotions, and energy; to hear the underlying beliefs and concerns, motivation, and commitment; and to hear the coachee's vision, values, goals, and greater PURPOSE. The coach listens "between the lines" to hear what the coachee is not saying. The coach focuses on the coachee's AGENDA without judgment and with NON-ATTACHMENT; integrates and builds on the coachee's thinking, creating, and learning; and encourages and reinforces self-expression and purposeful exploration. *See also* BOTTOM-LINING, COACHING PRESENCE, INTUITION, PARAPHRASING, REFLECTING, SUMMARIZING, VENTING

ADVANCED COACHING Invites the coachee to reframe life as a develop-mental journey, see creative potential within current reality, and find meaning, purpose, and a powerful sense of self. It reflects a transpersonal psychology which recognizes and responds to a coachee's yearning for something beyond the personal, material, and everyday, and adds a deeper sense of will, personal responsibility, and serving something greater than the self. It is transform-ational not transactional, emphasizes exploration, and embraces the whole of the coachee – their greatness and gifts as well as limiting beliefs and patterns.

The coach has full trust in the process, and is not afraid to ask questions that connect a coachee to their hidden drives and obstacles. It is an empowering process which enables the coachee to discover who they are and operate from their core – their source of deepest values and qualities – a wellspring of real personal power, creativity, and actualization. *See also* COACHING

AGENDA   The coachee chooses the focus of the coaching and the coach attends to this agenda throughout, with NON-ATTACHMENT to the outcome. Holding attention on the "big picture" coaching plan or PURPOSE, desired outcomes, and ACTIONS agreed. In masterful coaching, the coach may challenge the coachee to go deeper to uncover the real issue, desire, and agenda. *See also* PARTNERING

AGREEMENT   Coach and coachee co-design at the start, and review regularly, their coaching agreement/alliance to determine what the coachee would like from the coaching interaction long term, whether there is an effective match between the needs of the coachee and the approach and methods of the coach, and what the coach and coachee's responsibilities are. At the start it is important to ensure that the coachee understands the nature of the coaching process, that they have options for responding to a REQUEST from the coach, to establish what is appropriate in the relationship, and to discuss specific parameters such as logistics, fees, and scheduling. *See also* AGENDA, ETHICAL GUIDELINES, PROFESSIONAL STANDARDS

ALLIANCE   *see* AGREEMENT

ANALOGY   An analogy can contain a METAPHOR or compare one thing as being *like* another, but goes further, adding reasoning or explanation to illustrate a concept or process. It can help the coachee understand something complex by comparing it with something familiar as an example, exploring resemblances and relationships in something they had perhaps not considered. Sigmund Freud said of analogies, "They can make one feel more at home." For example, an analogy you could help a coachee to arrive at might be: "I want my next bid to stand out from the rest – to sparkle like a diamond, to be strong under scrutiny and crystal clear in what I offer, yet reflecting different ideas depending on what the buyer wants to see." *See also* CLARIFYING

APPRECIATION   The coach communicates to the coachee something that they appreciate about them, which can raise their self-belief and confidence, and help them know themselves more fully. Appreciation is a sincere form of ACKNOWLEDGMENT.

ARTICULATE THE REALITY   The coach says what they see is going on, e.g., an action the coachee has taken and the effect it is having on them, to validate or add insight. *See also* REFLECTING/MIRRORING, SUMMARIZING

AUTHENTICITY   The coach needs to be comfortable with their own authenticity. When the coach honestly admits they don't know where to go next in the conversation, or tells a story of something they have struggled with, the coachee senses the coach being *real* and will feel more comfortable being vulnerable or admitting struggles, doubt, and failures.

AWARENESS   Self-realized, high-quality, relevant input, gained through the mind, the senses, and the emotions. Awareness may be of self, of others, of things, or of circumstances. Coaching is about facilitating the coachee's ability to have access to accurate self-perception, raising awareness in relevant areas in order to enhance their own capacity for growth and performance. It leads to enhanced learning, achievement, and enjoyment. Awareness is the basis from which RESPONSIBILITY, self-belief, and self-motivation can emerge. *See also* EMOTIONAL INTELLIGENCE

BODY WISDOM   Awareness of sensations in the body from physical activity or emotional charge, which guides one to act or get curious about what is happening for the coachee. *See also* INTUITION

BOTTOM-LINING   The coach helps the coachee express the essence of their communication quickly, without engaging in or getting caught up in long descriptions. Mastery of the core competency of ACTIVE LISTENING enables the coach to "bottom-line" what they heard from the coachee to enhance clarity and move the conversation forward.

BRAINSTORMING   The coach offers to brainstorm options with the coachee, with NON-ATTACHMENT to the ideas offered. Both coach and coachee contribute. As the coach encourages the coachee to come up with ideas, this becomes an opportunity for the coach to encourage the coachee's creativity and resourcefulness.

CELEBRATING   Encouraging and allowing time for the coachee to own what they do, to really feel celebration in their body for their success, and to appreciate their capabilities for future growth, gives them a way of actually experiencing their own success, as opposed to rushing through a succession of challenges. Celebration is one antidote to burnout.

CHALLENGING   The coach invites the coachee to stretch beyond their comfort zone, and challenge assumptions, limiting beliefs, and PERSPECTIVES to provoke new insight and possibilities. The artful coach is able to challenge without judgment or criticism.

CHAMPIONING The coach sees the potential in the coachee and believes the coachee is capable and resourceful. The coach manages their own limiting beliefs, suspending judgment, and watching for and challenging the coachee's limiting beliefs.

CHECKING IN ON PROGRESS The coach holds the coachee's attention on their AGENDA and their coaching plan, and ACKNOWLEDGES them for awareness/insight gained and for what they have done. The coach positively CHALLENGES them for what they have not done, and remains open to adjusting measures and ACTIONS. The coach develops the coachee's ability for self-feedback. *See also* ACCOUNTABILITY, COACHING FEEDBACK, PLANNING

CLARIFYING The coach expresses succinctly the essence/core of what has been said/heard and adds anything noticed intuitively from observing emotions or discrepancies in word and expression of face or body, to generate insight and clarity for the coachee. Clarifying creates a checkpoint to ensure the coach has heard deeply and understood the meaning of the coachee's message e.g., "It sounds like . . . What is it for you?" A coach with great intuition will often get the response "That's it!" from the coachee. *See also* PARAPHRASING, REFLECTING/MIRRORING, SUMMARIZING

CLEARING *see* VENTING

CLOSED QUESTIONS Any question that can be answered with a simple "Yes" or "No." *See also* OPEN QUESTIONS, POWERFUL QUESTIONING

COACHING Supporting people to grow themselves and their performance, clarify their PURPOSE and vision, achieve their goals, and reach their potential. AWARENESS and RESPONSIBILITY are increased through inquiry, purposeful exploration, and self-realization. Coaching focuses on the present and future, is a complete partnership between coach and coachee, and sees the coachee as whole (not broken or needing fixing), resourceful, and able to find their own answers. *See also* ADVANCED COACHING, COACHING MINDSET

Coaching is unlocking people's potential to maximize their own performance. It is helping them to learn rather than teaching them.

ICF Definition of Coaching: *"Partnering with clients in a thought-provoking and creative process that inspires them to maximize their personal and professional potential."*

COACHING FEEDBACK The coach draws out self-feedback from the coachee, focusing on the goal, not the obstacle, so that interferences can fall to the side, learning and new insights can occur, and potential can come through. Effective feedback, whether self-feedback or from the coach's observations, enables the coachee to identify major strengths and major areas for learning and growth.

COACHING MINDSET The coach believes that the coachee is capable, resourceful, and full of potential. Believing in the dormant capability of a person will build their self-belief and self-motivation and enable them to flourish. And with that mindset, you can coach them to make their own powerful choices and find enjoyment in their performance and their success.

COACHING PRESENCE To create a spontaneous and deep relationship with the coachee, the coach needs to be fully conscious and flexible. This requires being open to not knowing, taking risks, and experimenting with new possibilities. The coach must be confident in shifting PERSPECTIVES and working with (and not getting caught up in) strong emotions, accessing their own INTUITION, and using humor to introduce lightness and lift energy. Being fully present with the coachee is the master competency of coaching. *See also* DANCING IN THE MOMENT

CODE OF ETHICS *see* ETHICAL GUIDELINES

CONSULTING Giving advice and guidance.

CONTRACTING *see* AGREEMENT

COUNSELING Personal problem-oriented support.

DANCING IN THE MOMENT The coach is fully present and follows the direction and flow of the coachee, noticing changes in energy and creating awareness within both coach and coachee from each moment.

DECLARATION The coach creates a space or environment for the coachee to make a commitment to effective action that will lead to the accomplishment of the desired future. This is much bigger than saying "Yes, I will do . . ." For example, "From this moment on I declare that I will step into a new style of leadership which fits with my own vision of who I am becoming." *See also* WITNESS

DEEPENING THE LEARNING The coach helps the coachee find the learning from a previous action or from current perspectives to set the stage for new action. The coach can invite the coachee to "do it now" while they are together, and give support and immediate CELEBRATION on the success of the action or the learning that emerged.

DESIGNING ACTIONS The coach helps the coachee to explore alternative ideas and solutions related to the coachee's AGENDA and to define the committed actions they will take to move toward their goal. *See also* ACCOUNTABILITY, BRAINSTORMING, CELEBRATING, REVIEWING ACTIONS

DIRECT COMMUNICATION   Using appropriate, respectful language which suits the coachee's learning style, the coach effectively shares with and invites from the coachee new PERSPECTIVES, thoughts, INTUITION, and feedback, with NON-ATTACHMENT to support the coachee's self-awareness and AGENDA. Direct communication is only effective when it is delivered without causing resentment or resistance in the coachee. *See also* ANALOGY, METAPHOR, REFRAMING

DISRUPTION   Finding a way to disrupt patterns that the coachee wants to let go of. This might be a disruption of an activity (yelling at one's employees) or a way of thinking ("I have to be perfect").

EFFECTIVE QUESTIONING   *see* POWERFUL QUESTIONING

EMBODY   Using the body to strengthen a commitment or deepen an understanding or experience, e.g., standing *as* a powerful presenter when working on becoming a powerful presenter, rather than just talking about it.

EMOTIONAL INTELLIGENCE   Coaching is emotional intelligence (EQ) in practice. EQ is a term coined by Daniel Goleman in his book of the same name. EQ can be described as the range of emotional, social, and personal competencies which influence our ability to cope with life's demands and pressures. It can be broken down into a number of areas and competencies, each of which has an impact on the way we approach tasks, activities, and interactions. Coaching is about developing and using our EQ. All change starts from within. Developing and accessing our EQ can shift our self-AWARENESS. This enables us to manage ourselves better and become more aware of others, thereby having a more positive impact and increased RESPONSIBILITY.

ENGAGED LISTENING   *see* ACTIVE LISTENING

ETHICAL GUIDELINES   The coach has ethical obligations to the coachee and must understand, communicate, and adhere to a set of ethical guidelines, e.g., ICF Code of Ethics and Professional Standards. *See also* STANDARDS OF CONDUCT

EVALUATION   To make an assessment or measurement of the outcome of the coaching in terms of its value added, both qualitative (behavior change) and quantitative (monetary impact).

FEEDBACK   *see* COACHING FEEDBACK

FOCUS   *see* HOLD THE FOCUS

GOAL SETTING   The coach and the coachee agree on what the desired outcome of the coaching will be, e.g., "I want to have an effective plan for getting to work half an hour early each day." This enables the coach to facilitate the conversation effectively in the time available to serve the coachee in the best way possible. *See also* Chapter 10, "G: Goal Setting"

GREMLIN   The personification of a belief that blocks us from moving forward. The coaching perspective is that the belief developed to keep us safe and that by becoming aware of it we can choose how it impacts our life. Rick Carson's book *Taming Your Gremlin* is excellent for clearing out the gremlins.

GUT FEELING   *see* INTUITION

HOLD THE FOCUS   The coach keeps the coachee's energy directed toward their desired outcomes. *See also* AGENDA

HOLD THE SPACE   The masterful coach honors the coachee's dynamic space and gives permission for their full freedom of expression of emotions, doubts, fears, and limiting beliefs, without judgment or overreaction.

INNER GAME   In the 1970s, tennis coach Timothy Gallwey developed a number of concepts which contributed to the development of coaching, including the importance of awareness of internal obstacles (our thoughts, feelings, and physical reactions, which are often self-created). Gallwey recognized the power of increased awareness in decreasing performance-limiting interference. He stated: "Our Performance equals our potential minus interference" or $P = p - i$.

INTUITION   Directly accessing and trusting one's inner knowing or "gut feeling," taking risks to communicate what you intuit. *See also* NON-ATTACHMENT

LISTEN FOR POTENTIAL   The coach focuses on the coachee's capabilities and believes that the coachee is capable, resourceful, and full of potential, rather than seeing the coachee as a problem or having a problem.

LISTEN WITH HEART   The coach listens to non-verbal messages such as voice tone, phrasing, facial expression, and body language. When we are listening attentively at the level of feeling and meaning (the intent), our body language and facial expression show this and encourage the speaker to open up to us.

LISTENING   *see* ACTIVE LISTENING

MEET THE COACHEE WHERE THEY ARE   The coach has empathy for the coachee's situation and respects where they are, not trying to influence them to be somewhere else. The coach speaks in the coachee's terms, using their type of language.

MENTORING   Sharing expertise and some guidance.

METAPHOR   Introducing symbolism and imagery – something which is not literal but a figure of speech – helps the coachee to explore emotions and associations from another context (something they know) and to draw on them to build a picture or sensation of what they are trying to express in words (what they don't know or understand). When coaches use metaphor, they aren't just asking the coachee to think of one thing being *like* another, they actually take the coachee a step further by inviting them to picture or sense that one thing *is* the other (X = Y, e.g., "When I give my presentation, I will be the diamond on the stage – my message will be crystal clear."). *See also* ANALOGY, CLARIFYING

MINDSET   *see* COACHING MINDSET

MIRRORING   *see* REFLECTING

MOVING THE COACHEE FORWARD   The coach can help move the coachee forward in many ways, including by BOTTOM-LINING, bringing the focus back to the goal, helping to create actions for the coachee, and making a REQUEST of the coachee. *See also* BRAINSTORMING, CHALLENGING, GOAL SETTING, PERSPECTIVES, VENTING

NLP (NEURO-LINGUISTIC PROGRAMMING)   A model of interpersonal communication chiefly concerned with the relationship between successful patterns of behavior and the subjective experiences (especially patterns of thought) underlying them, co-founded by Richard Bandler and John Grinder in the 1970s.

NON-ATTACHMENT   The coach remains on the coachee's AGENDA and does not try to influence or have an opinion about the outcome. *See also* PARTNERING

OPEN QUESTIONS   Broad, open-ended questions, e.g., "What do you really want?," "What other options do you have?," evoking clarity and insight. *See also* CLOSED QUESTIONS, POWERFUL QUESTIONING

PARAPHRASING   The coach repeats what is said but uses slightly different word(s) which do not change the substance or meaning, to show the coachee that they are listening to their words (the content), validate what they have said, and help them to replay and perhaps revise what they said. *See also* CLARIFYING, REFLECTING/MIRRORING, SUMMARIZING

PARTNERING   The coach ensures that the coach–coachee relationship is one of equals, by being beside the coachee when coaching rather than walking ahead or standing opposed. *See also* AGENDA, DANCING IN THE MOMENT, NON-ATTACHMENT

PERMISSION   By asking if the coachee is happy to be coached in sensitive, intimate, or new areas, or before offering a hard truth or speaking to a gut feeling, the coach creates a safe environment, helps to build TRUST, and makes sure the coaching remains in partnership.

PERSPECTIVES   The coach communicates other points of view which expand the way the coachee sees something, allowing them to examine their viewpoint and inspiring commitment to shift to a more resourceful place with possibilities. *See also* BODY WISDOM, REFRAMING

PLANNING   The coach creates an effective coaching plan which integrates the whole of the coachee, addressing their AGENDA, concerns, and major areas for learning and development, and with targets which are measurable, achievable, challenging, and timeframed, and have the potential to move the coachee toward their desired outcome. *See also* GOAL SETTING

POWERFUL QUESTIONING   The coach first asks broad, inclusive questions which compel attention, thought, and observation, and then tighter questions to increase the quality of focus, clarity, detail, and precision and evoke discovery, insight, new learning, commitment, or action toward the coachee's desired outcome. Powerful questioning reflects curiosity and ACTIVE LISTENING, follows the coachee's AGENDA with NON-ATTACHMENT, challenges their assumptions, creates a feedback loop, and carries no judgment, blame, or criticism.

PRESENCE   *see* COACHING PRESENCE

PROFESSIONAL STANDARDS   Coaches must conduct themselves at all times in a professional manner and understand and model appropriate professional standards, e.g., ICF Code of Ethics and Professional Standards. *See also* ETHICAL GUIDELINES

PSYCHOTHERAPY   Therapeutic support which explores blocks and past influences, particularly the emotional past. Coaches should clearly communicate to their coachees the distinction between coaching and psychotherapy, and be able to refer coachees to a professional psychotherapist as needed.

PURPOSE   The greater purpose or "why" that a person acts from is as important as "how" they act or "what" they do, and is the unifying and integrating factor in real change.

QUESTIONING   *see* POWERFUL QUESTIONING

REFLECTING/MIRRORING   The coach expresses a summary of what they think they heard the coachee say, using the coachee's exact wording for key concepts. This "mirroring" enables the coach to check for understanding, and gives the coachee the opportunity to hear their own words and, if necessary, revise what they said so their meaning is accurately expressed. *See also* CLARIFYING, PARAPHRASING, SUMMARIZING

REFRAMING   The coach helps the coachee to understand things from a new perspective. An example of reframing might be, "So, you could consider yourself the victim of the current circumstances, or another way to look at it might be . . ." *See also* CLARIFYING

REITERATING   *see* REFLECTING/MIRRORING

REQUEST   The coach invites the coachee to take specific action on something, e.g., "I would like you to complete X task by Y date," and allows the coachee to say "Yes I will," "No I won't," or make a counter offer. Ways of responding to a request are usually set up in the AGREEMENT. *See also* MOVING THE COACHEE FORWARD

RESPONSIBILITY   The personal choice to take ownership and to commit to take action. It cannot be imposed; it must come from inside. Coaching is about building AWARENESS and responsibility in order to grow people and performance. Increased responsibility leads to enhanced potential, confidence, and self-motivation. It is the basis from which uniqueness, self-belief, and ownership can emerge. *See also* EMOTIONAL INTELLIGENCE

REVIEWING ACTIONS   The coach helps the coachee to increase their learning and awareness, identifies possible blocks, and offers further support and challenge to meet the goal. When actions and their results are reviewed, action learning takes place. When results are not what the coach and coachee expected or desired, the coach may challenge the coachee to recognize if there is a separation between what they are stating and what they are doing. It is not about blame or criticism, but helping the coachee to see current reality accurately. *See also* ACCOUNTABILITY, CELEBRATING, DEEPENING THE LEARNING, DESIGNING ACTIONS

STANDARDS OF CONDUCT   *see* PROFESSIONAL STANDARDS

STRUCTURED/STRATEGIC DAYDREAMING   The coach challenges the coachee to create a powerful vision of the future which will motivate them to pursue their own fulfillment. *See also* GOAL SETTING

SUMMARIZING   Repeating back what the coachee said but more briefly, without changing substance or meaning, shows the coach is listening to their words (the content), checks that the coach has understood, helps the coachee to replay and perhaps revise what they said, validates what they have said, and enables the coach to interrupt smoothly when the coachee talks too much or repeats themselves. *See also* CLARIFYING, PARAPHRASING, REFLECTING/MIRRORING

SYSTEMS COACHING   The coach recognizes, considers, and connects all elements of the system in operation for the coachee. This may include human dynamics as well as workflow, hierarchy, business units involved, causal factors, and overall patterns present in the system. Systems coaching can be very powerful for a coachee who is struggling with elements of a system that are outside their control. *See also* WHOLE SYSTEM APPROACH

THERAPY   *see* PSYCHOTHERAPY

TRUST   Coaching relies on a deep and trusting connection between the coach and coachee, built on intimacy, mutual respect, and genuine concern for the coachee's welfare and future. Building a trusting relationship between coach and coachee requires a safe, supportive environment as well as clear agreements, personal integrity, honesty, and sincerity. *See also* AUTHENTICITY, CHAMPIONING, PERMISSION

VALUES   The guiding principles you hold most dear and for which you are willing to stand. Identifying and understanding the core values of the coachee is foundational for the coaching relationship. The coach can help the coachee to enhance enjoyment, performance, and overall wellbeing by declaring their values and working to live their values every day, e.g., by asking: "How can you live your value of integrity at work every day?"

VENTING   The coach allows the coachee to clear an emotional state of being, without judgment and with NON-ATTACHMENT, so that they are able to move on to the next step. The coach does not use any of this material to start a coaching conversation. The coaching starts afresh after venting.

VISIONING   A process by which the coach helps the coachee to imagine what they want as if it has already happened or it has already been accomplished. Creating a powerful vision that can actually be pictured as "desired future" by the coachee is the first step to building forward momentum toward where the coachee wants to go.

WHOLE-SYSTEM APPROACH   Recognizes the interconnectedness of people, processes, organizations, and the communities they touch. Actively engages the ability to work with and develop the inherent systemic potential.

WITNESS   The coach is a non-judgmental, objective witness to the coachee's life which creates space for creativity and reconnection with values and dreams to occur.

APPENDIX 2:
Coaching Question Toolkit

This toolkit gathers together all the questions that we at Performance Consultants consistently find helpful in coaching, in bags labeled according to topic. We invite you to dip into each bag as you need. The golden rule is to be clear and brief. Sometimes the most powerful questions lead to a long silence, so don't feel the need to jump in with another question if there is a long pause. Silence really is golden. Most of the questions listed here are great in team situations too if you replace "you" and "your" with "we/us" and "our." While coaching is not all about asking questions, that is the single most important skill to master for a novice coach. The reason is that it is with this skill that you start tapping into the wisdom of others. And everything is situational, so any question could work given the right intention and circumstances.

As your confidence grows, follow your intuition and allow powerful questions to flow. Instead of being tempted to work out your next question, trust that you will know instinctively what to ask next in the moment.

Question Bag 1: Self-coaching

Use this sequence of questions when you want to work on a specific challenge as an individual or team. Identify something you would like to achieve, improve, or perhaps resolve at work. Write down your answers to each of these questions, interpreting them in the way that seems appropriate to you. The questions follow the GROW sequence: Goals, Reality, Options, Will:

- What would you like to work on?
- What would you like to have after answering this set of questions (e.g., a first step/strategy/solution)?
- What is your goal related to this issue?
- When are you going to achieve it?
- What are the benefits for you in achieving this goal?
- Who else will benefit and in what way?
- What will it be like if you achieve your goal?

- What will you see/hear/feel?
- What action have you taken so far?
- What is moving you toward your goal?
- What is getting in the way?
- What different kind of options do you have to achieve your goal?
- What else could you do?
- What are the principal advantages and disadvantages of each option?
- Which options will you choose to act on?
- When are you going to start each action?
- What could anyone else do to give you support and when will you ask for it?
- How committed are you, on a scale of 1–10, to taking each of these actions?
- If it is not a 10, what would make it a 10?
- What will you commit to doing? (*Note*: It is also an option to do nothing and review at a later date.)

Question Bag 2: Conscious working agreements

Follow this sequence to set up conscious working agreements with an individual or team. Each person answers each question. If it is a large team, team members respond until the whole team feels that particular question has been answered and there is nothing else to add.

After a while, pick the ones that work for you to create your own set of questions for this purpose.

- What would the dream/success look like for us working together?
- What would the nightmare/worst-case scenario look like?
- What's the best way for us to work together to achieve the dream?
- What do we need to be mindful of to avoid the nightmare?
- What attitudes do you and I want to bring to this conversation?
- What permissions do you and I want?
- What assumptions do you and I have?
- What will we do when things get hard?
- What is working/not working?
- What do we need to change to make the relationship more productive/positive?
- How can we both take responsibility for making this work?

Question Bag 3: Asking permission

This bag contains different ways to ask permission – dip in as needed.

- Can I add to what you've just said?
- Would you like to brainstorm this with me?
- Is it OK if I use a coaching approach?
- Can I ask you . . .?
- Would it be helpful if I tell you what I'm hearing when you say that?
- Can I make a suggestion?
- What permissions do we want for this conversation?

Question Bag 4: The Top 10 powerful questions

This question bag consists of my top 10 – a list of simple yet profound questions that you can have at your fingertips.

1. If I wasn't here, what would you do? (My all-time favorite question which I use to prove to the cynical that coaching doesn't take time, it takes one powerful question!)
2. If you knew the answer, what would it be? (Not as daft as it sounds, since it enables the coachee to look beyond the blockage.) If you did know? (In response to "I don't know.")
3. What if there were no limits?
4. What advice would you give to a friend in your situation?
5. Imagine having a dialogue with the wisest person you know or can think of. What would they tell you to do?
6. What else? (This used at the end of most answers will evoke more. This followed by plain silence can also evoke more by allowing a coachee space to think.)
7. What would you like to explore next?
8. I don't know where to go next with this. Where do you want to go?
9. What is the real issue? (Sometimes used to help the coachee get out of the story and "bottom-line.")
10. What is your commitment on a scale of 1–10 to doing it? What can you do to make it a 10?

Question Bag 5: GROW

This bag contains sets of questions for each stage of the GROW model – dip in as needed.

GOAL

The Goal for the conversation

- What would you like to achieve in this conversation?
- What is the aim for this conversation?
- It sounds like you have two goals. Which would you like to focus on first?
- What would make this time well spent for you?
- What would be the most helpful thing for you to take away at the end of our conversation?
- We have half an hour for this, where would you like to have got to by then?
- If you had a magic wand, where would you like to be at the end of this?

The Goal for the issue

- What's the dream?
- How would you like it to be?
- What does that look like?
- What will you be saying to yourself?
- What will that enable you to do?
- What will other people be saying to you?
- What will you have that you don't have now?
- Imagine three months from now, all obstacles are removed, and you have achieved your goal:
    - What do you see/hear/feel?
    - What does it look like?
    - What are people saying to you?
    - How does it feel?
    - What new elements are in place?
    - What is different?
- What would be an inspirational goal for you?
- What outcome are you looking for?
- What will it bring you personally?
- What stretch will you need to achieve this goal?

- What is the timeframe?
- What milestones can you identify? What are their timeframes?
- How would you break this goal down into smaller pieces?
- What would it mean to you to achieve this?
- What is important to you about this process?
- What more do you want?
- What would a great outcome be for you from this?
- What would a successful outcome look like?
- What would a successful task completion look like?
- What are you working toward here?
- When do you need to have achieved this outcome?

REALITY

- What is happening at the moment?
- How important is this to you?
- On a scale of 1–10, if an ideal situation is 10, what number are you at now?
- What number would you like to be at?
- How do you feel about this?
- What impact is this having on you?
- What is on your shoulders?
- How does this affect other areas of your life?
- What are you doing that takes you toward your goal?
- What are you doing that is getting in the way of your goal?
- How much . . .?
- How many . . .?
- Who else does it affect?
- What is the present situation?
- *Exactly* what is happening now?
- What is your main concern here?
- Who else is involved/affected?
- How much control do you have personally over the outcome?
- What action(s) have you taken so far?
- What has stopped you from doing more?
- What internal resistance do you have to taking action?
- What resources do you already have (skill, time, enthusiasm, support, money, etc.)?
- What other resources are needed?

- What is the *real* issue here?
- What are the main risks here?
- What resources do you already have?
- What is your plan so far?
- What can you count on yourself for here?
- What are you most/least confident about?

OPTIONS

- What could you do?
- What ideas do you have?
- What alternatives do you have?
- Is there anything else?
- If there were anything else, what would it be?
- What has worked in the past?
- What steps could you take?
- Who could help you with this?
- Where could you find out the information?
- How could you do that?
- What are the different ways in which you could approach this issue?
- What else could you do?
- What would you do if you had more time/control/money?
- What would you do if you could start again, with a clean sheet?
- Who do you know who would be good at this? What would they do?
- Which options would give the best results?
- Which solution appeals to you most?
- What could you do to avoid/reduce this risk?
- How could you improve that situation?
- So now, how do you want to do that?
- What do you think?
- What else could work here?
- What ideas do you have that might work here?
- What would help you to remember?
- What would a permanent solution look like?
- What could you do to avoid this happening again?
- What choices do you have?
- I have some experience in this area, would it help if I made a suggestion?

WILL

Stage 1: Accountability Set-up – define actions, timeframe, and measures of accomplishment

- What will you do?
- How will you do that?
- When will you do it?
- Who will you talk to?
- Where will you go?
- Is there anything you need to put in place before that?
- How committed are you to taking that action?
- What will it take for you to commit to that?
- Which option(s) do you choose?
- To what extent will this meet the goal you have?
- How will you measure success?
- What is the first step?
- When precisely are you going to start?
- What stops you starting earlier?
- What could happen to hinder you taking this action?
- What personal resistance do you have, if any, to taking this action?
- What will you do to minimize these factors?
- Who else needs to know what your plans are?
- What support do you need? From whom?
- What will you do to get that support?
- What could I do to support you?
- What can you do to support yourself?
- What is your commitment to taking this action (e.g., on a scale of 1–10)?
- Who will take that action?
- What's the next step for you?
- When will you take that first step?
- What time will that be finished by?
- What is your commitment to this action?
- What might happen to prevent you from taking this action?
- Who else can you call on to help you?
- What else do you need?
- What specific actions will you take?
- How will you know it has worked?
- How will I know (accountability)?
- What is/are the best option(s)?

- What changes will you make?
- What will you do to make sure that happens?

Stage 2: Follow-up and Feedback – review how things went and explore feedback for learning

See Question Bag 6 for questions to check in on progress and Question Bag 7 for questions to explore feedback for learning.

Question Bag 6: Follow-up

These questions are for checking in during the **will** phase of coaching – after a goal has been set but before it has been achieved.

- Where are you with this project/goal?
- What has happened so far/since we last spoke about this?
- How is it going?
- How do you feel about where you are with this?
- What do you think about your progress?
- What have you achieved?

One of three things will have happened and the following questions are grouped accordingly. Dip in as appropriate.

THE COACHEE SUCCEEDED
- What's working well and why?
- What are you most pleased with?
- What are you most proud of?
- What successes have you had?
- What led to this success?
- What's enabled you to get this far?
- What skills, qualities, or strengths of yours contributed to this?
- What behaviors were most effective?
- Congratulations! Take a moment to celebrate.
- What do you want to celebrate in yourself?
- What did you learn?
- What challenges did you overcome and how?
- What new strengths did you find?
- What capability did you grow?
- What's next for you?

THE COACHEE DID NOT SUCCEED

- What happened (short story)?
- What did you learn from that?
- What's not going well and why?
- What challenges have you had?
- How have you dealt with challenges?
- What new strengths did you find?
- What development areas did you find?
- What do you want to celebrate in yourself?
- What do you want to do next time?
- How will you move on from this?
- What gaps in skills, knowledge, or experience would you like to develop?
- What behaviors would you change next time?
- What development areas would you like to work on?
- What's the biggest block?
- What's the most effective thing you could do to overcome this block?

THE COACHEE DID NOT DO IT

- What happened?
- What kept you from doing it?
- What does it mean to you?
- What did you learn about yourself?
- What will you do?

All of the above questions are about creating learning. See Question Bag 7 for questions to capture and deepen that learning.

Question Bag 7: GROW Feedback Framework

Dip into the following questions as needed. Remember, the golden rule for feedback is that in each step of the framwork the coachee shares first and the coach adds their perspective second.

GOAL: SET INTENTION

Coachee shares – ask your coachee questions that focus attention and raise energy

- What do you/we want to get out of this?
- What would be helpful for you?

Coach shares – add your goal

- I want . . .

REALITY: RECOGNIZE

Coachee shares – ask your coachee questions focused on the positive

- What is going/went well?
- What did you like about what you did/how you did it?
- What worked well?
- What behaviors were most effective?
- What are you most proud of?
- What specific strengths did you use?
- What behaviors were most effective?
- What do you think contributed most to your success?

Coach shares – add what you feel worked well

- I like/liked . . .
- I found what worked well was when/how you . . .
- I felt that you consistently surpassed agreed goals and expectations by . . .
- I recognize the effort you put into . . . even though the goal hasn't been met fully . . .
- Strengths that I see include . . .

OPTIONS: IMPROVE

Coachee shares – ask your coachee questions to raise responsibility for improving performance

- If you could do it again, what would you do differently?
- What strengths would you want to use more of in the future?
- What behaviors would you change next time?
- What got in the way of you achieving/exceeding . . .?
- How would you overcome this next time?
- What would enable you to achieve greater frequency/consistency/quality in the future?
- Where specifically over the past year would additional skills or experiences have been helpful?
- What important skills or experiences are you missing that will prepare you for future opportunities?
- If you got off track, what happened? What can you do to improve this situation?

Coach shares – add what you feel your coachee needs to do to stretch further

- Can I make a suggestion?
- I feel you could achieve this goal by . . .
- I feel you could stretch yourself by . . .
- How about . . .?
- Ways to further leverage your strengths would be to . . .
- The reason this development area is important is . . .

WILL: LEARN

Coachee shares – ask your coachee questions that reinforce learning and agree next steps

- What is the learning here?
- What did you learn that you can apply going forward?
- What are you learning about yourself?
- What are you learning about others?
- What do you now know about this goal/project that you didn't previously?
- What else can we learn?
- What will you/we do differently next time?
- Where else would you apply this learning?

Coach shares – add what you are learning and what you will do differently

- I am learning . . .
- I will do . . .

APPENDIX 3:
Some Solutions to the Nine Dot Exercise

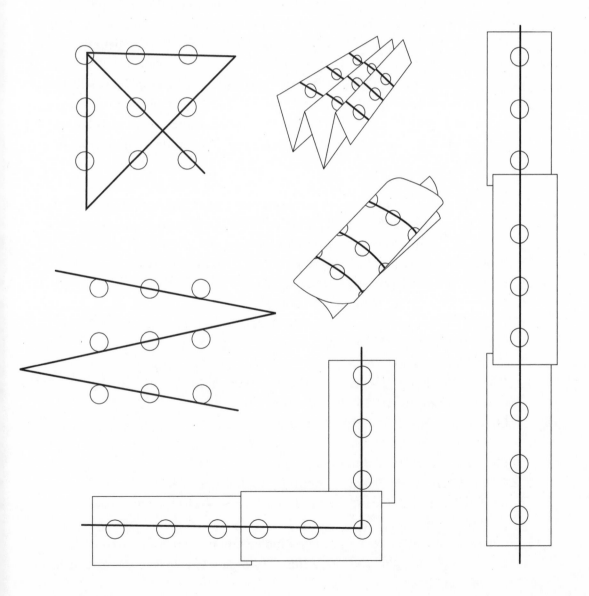

Bibliography

I have come to the firm belief that in this day and age, and with the responsibility they have, coaches have to be more than an empty vessel, a mirror, or a slave to their clients' agenda. They should be well informed and up to date with global affairs and trends, especially about environmental and economic degradation, social justice and social distress, psychotherapy and spirituality. That is a tall order, so I have added just a few books to my recommended bibliography covering these broader realms. I have deliberately avoided adding any new books on coaching, for there are too many to list and most have much to offer. My emphasis here is on broadening the vision of coaches and leaders beyond the conventional boundaries of coaching.

Barrett, Richard (1998) *Liberating the Corporate Soul*, Butterworth-Heinemann.

Barrett, Richard (2006) *Building a Values-Driven Organization*, Elsevier.

Barrett, Richard (2014) *Evolutionary Coaching*, Lulu.

Bennis, Warren (1989) *On Becoming a Leader*, Addison-Wesley.

Bridges, William (2004) *Transitions*, Da Capo Press.

Browne, John (2016) *Connect*, WH Allen.

Canadian Union of Public Employees (CUPE) (2003) *Enough Workplace Stress*, Canadian Union of Public Employees.

Canfield, Jack (2005) *The Success Principles*, Element.

Carson, Rick (2007) *Taming Your Gremlin*, William Morrow.

Chang, Richard (2001) *The Passion Plan,* Jossey-Bass.

Childre, Doc, Howard Martin, & Donna Beech (2000) *The Heartmath Solution*, HarperCollins.

Collins, Jim (2001) *Good to Great*, Random House Business.

Colvin, Geoff (2008) *Talent Is Overrated*, Nicholas Brealey.

Conference Board (2016) *The Conference Board CEO Challenge® 2016*, Conference Board.

Correa, Cristiane (2014) *Dream Big*, Kindle edition, Primeira Pessoa.

Covey, Stephen (1989) *The Seven Habits of Highly Effective People*, Simon & Schuster.

Day, Laura (1997) *Practical Intuition*, Broadway Books.

Dispenza, Joseph (2009) *Evolve Your Brain,* Health Communications.

DuPont (2015) "The DuPont Bradley Curve infographic," www.dupont.com/products-and-services/consulting-services-process-technologies/articles/bradley-curve-infographic.html.

DuPont Sustainable Solutions (2015) "The DuPont Bradley Curve | DuPont Sustainable Solutions," https://www.youtube.com/watch?v=tMoVi7vxkbo.

Einzig, Hetty (2017) *The Future of Coaching*, Routledge.

Emerald, David (2016) *The Power of TED (The Empowerment Dynamic)*, Polaris.

European Foundation for the Improvement of Living and Working Conditions (Eurofound) and the European Agency for Safety and Health at Work (EU-OSHA) (2014) *Psychosocial Risks in Europe*, Publications Office of the European Union.

Ewenstein, Boris, Bryan Hancock, & Asmus Komm (2016) "Ahead of the curve: The future of performance management," *McKinsey Quarterly*, May.

Ford, Debbie (2004) *The Right Questions*, HarperOne.

Foster, Patrick & Stuart Hoult (2013) "The safety journey: Using a safety maturity model for safety planning and assurance in the UK coal mining industry," *Minerals*, 3: 59–72.

Gallwey, Timothy (1986) *The Inner Game of Golf*, Pan.

Gallwey, Timothy (1986) *The Inner Game of Tennis*, Pan.

Gallwey, Timothy (2000) *The Inner Game of Work*, Texere.

Gladwell, Malcolm (2000) *The Tipping Point*, Little, Brown.

Gladwell, Malcolm (2008) *Outliers*, Little, Brown.

Goleman, Daniel (1996) *Emotional Intelligence*, Bloomsbury.

Goleman, Daniel (1999) *Working with Emotional Intelligence*, Bloomsbury.

Goleman, Daniel (2006) *Social Intelligence*, Random House.

Goleman, Daniel, Richard Boyatzis, & Annie McKee (2002) *Primal Leadership: Learning to Lead with Emotional Intelligence*, Harvard Business School Press.

Goleman, Daniel, Richard Boyatzis, & Annie McKee (2002) *The New Leaders*, Little, Brown.

Hackman, Richard, Ruth Wageman, & Colin Fisher (2009) "Leading teams when the time is right," *Organizational Dynamics*, 38(3): 192–203.

Harris, Alma (2003) "Teacher leadership, heresy, fantasy or possibility?" *School Leadership and Management*, 23(3): 313–324.

Hartmann, Thom (1998) *The Last Hours of Ancient Sunlight*, Three Rivers Press.

Harvard Business School (2009) "Jorge Paulo Lemann, A.B. 1961; Carlos A. Sicupira, OPM 9, 1984; Marcel H. Telles, OPM 10, 1985," *Alumni Stories*, https://www.alumni.hbs.edu/stories/Pages/story-bulletin.aspx?num=1990.

Hawken, Paul (2007) *Blessed Unrest*, Viking.

Hawken, Paul, Amory B. Lovins, & Hunter Lovins (2000) *Natural Capitalism*, Earthscan.

Hay Group (2010) "Growing leaders grows profits," *Developing Leadership Capability Drives Business Performance*, November.

Heifetz, Ronald, & Marty Linsky (2002) *Leadership on the Line*, Harvard Business School Press.

Hemery, David (1991) *Sporting Excellence*, Collins Willow.

Hill, Andrew (2017) "Power to the workers: Michelin's great experiment," *The Financial Times*, 11 May.

Homem de Mello, Francisco S. (2015) *The 3G Way*, 10x Books.

Hopkins, Andrew (2008) *Failure to Learn*, CCH.

International Coach Federation and Human Capital Institute (2014) *Building a Coaching Culture*, Human Capital Institute.

James, Oliver (2008) *The Selfish Capitalist*, Vermilion.

Kahneman, Daniel (2002) "Daniel Kahneman – Biographical," www.nobelprize.org/nobel_prizes/economic-sciences/laureates/2002/kahneman-bio.html.

Katzenbach, Jon, & Douglas Smith (1993) *The Wisdom of Teams*, Harvard Business Press.

Kegan, Robert, & Lisa Laskow Lahey (2009) *Immunity to Change,* Harvard Business School Publishing.

Kegan, Robert, Lisa Laskow Lahey, Matthew L. Miller, & Andy Fleming (2016) *An Everyone Culture*, Harvard Business Review Press.

Kimsey-House, Henry, Karen Kimsey-House, Phillip Sandahl, & Laura Whitworth (2011) *Co-Active Coaching*, Nicholas Brealey.

Kline, Nancy (1998) *Time to Think,* Octopus.

Knight, Sue (2002) *NLP at Work*, Nicholas Brealey.

Laloux, Frederic (2014) *Reinventing Organizations: A Guide to Creating Organizations Inspired by the Next Stage in Human Consciousness*, Nelson Parker.

Landsberg, Max (1997) *The Tao of Coaching*, HarperCollins.

Lee, Graham (2003) *Leadership Coaching*, Chartered Institute of Personnel & Development.

Maslow, Abraham (1943) "A Theory of Human Motivation," *Psychological Review*, 50, 370–396.

Maslow, Abraham (1954) *Motivation and Personality*, Harper.

Mehrabian, Albert (1971) *Silent Messages*, Wadsworth.

Mindell, Arnold (1998) *Dreambody*, Lao Tse Press.

Mitroff, Ian, & Elizabeth A. Denton (1999) *The Spiritual Audit of Corporate America*, Jossey-Bass.

Monbiot, George (2006) *Heat*, Penguin.

Moss, Richard (2007) *The Mandala of Being*, New World Library.

Neill, Michael (2009) *You Can Have What You Want*, Hay House.

Nicholas, Michael (2008) *Being the Effective Leader*, Michael Nicholas.

Peltier, Bruce (2009) *The Psychology of Executive Coaching*, Routledge.

Perkins, John (2007) *The Secret History of the American Empire*, Dutton.

Pilger, John (1998) *Hidden Agendas*, Vintage.

Renton, Jane (2009) *Coaching and Mentoring*, The Economist.

Rock, David, & Linda Page (2009) *Coaching with the Brain in Mind*, John Wiley.

Roddick, Anita (2001) *Business as Unusual*, Thorsons.

Rogers, Jenny (2016) *Coaching Skills*, Open University Press.

Russell, Peter (2007) *The Global Brain*, Floris Books.

Schutz, William, C. (1958) *FIRO: A Three-Dimensional Theory of Inter-Personal Behavior*, Rinehart.

Seligman, Martin (2006) *Learned Optimism,* Vintage Books.

Semler, Ricardo (2001) *Maverick*, Random House.

Senge, Peter (2006) *The Fifth Discipline,* Random House Business Books.

Senge, Peter, C. Otto Scharmer, Joseph Jaworski, & Betty Sue Flowers (2004) *Presence*, Nicholas Brealey.

Sisodia, Raj, David Wolfe, & Jag Sheth (2014) *Firms of Endearment*, Pearson Education.

Spackman, Kerry (2009) *The Winner's Bible*, HarperCollins.

Speth, James (2008) *The Bridge at the Edge of the World*, Yale University Press.

Tolle, Eckhart (2001) *The Power of Now*, Mobius.

Tolle, Eckhart (2005) *A New Earth*, Penguin.

Whitmore, Diana (1999) *Psychosynthesis Counselling in Action*, Sage.

Zohar, Danah, & Ian Marshall (2001) *SQ: Spiritual Intelligence*, Bloomsbury.

Acknowledgments

Any book of this nature will be the product of the author's exposure to and learning from many experiences and many people. Tim Gallwey must undoubtedly head the list as the creator of the Inner Game, the bedrock of the finest coaching. Earlier editions of this book identified many other contributors and supporters. I will not repeat their names here, but rather draw attention to two main stems of influence during the run-up to this edition.

The first is our clients – we have a saying at Performance Consultants, "We grow through our clients." Our client partnerships are how we stay on the cutting edge of our industry – we explore their world and create solutions to fit their needs. This work has informed much of the revision of this book, and I am eternally grateful to all those individuals who had a vision and brought us into their organization to make it a reality. To my mind, these people are like the "imaginal cells" in a caterpillar that lead the transformation into a butterfly. After all, coaching is behavior change and no quick fix; vision and long-term partnership transform organizations. I will mention a few long-term partners here. Our partnership with Medtronic started with the vision of John Collingwood and Pamela Siliato who have since moved on to new opportunities outside Medtronic. The work continues with the leadership of Cheryl Doggett and Karen Mathre as part of the newly formed Global Learning and Leadership Excellence Center of Expertise. Their mission is to deepen and expand the coaching capabilities across the organization, building upon the great work while maintaining the integrity of its foundation. At Linde, James Thieme and Kai Gransee had the vision to transform safety performance through teaching a coaching style – the work that inspired The Performance Curve. Lena Glenholmes and Rodrigo Avelar de Souza at Louis Vuitton are transforming the global retail experience.

The second is the extraordinarily talented individuals at Performance Consultants who work with our clients around the world. David Brown, my CEO, singled me out many moons ago, kicked me off my easy chair of life, challenged my reservations, and projected me into the unlimited arena of new possibilities and into many countries all over the world. Tiffany Gaskell led the team that contributed their expertise and knowledge to bring this edition up to date. Creator of The Performance Curve and our evaluation tool Coaching for Performance ROI, Tiffany's vision for the impact coaching can have in organizations has taken our work to a whole new level. Frances MacDermott, our Chief Learning Officer who has a background in publishing, brought incredible thought and rigor to all our incredible materials featured in this text and added extraordinary depth. Kate Watson leads the global team's focus on the cutting edge of organizational transformation – the hard as well as the soft components in culture, which we call emotionally intelligent change management. Carolyn Dawson created the new dialogues that give such fantastic insight into what a coaching style looks like in practice in the workplace, and has been an invaluable sounding board throughout the project. Rebecca Bradley, Master Certified Coach and long-time Assessor for the International Coach Federation (ICF), contributed her expertise to the coaching dialogues and Glossary. Rebecca Jones brought her talents to the creation of the The Performance Curve survey. Sunčica Getter and Anne-Marie Gonçalves Desai brought their expertise in team coaching to make Chapter 16 so practical, ably edited by Adina Bratescu. Jon Williams, who actually came from a client, Lloyds Bank, now works with us and specializes in coaching for safety performance and coaching for Lean performance, which are outlined in Chapters 17 and 18 together with their coaching dialogues. Hetty Einzig, who I have worked with the longest and who is one of the most talented facilitators of her time, has cast her expert editorial eye over the manuscript, her background in psychology ensuring rigor and depth. Nadia Terribilini, the youngest member of the team, added her unique perspective. And the person who made sure we all delivered is Tamsin Langrishe, who led the project and also challenged content where appropriate.

Then I want to thank the literally thousands of people I have met in the coaching profession who have had faith in the role I have attempted to play in promoting the emerging significance of coaching within all our institutions and lives. I feel humbled by the awards you have given me, including an ICF President's Award and an Honorary Doctorate from the University of East London.

Finally, special thanks to my publishers. Nicholas Brealey first had the foresight to publish me. Sally Osborn worked with me on the previous editions also, and has added even greater polish to this one. Holly Bennion, Ben Slight, Caroline Westmore, and the team at Nicholas Brealey Publishing have helped to shape this Fifth Edition. I believe this new edition reflects how coaching in the workplace has evolved since I first introduced it in the early 1980s, and lays the foundation for its future significance.

About the Authors

Sir John Whitmore

Sir John Whitmore was the pioneer of coaching in the workplace and Co-Founder of Performance Consultants International, the market leader in coaching globally. He was the first to take coaching into organizations in the early 1980s and co-creator of the GROW model, the most used coaching model in the world. Honoured for his lifetime's work with the President's Award from the International Coach Federation, Sir John's global contribution to coaching and leadership has helped to drive organizational transformation. Through his books – most notably *Coaching for Performance* – workshops and speeches, he defined the principles of performance coaching and midwifed its birth. *Coaching for Performance* is widely considered to be the bible of coaching and it has inspired millions of managers, leaders, and coaches across four decades to bring the best out of themselves and others. This book was completed before his death in 2017, and his extraordinary legacy is continued by his colleagues.

Performance Consultants International

Co-founded by Sir John Whitmore, for over four decades Performance Consultants have been at the forefront of creating high-performance cultures in organizations through people and leadership. Their mission is to transform the relationship between organizations and employees. Their stance is simple: organizations are sitting on a great untapped reservoir of potential – that of their people. They partner with organizations globally on effective leadership development, coaching, and culture transformation. Market leaders in their field, Performance Consultants invite organizations to improve performance through their leaders and thereby reap rewards for people, profit, and planet. They are able to demonstrate an average 800% return on investment for their clients. Their flagship development program named after this book is Coaching for Performance. It is considered the industry gold standard and is delivered in over 40 countries and more than 20 languages.

Would you like your people to read this book?

If you would like to discuss how you could bring these ideas to your team, we would love to hear from you. Our titles are available at competitive discounts when purchased in bulk. Bespoke editions featuring corporate logos, customised covers or letters from company directors in the front matter can also be created in line with your special requirements.

We work closely with leading experts and organisations to bring forward-thinking ideas to a global audience. Our books are designed to help you be more successful in work and life.

For further information, or to request a catalogue, please contact:
business@johnmurrays.co.uk or
sales-US@nicholasbrealey.com (North America only)

Nicholas Brealey Publishing is an imprint of
John Murray Press.

Going further with

At www.coachingperformance.com you will find a wealth of state-of-the-art resources and information about our gold standard Coaching for Performance offers, including solutions for creating and sustaining high-performance cultures that can be tailor-made for your organization

If you wish to develop your skills further or play a part in transforming your organization, Performance Consultants International can help. Working in over 40 countries and 23 languages, our team is dedicated to creating transformational organizations with high-performance cultures where people can thrive

e-Learning
Flexible self-paced learning, wherever you are, whenever you want.
Our top-quality blended learning delivered direct to you

Surveys and Evaluations
Find out where your culture is on The Performance Curve. Evaluate a Return on Investment (ROI) of leadership development

Consultancy
Create and sustain a high-performance culture. Partner with our world-class transformation consultants

Coaching for Performance

Workshops and Programs
The gold standard for leaders and managers who want to develop a high-performance coaching leadership style. Blended learning programs with consistently outstanding feedback

Leadership Development
Developing authentic leadership and delivering an average 800% ROI. A blend of in-person workshops, 1:1 coaching, and evaluation

1:1 Coaching
For leaders and managers looking to accelerate results and fulfil their potential. Fast-track, tailor-made leadership development delivering an average 800% ROI

International Coach Federation

ICF Coach Certification Pathway
For internal and external coaches seeking an ICF coaching credential via a Public or Corporate program

www.CoachingPerformance.com